T0407867

EMPIRE CRUISE

THE SPECIAL SERVICE SQUADRON
1923-24

DANIEL KNOWLES

FONTHILL

Fonthill Media Language Policy

Fonthill Media publishes in the international English language market. One language edition is published worldwide. As there are minor differences in spelling and presentation, especially with regard to American English and British English, a policy is necessary to define which form of English to use. The Fonthill Policy is to use the form of English native to the author. Daniel Knowles was born and educated in the United Kingdom; therefore, British English has been adopted in this publication.

Fonthill Media Limited
Fonthill Media LLC
www.fonthill.media
office@fonthillmedia.com

First published in the United Kingdom and the United States of America 2024

British Library Cataloguing in Publication Data:
A catalogue record for this book is available from the British Library

Copyright © Daniel Knowles 2024

ISBN 978-1-78155-898-0

The right of Daniel Knowles to be identified as the author of this work has been asserted by him in accordance with the Copyright, Designs and Patents Act 1988.

All rights reserved. No part of this publication may be reproduced, stored in a retrieval system or transmitted in any form or by any means, electronic, mechanical, photocopying, recording or otherwise, without prior permission in writing from Fonthill Media Limited

Typeset in 10.5pt on 13pt Sabon
Printed and bound in England

Contents

Acknowledgements		4
Introduction		5
1	Planning the Cruise	9
2	The Ships of the Squadron	27
3	Admirals and Captains	41
4	'The "Floating Power" of Britain'	50
5	'The Warmest Tribute in its Power'	74
6	'The Navy Means Everything'	85
7	'We Only Did Our Duty'	184
8	'We Surrender Our City Unto You'	208
9	South America	260
10	'A Halo of Splendour'	266
11	Return of the Squadron	294
Epilogue		297
Endnotes		302
Bibliography		310
Index		314

Acknowledgements

Projects such as this book can never be achieved without a considerable amount of help and assistance for which I am extremely grateful. First of all, I am very grateful to all the staff at the National Archives in Kew for their assistance with official documentation relating to the cruise.

Sourcing the many photographs that have been included in the book has been a journey, which like the ships of the Special Service Squadron, led me around the world. In Canada, I am indebted to Jeannie Hounslow of the City of Vancouver Archives for her invaluable assistance with information on the photographs contained within the archives. I wish also to extend my sincere thanks to Catherine Lavoire of the Bibliothèque et Archives nationales du Québec and to Kimberley Head, the archives specialist at Saanich Archives, British Columbia, for her assistance. I wish also to extend my gratitude to Carol Smith and Pena Atanasoff at the State Library of Western Australia, Susan Kennedy at the City of Sydney Archives, Lisa Crunk of the Naval History and Heritage Command, and Steve Locks for their assistance and advice.

Finally, I would like to take this opportunity to thank my friends and family, in particular my parents Tracey and Gary and sister Natalie, for their continued support and encouragement.

Introduction

On 22 May 2021, the UK Carrier Strike Group set sail from Britain to 'fly the flag for Global Britain'.[1] The largest and most powerful European-led maritime force in two decades (centred around the largest ship ever constructed for, and flagship of, the Royal Navy, the aircraft carrier HMS *Queen Elizabeth*), the Carrier Strike Group embarked upon a twenty-eight-week deployment to project British influence and signalling power while engaging with allies and reaffirming Britain's commitment to addressing security challenges around the globe.[2] During the course of the deployment, the Carrier Strike Group covered 29,920 miles, visited more than forty countries, and partook in more than seventy engagements including engagements and exercises to celebrate the fiftieth anniversary of the Five Power Defence Arrangement.

The celebrations of the fiftieth anniversary of the Five Power Defence Arrangement saw joint air and naval displays involving ships and aircraft from Britain, Australia, New Zealand, Malaysia, and Singapore. During the course of its journey, the Carrier Strike Group conducted exercises with American, French, Dutch, Australian, New Zealand, Singaporean, and Indian forces and made port calls at Gibraltar, Italy, Crete, Oman, Japan, and Guam. Elements of the strike group also conducted freedom of navigation exercises in the Black Sea and through the disputed areas of the South China Sea.

The deployment of the Carrier Strike Group was an important move as it came at a time when Britain was reconsidering its place in the world following the decision to leave the European Union. The strike group over-delivered on expectations of a UK naval presence in the Indo-Pacific region. Despite the planning and the success of the deployment, many of the countries on the strike group's itinerary placed constraints on activities ashore designed to increase engagement and to foster goodwill as they continued to deal with the effects of the COVID-19 pandemic.

The deployment of the UK Carrier Strike Group on a flag-waving exercise to the Indo-Pacific had echoes of an earlier era. Indeed, almost a century earlier, in 1923, a Royal Navy battle group known as the Special Service Squadron had embarked on a similar mission around the British empire. Coming at a time when Britain was

The UK Carrier Strike Group in the South China Sea. (*Royal Navy*)

once more looking to reaffirm her commitments to addressing security challenges around the globe, the Special Service Squadron sought to project British power and influence across the empire and the world in the wake of the First World War.

This book focuses on the cruise of the Special Service Squadron, which came to be known informally as the 'Matelot's world booze'. In this, a comprehensive overview of the events involving the squadron during the course of the cruise has sought to be portrayed and a fair description of the events aboard each of the vessels involved provided. It must be noted, however, that this has not been possible owing to the weightedness and availability of source material. Many of the contemporary accounts of the cruise of the Special Service Squadron focus on the battlecruisers, in particular HMS *Hood*. The cruise of the Special Service Squadron occurred at a time when the historical value of the voices of the lower deck was not considered to be as great as those of senior officers.

While the cruise involved several ships, the squadron was centred around HMS *Hood*. First, she was the flagship of the squadron; flagships often command attention within a squadron. Secondly, at the time of the cruise, she was the largest and fastest vessel in the world. Discounting the squadron as a whole, the *Hood* was a spectacle in her own right. It may therefore be said that it is no surprise that so much of the available material focuses on the cruise from the perspective of HMS *Hood*. Despite this, an attempt has been made throughout to provide a fair overview of the cruise.

Not only is this book the story of the cruise of the Special Service Squadron, it is also a photographic record. As many photographs as possible have been included over the following pages in order to illustrate the ships at different points of the voyage and the activities that the men of the squadron engaged in and to reflect on the local populations and receptions to the squadron. It may be noted here that the vast majority of the photographs that have been taken and which are included over the ensuing pages of this book feature or were taken aboard HMS *Hood*. The quality of the photographs vary throughout. The vast majority of the photographs are amateur photographs taken by visitors to the ships. While some of the photographs included in this book are of poor quality, they have been reproduced because of their interest. Every effort has been made to improve the quality of images which were damaged, creased, under-exposed, or over-exposed. It should be borne in mind that the quality of general photographic materials in the early 1920s were not of the highest standard and that processing facilities were also lacking. Many photographs have been reproduced here because of their human interest—telling a photographic story that might not otherwise be told. Therefore, images have been reproduced here that might otherwise have been rejected because of their poor condition.

While a story of a great undertaking, it is also a story in some respects of tragedy as not all of those who embarked upon the cruise in 1923 returned back to Britain. At the same time, the cruise may be viewed as a metaphor for the decline of British imperialism.

Over the course of the cruise, millions of people visited the ships. In most cases, the photographs used to illustrate the Special Service Squadron in various locations are from specific photographic collections, taken by one or two individuals. Given the number of people who visited the ships, it has to be assumed that many more thousands of photographs of the Special Service Squadron exist which would provide a further insight into the cruise.

1

Planning the Cruise

During the interwar period, perceptions of the Royal Navy both at home and aboard were conditioned by four principal factors: international competition, technological change, operational overstretch, and economic constraints.

The end of the First World War saw the world's major naval powers—Great Britain, the United States, and Japan—embark upon a new naval arms race, the likes of which had contributed to the so-called 'War to End All Wars'. At the end of the war, Japan remained the dominant power in Asia, as she had been ever since the annihilation of the Russian Fleet at the Battle of Tsushima in 1905.[1] Japanese naval ambitions were based on the Eight-Eight Plan, which envisaged a fleet of eight modern battleships alongside eight modern battlecruisers in service at any one time to help pursue and secure its future ambitions in the Pacific.[2]

Following the First World War, the United States possessed the second largest naval fleet in the world. With an expanding economy and industrial base, the United States was well on the way to becoming the world's most powerful nation and a major player on the world's stage. This intent was broadcast to the world in 1907 when President Theodore Roosevelt engaged in a flag-waving exercise by sending a force that became known as 'The Great White Fleet' on a fourteen-month-long world cruise. From Hampton Roads, Virginia, the Great White Fleet visited Trinidad, Brazil, Chile, Peru, Mexico, Hawaii, New Zealand, Australia, the Philippines, Japan, China, Ceylon, Egypt, and Gibraltar. The voyage of the Great White Fleet was an immense success:

> Theodore Roosevelt's battleships captured the imagination of the world. The cruise proved an immense public relations success for the Navy. Relations were fostered with nations that hitherto had been little more than names on a map; while relations with the familiar capitals were enhanced. The cruise highlighted such deficiencies in American battleship design as the placement of armour and ammunition hoists. The lack of American logistical support was also laid bare, ramming home the lesson that without an adequate home-grown merchant marine, control of the seas was all but impossible.... It demonstrated America's ability to transfer power from the Atlantic

The Great White Fleet began a fourteen-month-long cruise in 1907 when President Roosevelt engaged in a flag-waving exercise to indicate America's intention to become a major international player. This photograph shows the battleships departing Hampton Road, Virginia, at the start of the cruise. (*NH 92091, US Naval History and Heritage Command*)

The USS *Connecticut* leading the Great White Fleet at sea in December 1907. (*NH 92067, US Naval History and Heritage Command*)

Planning the Cruise

Ocean to the Pacific. Valuable lessons learned in the projection of sea power would later pay handsome dividends in two global conflicts. But of greater importance is that Roosevelt's gambit elevated the United States to the ranks of a global powers.[3]

In 1915, US naval administrators began to press for a navy that was second to none. President Woodrow Wilson supported this proposition which in August 1916 was approved by Congress. The construction program proposed the construction of six battleships and six battlecruisers. The entry of the United States into the First World War brought about a shift in priorities in the country's shipyards. In order to wage war against Germany and her U-boats, the production of anti-submarine vessels was necessary while a vast fleet of merchant ships was required to transport supplies to Britain and mainland Europe. This compelled the United States to suspend its capital ship-building program with the result that only one battleship, the USS *Maryland*, was laid down during the period of the First World War; it would not be until the 1920s that construction on the bulk of the new fleet would ultimately begin.[4]

In 1919, the United States announced further plans for capital ship construction. In order to keep pace with the United States, Japan proposed to construct a further four battleships and four battlecruisers between 1920 and 1922.[5] The first four ships—battlecruisers to be named *Amagi*, *Akagi*, *Atago*, and *Takao* armed with ten 16-inch guns in five twin turrets and capable of 30 knots—were laid down as planned while an unnamed class of ships, referred to simply as the No. 13 class, was projected to be laid down in 1922. The ships of the No. 13 class, it was planned, would have been armed with 18-inch guns and would have displaced 47,500 tons.[6]

Meanwhile, with access to a wealth of data gathered from wartime experience and experiments conducted against German battleships, Great Britain was keen to modernise her fleet in order to ensure the continuing dominance of the Royal Navy. To achieve this, four new battlecruisers, referred to as the G3, armed with 16-inch guns and displacing 48,400 tons, were designed and ordered in late 1921. The G3 battlecruisers were to be followed in 1922 by four battleships designated N3, which were to be armed with 18-inch guns and which were projected to displace 48,500 tons.[7]

All of the new post-war capital ships proposed by Britain, the United States, and Japan were heavily armed and armoured. The distinction between each of the proposed ships was speed; some of the proposed vessels retained the existing battle fleet standard of 21–23 knots while others were planned to be able to attain a minimum of 30 knots. Having planned their respective building programs, Britain, the United States, and Japan, somewhat ironically, all had good reasons for wishing to abandon their building programs, not least of which were financial.

The First World War had imposed immense strains upon British society and the economy. Not only was there a huge loss of life among the British population leading to claims of a lost generation, but there had also been a great financial strain.[8] Economic historians have claimed that the First World War cost the

British taxpayer £20 billion (a figure which is in excess of £1.4 trillion today). The Dominions—including Australia, New Zealand, Canada, South Africa, and India—contributed £3 billion financially. Nevertheless, by the end of the war, the British Treasury was exhausted. Moreover, the war had served to weaken ties between Britain and the empire.[9] Britain spent more on the war per capita than any other combatant. By 1918, she boasted not only the largest navy in the world, but also the largest functioning army and air force in the world, something she could not afford. The British Treasury had loaned great sums of money to Britain's allies and had borrowed heavily from the United States on their behalf. Many of Britain's overseas assets had been sold and much of the country's merchant fleet had been sunk. The United States, formally Britain's largest debtor, was now her largest creditor and London had to cede to New York its international financial primacy.

Nevertheless, Britain emerged from the war much less damaged than any other European combatant. Living standards rose and, as a result of state intervention, there was an improvement in the general health of the populace. New industries arose to replace German imports which were to be the basis of much of Britain's interwar economy. What made this possible was Britain's accumulated wealth, the wealth of the Dominions, and the ability to pay for the majority of the war effort out of taxation rather than inflation, as well as its credit-worthiness in the United States.[10]

This wealth was augmented by territorial gains from the war which bolstered the size of the British empire by 1,400,000 sq. miles and 13 million new subjects. Key territorial gains included the effective acquisition of the oil-rich territories of the Middle East as the former German and Ottoman colonies in Palestine, Transjordan, and Iraq were ceded to Britain as mandates alongside parts of Cameroon, Togo, and Tanganyika. Yet, in a remarkably short time, Britain would begin to regret the war. Britain acquired responsibilities that she was no longer strong enough to meet and the old international financial and trading system which Britain felt to be essential for her own prosperity was still in ruin.[11] Throughout the 1920s, therefore, the main aim of British foreign policy was the reconstruction of as much of that system as was possible.[12]

For the Royal Navy, the end of the First World War meant that it had to begin to immediately reinforce its stations in the far-flung corners of the world and sustain Britain's global commitments, in particular in areas where nationalist uprisings threatened. Before that, however, the Royal Navy had unfinished business to attend to which required old-style gunboat diplomacy. Following escorting the German High Seas Fleet into captivity at Scapa Flow in the Orkney Islands, the Royal Navy had dispatched a number of warships to participate in what became known as the Intervention War against communist factions in Russia.[13] Following the signing of the Treaty of Versailles, German naval ambitions had been crushed and the Royal Navy looked to be the undisputed master of the world's oceans. The reality, however, was somewhat different.[14] Following the war, the British empire was to be increasingly challenged as the world's premier power and *Pax Britannia* was effectively at an end.[15]

Planning the Cruise 13

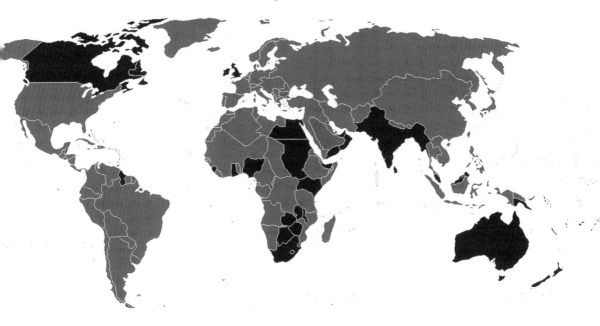

The British empire in 1914.

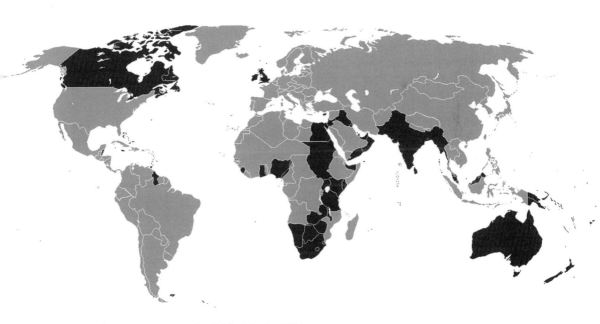

The British empire at its territorial height in 1921.

By the early 1920s, most of the skirmishes associated with the end of the First World War and its conclusion had ended whereupon the Royal Navy returned to what may be described as 'ordinary' duties of showing the flag, policing the world's oceans and maintaining British interests aboard, although there remained areas where gunboat diplomacy was required.

While this was ongoing, the Admiralty faced the urgent problem of drastically cutting the size of the overall fleet which far exceeded peacetime needs. Thousands of 'hostilities only' seamen alongside a large number of career mariners were let go as the commitments of the Royal Navy were severely pruned in bankrupt Britain. Dozens of obsolete ships and submarines were sold for scrap while work on various other types of ship ordered during the war was halted with many being scrapped. Of what was left, half of the remaining fleet was placed into reserve. This was a challenge which was keenly felt by the navy, which since the beginning of the twentieth century had been portrayed to the British public and to the empire as the most powerful navy in the world and the shield of the empire on which the sun never set.[16]

The post-war economic climate that existed in Britain left little resource or appetite for the grandiose naval reviews of the pre-war period. The loss of life associated with the conflict rendered the reviews too 'morally problematic'.[17] Due to this, alongside relief that the war and bloodshed was over, there was an evident distancing from the navy's previous policy and aversion to acts of naval pageantry which would continue into the early 1920s in line with a critical re-evaluation of the First World War and the militarism which was perceived to have led to the outbreak of the conflict. As such there could be 'no return to the vast international naval spectacles of the pre-war years'.[18]

Within the complex economic, political, and social situation faced by Britain in the aftermath of the First World War, the Royal Navy was slow to reassert its place in the post-war world and the need to reinforce its position overseas was not immediately recognised; the propaganda machine that had carried Britain through the war and had kept the Royal Navy foremost in the minds of the populace was quickly dispensed with at the end of the war, having been regarded by many in authority as an 'abhorrent necessity' that could now be abolished alongside wartime protocols.[19] Overt propaganda in the form of dispatching fleets to trouble spots was frowned upon by naval elites, such overseas missions being viewed initially by the Admiralty as worthwhile ventures but as being of greater benefit to diplomats. There existed a belief that the navy should return to being something of a silent service.

At the same time, however, naval pageantry was in a sense re-introduced and remained an important development which allowed for the 're-opening of the naval theatre'.[20] In particular, 'showing the flag', it was strongly argued, would demonstrate the continued power of the Royal Navy while also providing economic benefits to the flagging British economy. Such ventures, it was believed, would help to secure orders for British shipyards in foreign markets, and would assist British economic prosperity and help to reassert Britain's imperial position.[21]

In its broadest form, 'showing the flag' was an event which showed the British flag aboard, in particular at an officially organised visit to a foreign port.[22] The term has been referred to as 'a euphemism frequently applied to the appearance of the White Ensign in seaports around the world'.[23]

With this in mind, in 1919, the Admiralty designated the principal preoccupation of the navy's destroyers as being 'showing the flag where it had not been since before the war' while also 'preserving order and protecting British subjects'.[24] While showing the flag exercises were to be a principal preoccupation of destroyers, the Admiralty was not adverse to the use of capital ships in such exercises when there was deemed to be a greater benefit. In 1919, the battlecruiser HMS *New Zealand*, which had been funded by the government of New Zealand as a gift for the British government, carried Admiral Sir John Jellicoe on his tour of the Pacific Dominions. That same year, the battlecruiser HMS *Renown*, fresh out of a refit, was dispatched on a voyage to Newfoundland, Canada, and the United States. This voyage was followed by a 210-day voyage to Australia and New Zealand. The most high profile cruise, however, was that of the *Renown* to India, Burma, Ceylon, and Japan carrying the prince of Wales (later King Edward VIII).[25] By and large, India notwithstanding, the reception given to the visiting prince and the *Renown* was joyous and the tour was deemed to be a success.[26] Officers such as Captain August Agar did not doubt the importance showing the flag exercises played in helping to project British power and prestige, later writing:

> When it became known that the flag being worn by the ship was the White Ensign of the Royal Navy ... any apprehension which those ashore may have previously felt were at once allayed. Instead of fear there was confidence and goodwill, because the White Ensign signified authority in support of law and order.[27]

The 'resurgence' of flag-waving exercises, if it may be so called, at this time was partly in response to anxieties over imperial unity. Admiral Sir David Beatty, the first sea lord, delivered a speech in Belfast in which the navy was reaffirmed as the quintessential representative of the might of the British empire. The speech reinforced the value of the navy in forging unity both nationally and imperially. During the course of his speech, Beatty stated:

> They [the navy] were not only a fighting service. They were an ambassadorial service. Wherever the white ensign flew there was security, there was a connecting link between those far-flung portions of the Empire and the Motherland, and it was their proud privilege in the navy to feel and to know that they were as much a peace service, in enabling the empire to band together, as they were a war service in protecting the empire.[28]

In an Admiralty memorandum dated 24 April 1923, written at the insistence of First Lord of the Admiralty Leo Amery, the chief of the naval staff, Admiral Sir Roger Keyes, drafted a memorandum to Admiral Sir David Beatty in which he proposed dispatching a squadron of ships around the empire. In the memorandum, Keyes stated:

I am considering the desirability, pending the proposed redistribution of Fleets, of sending a really representative Squadron of our most modern ships round the Empire (a) in order to follow up any agreements for co-operation at the Imperial Conference by creating Dominion interest and enthusiasm so that such agreements may be really carried out; (b) to let the local forces in Australia and elsewhere not only see our standard of work etc. but have an opportunity of doing joint exercises etc., and getting in touch generally, as a prelude to some more permanent system of interchange and co-operation; (c) to give our own ships more experience of long distance cruises and of waters practically unvisited by the Navy at large for nearly 20 years.

I discussed this idea with C.-in-C. Atlantic Fleet (whose ships would presumably be the ones borrowed for the purpose) and I attach a rough estimate of the route, fuel, consumption etc., made by his staff. My present idea is that the Squadron composed of say *Hood* and *Repulse* and a Squadron of modern light cruisers should during or immediately after the Conference, say some time in November, go (1) to South Africa, staying there three or four weeks; (2) India—Bombay or Trincomalee—stopping for a few days only; (3) Singapore (4) Australia and New Zealand where they should spend say two or even three months doing joint exercises etc.; (5) Vancouver (6) Panama Canal, and W. Indies and Bermuda; (7) Eastern Canada and Newfoundland for say a month before returning home.

I should like you to consider the possibility of getting part or whole of the China Squadron and possibly one or more of the Australian ships to meet our Fleet at Singapore and proceed together to Australia (with a view to future closer association between China Squadron and Australian Navy); also of leaving one of our cruisers behind in Australia for 6 months and taking and Australian cruiser with our Fleet to Canada and W.I.—this not only as experience to Australians but in order to show Canada what Australians are doing. There is also the question of paying courtesy visits en route at San Francisco and Seattle on the U.S. West Coast and one or more U.S. east coast ports.

There will, of course, have to be a supplementary estimate for fuel and I should like this worked out both for our ships and for the Australian ships (they would naturally find their own supplementary).

If an Australian ship came home with our Fleet via Canada, she might then be attached to A.F. for a while and go back via [the] Mediterranean. This bigger scheme would, I think, supersede the present proposal for an exchange of cruisers with Australia if that is only to come off towards the end of the year.[29]

To Amery, the cruise would serve to strengthen imperial unity:

The British Empire is an Oceanic Commonwealth. It has grown by sea-power and seafaring ... in the long run an ocean-wide system of defence of naval powers such

Planning the Cruise 17

as those which are coming to the front to-day, cannot be maintained indefinitely by the resources of this small island alone. The naval problem, like all our other problems, can only be solved by the co-operation of all the partner nations in the British Empire.[30]

Admiral Beatty readily agreed that the proposed endeavour would be 'a good advertisement' and insisted that the loss of several important vessels from European waters to conduct the cruise would be more than outweighed by the political impact the cruise would have throughout the empire. With approval from the Cabinet, planning got underway for the cruise. The Admiralty began to work with the Treasury, the Foreign Office, the Colonial Office, and the governments of the Dominions to navigate the complex logistical arrangements that the event necessitated.[31]

While Amery proposed sending a representative squadron of the Royal Navy's most modern vessels on the voyage, it was thought by some within the Admiralty that this show of strength would be counterproductive at a time when the Dominion navies were being encouraged to contribute more to imperial defence. The initial suggestion that was put forward in a minute written on 24 March 1923 was 'for a Squadron say of *Hood* and *Repulse* and a squadron of modern light cruisers'.[32] By mid-May 1923, the Admiralty had settled on a provisional list of seven vessels: HMS *Hood* and *Repulse* and the *Danae*-class light cruisers HMS *Danae*, *Delhi*, *Dauntless*, *Dragon*, and *Dunedin*. Debate over the composition of the force, however, continued. One Admiralty minute dated 6 June 1923 voiced the concern:

Whilst it would be of value to the Empire to see our newest and largest ships with a view to obtaining the active co-operation of the Dominions in providing navies of their own it is possible that if battle cruisers are sent, it may produce an entirely opposite effect and might discourage rather than stimulate the Dominions from making an increased naval effort. They might reason in this way:—'We cannot hope to maintain ships of such size ourselves, and if we cannot have the best and biggest, we will not have anything at all'.[33]

Attached to the minute was a note written by Commander C. A. Spooner, a Royal Navy officer who had recently returned from service on the Australian Navy Board. The note written by Spooner argued:

I assume that at the forthcoming Imperial Conference, Australia may be advised, *inter alia*, that, as her present squadron is obsolete, it should be replaced by new ships at an early date. I assume also, that such a policy would be acceptable to the present Australian Government and that they would be able to advance it with a good chance of success.

If Australia was considering a replacement programme for her cruisers, the new ships would presumably be at least as heavily armed as *Hawkins*, and I believe that a visit by a ship of that class, or a modern Light Cruiser Squadron, would prove a useful incentive.

Further, I believe that a visiting squadron would have a good effect on the R.A.N. [Royal Australian Navy] ships, especially if it was mainly a business visit and included combined exercises and practices. Incidentally, it would direct public attention to the importance of oil fuel supplies. (The R.A.N. squadron is mainly coal burning.)

I am doubtful whether the visit of a squadron containing Capital Ships would have as good a general effect. It will be beyond the financial capacity of Australia to acquire or maintain capital ships for many years to come, and their presence may tend to discourage proposals to build lesser ships, which might appear to the public, to be of doubtful value in comparison.

Furthermore, a visit of capital ships to Australia might give rise to undue confidence in the power and mobility of the British Fleet, and might tend to stifle an inclination to improve the local navy, which latter is the only form of Empire naval contribution that it is wise to advocate. The visit of H.M.S. *Renown* in 1921 appeared to me to make Australians dissatisfied with their own ships and to question the wisdom of retaining them, but it did not occasion any public agitation for their replacement.

A visiting British squadron to Australia should encourage recruiting for the R.A.N., especially if an arrangement had been concluded for a regular exchange of R.A.N. ships with other stations, thus providing foreign service for Australian personnel, and avoiding the stagnation which is the worst feature of a small navy.[34]

Admiral Sir Roger Keyes, upon reading Spooner's memo, stated that he was in favour of limiting the cruise to a squadron of light cruisers if it was to go ahead. Despite this, the battlecruisers were seen by those with a vested interest in the cruise—some members of the Admiralty, the Treasury, the Foreign Office, and the Colonial Office—as essential to the nature of the modern navy as they were big, impressive, and powerful vessels which showcased British might. It was therefore decided that the ships most capable of projecting British power should make up the squadron. Subsequently, the Admiralty noted:

> The Dominions will want the best we have got, and we want to make them feel something of what the Navy is like. But … we might consult them as to what they would like themselves, holding ourselves in readiness to send the Battle Cruisers if they wish to have them.[35]

From the early planning stages, it was understood that the centrepiece of the cruise would be the battlecruiser HMS *Hood*. In the opinion of the Admiralty, the *Hood* was the natural choice to serve as the flagship of the squadron as she was the most modern and powerful battlecruiser in service anywhere and was also the largest warship in the world.[36]

It may be said that the selection of HMS *Hood* for inclusion in the squadron was 'a necessity' for she was one of the most visible elements of British naval prestige. Furthermore, as Ralph Harrington has stated, 'The appearance of the biggest warship in the world off the shores of imperial cities across the globe was naturally intended to provoke awe in those who beheld her'.[37] The other ships that took part in the cruise, while worthy in their own right, were chosen as suitable escorts for the *Hood*, representing the most modern of their class to ensure that the world saw the best of the Royal Navy.[38]

Not only were the light cruisers of the *Danae*-class modern light cruisers, there were links to the proposed destinations to be visited by the squadron. The Royal Navy has long named its ships after towns, cities, counties, and countries and has sought to establish links between the navy and namesake communities through the use of visiting vessels. HMS *New Zealand* had been used to carry Jellicoe on his tour of the Pacific, which included a visit to New Zealand. Admiralty records do not suggest that the light cruisers selected to make up the squadron were selected due to their names, however, including the cruisers HMS *Delhi* and *Dunedin* may have been a politically conscious and shrewd move as it was proposed that the squadron would visit India and that ships would be sent to Dunedin, New Zealand. Rather than suggest they were chosen for their names, Admiralty records only indicate that the ships were selected because they were modern vessels of a suitable class and would be available.[39]

While discussions had surrounded which ships the Royal Navy should dispatch on the tour, Amery had decided that following the squadron's proposed visit to Australia, a cruiser of the Royal Australian Navy would join the cruise 'in order to show Canada what the Australians are doing'.[40]

Canada was a key concern for Britain at the time. During the First World War, Canadian politicians had come to believe that the close collaboration achieved by the Imperial War Cabinet would lead to some sort of more permanent arrangement for shaping imperial policies of common concern. Mackenzie King, who became prime minister of Canada in December 1921, had other ideas. To King, the independence of Canada was to preclude any form of co-operation either in diplomacy or in defence which might prejudice Canada's decision whether or not to go to war should a similar situation to that which existed in 1914 again occur.[41] At the same time, fears of United States expansionism and the frictions which developed as a result led to acceptance of Canada's role as a North American country and a determination to avoid becoming embroiled in any issues in which the United States might find itself on the opposing side. In turn it became an assumption of Canadian defence policy that no great armaments were required for Canada's own defence and that the country's resources could be saved for more pacifist forms of investment.

The arguments upon which this policy was based centred around national unity, the dangers to which had been highlighted by the dispute which had erupted in 1916 and continued until the end of the First World War over conscription. It was therefore believed that the fewer foreign entanglements in which Canada became embroiled, the easier relations would be between British and French Canadians.[42]

From the point of view of British statesmen and defence chiefs, the situation was different. In public, there was increasing commitment to the Balfour-style commonwealth with an emphasis on equality of status which made it difficult to openly object as Canada explored the potentials of the new situation. In private, however, they were aware of the new situation in a world in which the dangers to Britain and the empire were always manifold and Britain's own resources inadequate to meet them alone. Conscious of the role the Dominions played during the war and of the need to maintain unity across the empire, the British government was not willing to embark upon policies willingly which might serve to divide Britain from the Dominions. Each of the Dominions was viewed separately, in light of their own external interests and of the degree of its dependence upon British strength, particularly naval strength. With respect to Canada, the Dominion's unwillingness to challenge important aspects of American policy or to accept risks made the situation a complex one. Within imperial councils, Canada, to some extent, came to represent the absentee voice of the United States, something which could be viewed as decisive on occasion.[43]

The 1923 Imperial Conference officially began on the morning of 1 October when the representatives met for the opening session at 10 Downing Street. Mackenzie King had arrived in London on 29 September and lost no time in entering into informal discussions with key British ministers ahead of the conference. On 1 October, he spoke with Leo Amery and subsequently told the editor of the *Manitoba Free Press*, J. W. Dafoe, who had been invited to accompany the Canadian delegation:

> [King] told him [Amery] of his emphatic objection to publication in Canada of memorandum prepared by Admiralty urging increased expenditures on [the] Canadian navy. [King] said it was an obvious attempt to influence Canadian opinion over heads of government and [that the] Canadian govt. resented this.... Amery seemed quite taken aback by King's declaration.
>
> King also told Amery that in [the] present state of public option about expenditure in Canada, no additional outlay on [the] navy was possible and that he need not expect he would consent to commitments suggested by the Admiralty. [He] told Amery it would be useless for him to make promises which he could not fulfil upon his return and that conditions forbade anything in the nature of a policy naval expansion.[44]

Following his discussions with King, Amery could be under no illusion as to the Canadian position. Nevertheless, Amery was noted for his tenacity of purpose and did not abandon his objectives. The strategy of conversion on which he settled was to invite the Dominion prime ministers and other representatives to Spithead to review the fleet ahead of the annual fleet manoeuvres. 'It was an inspection', Amery later wrote, 'under realistic conditions, a grey day and a gale blowing'.

> A gleam of sunlight on the long lines of ships of war, as *Princess Margaret* ran down between them, added to the impressive sense of power. Standing on the bridge with the Prime Ministers, I could not help saying to Mackenzie King: 'That is why you

Planning the Cruise 21

are Prime Minister of Canada and not, at best, one of the Senators for the American State of Ontario'.[45]

While discussions were ongoing regarding the composition of the squadron, discussions were also underway regarding the ports to be visited by the squadron.

During the early planning stages of the cruise, it had been proposed that the squadron would make a port call at Bombay, India. At the time, India possessed the most organised anti-colonialist nationalist movement in the world and therefore posed a significant problem for the British authorities who were seeking to project an image of imperial unity and peace. Anti-colonialist discontent was widespread with intense anger over the treatment of Indian workers in Kenya and the incarceration of Mahatma Gandhi for six years for sedition. Meanwhile, the Indian National Congress was calling for a boycott of the British Empire Exhibition which was scheduled to be held in the summer of 1924.

Moreover, the 1921 visit of the prince of Wales aboard HMS *Renown* had been an unmitigated public relations disaster in India. Gandhi had organised a national strike and a boycott of the festivities; riots broke out in the streets of Bombay which resulted in twenty deaths with hundreds more injured. The events were covered in excruciating detail by the British and foreign press.[46] The Admiralty thus decided to quietly remove the squadron's visit to the jewel in the crown of the British empire from the itinerary in favour of a stopover in Ceylon. The Admiralty justified the selection of Trincomalee in favour of Bombay 'as it appears desirable to favour Ceylon rather than India, in view of the desire to encourage interest in the development of Colombo and Trincomali [sic.] for naval purposes'.[47]

That same memo, dated 30 March 1923, went on to detail thoughts on other potential ports of call:

> ... Mombasa, Esquimalt, Seattle, Tacoma, Bermuda and Boston are considered impracticable for Battle Cruisers, and it is proposed that they should be visited by Light Cruisers only.
>
> (d) Georgetown, Demerara, which is mentioned by the C-in-C., Atlantic Fleet, has been omitted, as Battle Cruisers could not approach within 17 miles of the town.
>
> (e) Dunedin, New Zealand, has been omitted owing to its unsuitability for the accommodation of a Squadron.[48]

Further debate on the ports to be visited ensued with the director of navigation, Captain Frederick Loder-Symonds, providing an analysis at the end of the first week of May as to the approaches to each anchorage, the depth of water in the proposed ports, and whether the battlecruisers and light cruisers would have to anchor inside or outside each harbour.

One port that would be visited by the squadron, it was decided, would be the protectorate of Zanzibar, which has been described an 'an unlikely destination for the Special Service Squadron'.[49] On the surface, that may have been the case, however, Zanzibar was in fact an important location for the squadron to make a port call and to demonstrate the continued power of the Royal Navy. On 20 September 1914, the protected cruiser HMS *Pegasus* was engaged by the German light cruiser *Königsberg* as she lay at anchor at Zanzibar. The guns of the *Königsberg* outranged those of the *Pegasus* and she scored telling hits on the British cruiser which began taking on water within eight minutes of the bombardment beginning. Outranged and outgunned, with no hope of fending off or of defeating the German cruiser, the commanding officer of the *Pegasus*, Captain John Ingles, decided to strike the ship's colours.[50] The striking of the colours aboard HMS *Pegasus* was the first occasion in over 100 years that a British ship had surrendered. To compound matters, the humiliating act was played out in full view of the citizenry of Zanzibar.

Retribution for HMS *Pegasus* was achieved on 11 July 1915 when the *Königsberg* was scuttled in the Rufiji delta after she was engaged by the monitors HMS *Mersey* and *Seven* which had been towed to the Rufiji from Malta for the purpose.[51] Despite the surrender and sinking of the *Pegasus* being addressed and the score with the *Königsberg* being settled, the Admiralty no doubt felt that British prestige at Zanzibar needed to be restored.

Another port of call for the squadron was to be Singapore. When the First World War broke out in Europe in 1914, Japan, despite opposition from the army which was by and large pro-German, decided to act in support of Great Britain in accordance with the Anglo-Japanese Alliance. Those in power in Japan recognised the opportunity that lay before them to enrich Japan at the expense of Germany and to gain a foothold in China without fear of active intervention by European powers. German concessions on the Shantung Peninsula were quickly captured along with German colonies in the Marshall, Caroline, and Mariana Islands. In 1915, Japan issued her 'Twenty-one Demands' to China, providing the world with the first warning of her desire to dominate China and the Far East politically and commercially. Both Britain and the United States reacted strongly to the demands prompting the Japanese to modify their demands, although she did wrest from China concessions both in the Shantung Peninsula and in southern Manchuria. The demands made on China marked a new and ambitious Japanese foreign policy.[52]

At the Paris Peace Conference, Japan was permitted to keep her concessions in China and was given a mandate under the League of Nations over the Mariana, Caroline, and Marshall Islands, excepting Guam which remained a possession of the United States. At the same time, Australia was given a mandate over the Bismarck Archipelago and northern New Guinea while New Zealand was given the German Samoan Islands. Finally, a mandate over Nauru was to be held jointly by Britain, Australia, and New Zealand.[53]

At the end of the First World War, the US and Japanese navies were left as the second and third largest navies respectively. With the growth of these two naval forces, the balance of power shifted from the Atlantic and Mediterranean to the Pacific. This was of particular concern to Britain for the growth of American and Japanese naval power and the change of focus to the Pacific threatened the sea communications between Britain, India, Australia, and New Zealand. It therefore became desirable that the Royal Navy station a fleet in the Far East.

With the end of the First World War, it was assumed that no major conflict was likely to be fought for approximately ten years. With this, and the financial constraints faced by Britain, the British government considered it neither necessary nor possible to maintain two fleets of adequate strength situated in the eastern and western hemispheres. As a compromise, it was decided that the Royal Navy would maintain fleets in the Atlantic and home waters, and in the Mediterranean from where they could be sent to reinforce the Far East if the need arose.

In order to implement this policy, a naval base with the facilities necessary for the maintenance of a modern fleet defended against likely forms of attack was required. At the time, no such base existed in the Far East; the only existing naval base in the area had been established in Hong Kong, where the docking and repair facilities were insufficient. Furthermore, in Hong Kong, only a limited scale of defence was deemed possible. Added to this, Hong Kong was situated too close to Japanese naval bases and airfields in Formosa and was remote from the nearest source of British reinforcement making it strategically unsound.

In 1921, the Committee of Imperial Defence examined the strategic situation in the Far East and concluded that no possibility existed of developing Hong Kong to be sufficiently secure against assault. Therefore, it was no longer considered as an adequate base for a British fleet in the Far East; an alternative and more suitable location was needed. Both Sydney and Singapore were considered as options. After examining both locations in detail, the committee recommended that Singapore was strategically the best situation for control of the lines of communication in the Indian Ocean and southern Pacific and so should be developed.[54]

At the time, only weak defences existed in Singapore, at the commercial port in Keppel Harbour. The defences around the harbour were designed to meet an attack by a squadron of cruisers and a raiding party of approximately two thousand men. Having reviewed the strategic placement of Singapore, the Committee of Imperial Defence decided that the challenges of defence did not appear to offer any particular difficulties. On 16 June 1921, the Cabinet accepted the recommendation of the committee for the development of Singapore. A few days later, at the Imperial Conference, the attendees were informed of the British government's decision.[55] The following year, the siting of the proposed naval base was considered. Two possible sites existed: the existing commercial port at Keppel Harbour or a site in the Johore Strait which was recommended by the Admiralty. The latter site recommended by the Admiralty was approved by the Cabinet in February 1923.[56]

The strategic situation in the Pacific was reviewed at the Imperial Conference of 1923. The review was conducted against the background of the Washington Naval Treaty with special attention paid to the need for a naval base in Singapore. The representatives of Australia, New Zealand, and India took a particular interest in the project and advocated work being started immediately, with agreement forthcoming that despite the financial considerations that the British government was being forced to make, the development work should proceed with as little delay as possible.[57] Against this backdrop, it was decided that the squadron would call at Singapore.

Australia, New Zealand, and Canada were all to be visited with the squadron making port calls at several cities in each country. When he learned of the proposed cruise, Sir Auckland Geddes, the British ambassador to the United States, wrote to the Admiralty with the suggestion that the squadron call at New York, Newport, and Rhode Island while sailing from the Caribbean to Canada, suggesting, 'The effect of the visit of two of His Majesty's ships of the size of the *Hood* and *Repulse* would, I am confident, create an excellent impression'.[58] The Admiralty, on the other hand did not share the same view as Geddes, suggesting instead that 'the presence of our latest battle-cruisers might only serve to stimulate naval ambitions [in the United States]'.[59] The Foreign Office shared the view maintained by the Admiralty and went so far as to point out that a 'visit to New York by two of the latest British capital ships' at a time when Congress was in the midst of discussing the naval budget of the United States could serve to act as 'propaganda in favour of an increase in naval power … as intense as ever in the United States' which would encourage the United States to engage in a naval arms race that Britain could not ignore but ultimately would not be able to win.[60] Instead, it was decided that while the battlecruisers would call into ports in the United States, they would be limited to calls at Hawaii and San Francisco, far removed from the centres of American naval and political power.[61]

Closely tied to the debate that surrounded the ports to be visited by the squadron were discussions regarding the weather, in particular in the West Indies. The issue of the weather was first raised on 9 May 1923 by Loder-Symonds when he noted that as the proposed scheduled then stood, the squadron would visit the West Indies during the hurricane season. In an effort to avoid the hurricane season, it was proposed that the cruise commence two months later than was originally proposed, with the ships departing Portsmouth in the middle of January 1924 to arrive in Jamaica in October when the hurricane season had passed. Such a proposal added further complications; one Admiralty memorandum questioned whether delaying the visit of the squadron to the West Indies until October would be at the detriment of the squadron's visit to Quebec. On 25 June, Admiral Sir Roger Keyes noted:

> The Hurricane Season in the West Indies is from June to October and it is, therefore, inadvisable for [the] Squadron to arrive there until well on in October or early November. As navigation in the Gulf of St. Lawrence is not considered safe after 15th November on account of ice, a visit to Montreal will be impracticable.… A revised programme has been substituted for the one originally attached. Attention has been paid to weather conditions so far as possible, but it is impracticable in a cruise of such dimensions to ensure good weather seasons being encountered everywhere.[62]

Discussion and debate regarding the weather would continue throughout June before it was finally decided that the squadron would embark upon the cruise in November 1923.

While the ships that would comprise the squadron and the ports to be visited had been decided upon, by October 1923, one month before the cruise was

Planning the Cruise 25

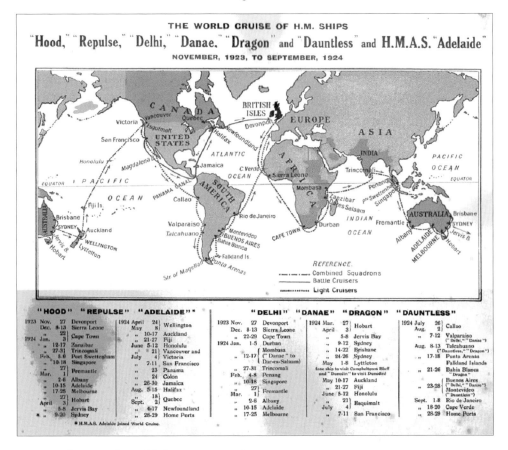

(*Empire Photographic Publishing, Steve Locks*)

scheduled to begin, there still remained details to be agreed upon, namely who would command the squadron, and the name that was to be given to the squadron.

In a memorandum on 9 October to Amery and the first, second, and fourth sea lords, the naval secretary, Rear Admiral Sir Michael Hodges, stated his thoughts that the squadron be 'placed under the command of Rear Admiral Field who should then have the status of a "Rear Admiral in Command of a large Independent Command".' The memorandum went on to detail the privileges that this command status would bestow upon Field, including direct dealings with the Admiralty, the adjustment of table money as desirable, and authorising the increase of allowances of staff members who have additional duties to undertake. The memorandum concluded with the line, 'The question of the title of the Squadron, i.e. Detached of Flying Squadron will need to be considered'.[63]

In reply, the head of the military branch within the department of the permanent secretary of the Admiralty wrote that it was agreed that Field would be appointed the commanding officer of the squadron and would be given the status of a flag officer in command of a detached squadron and that for the purpose of the cruise, he would serve as vice-admiral commanding. On the subject of the name of the squadron, it was recorded:

> The question arises of a suitable title for the combined squadron. Titles traditional in the Royal Navy for squadrons sent on detached service are 'Particular Service Squadron' or 'Special Service Squadron'. Of these the latter is considered preferable.
>
> 3. Should it be considered necessary to give a title more definitive of the object of the cruise, 'Empire Cruise Squadron' is suggested. The designation 'Imperial Cruise Squadron' would be more euphonious, but would be technically incorrect, as the ships and ships' companies participating in the cruise will be British, and particular care has always been taken to avoid the use of the word 'Imperial' in circumstances in which Dominion susceptibilities might be aroused. It seems desirable to avoid using any title which might be in the least controversial, and on the whole the designation 'Special Service Squadron' is suggested as the most suitable.[64]

So it was that the combined squadron would embark on the cruise under the title of the Special Service Squadron.

On 24 October, Field was officially informed of his appointment as the admiral selected to head up the cruise:

> I am commanded by My Lords Commissioners of the Admiralty to acquaint you that they have selected you to assume Command of the Battle Cruiser Squadron and the 1st Light Cruiser Squadron, during the forthcoming World Cruise.
>
> 2. These Squadrons will be constituted a detached Squadron with the title of 'Special Service' Squadron on 5th November, on which date you are to assume Command of the combined Squadron. You will be given the Acting rank of Vice Admiral to date 5th November and you are to hoist your Vice Admiral's Flag in H.M.S. *Hood* on that date accordingly.
>
> 3. A further communication will be made regarding your Court Martial Warrant, Table Money, Flag and other allowances etc.
>
> 4. On and after the 5th November official correspondence intended for you will be addressed to the Vice Admiral Commanding Special Service Squadron. The title Rear Admiral Commanding, 1st Light Cruiser Squadron will remain unchanged and correspondence will be addressed accordingly.[65]

With Field formally appointed to command the cruise, the final preparations were made. As part of the final preparations, some of the ships that were to comprise the Special Service Squadron were taken in hand for minor refits and repairs to be made. HMS *Dauntless* underwent a minor refit at Chatham in October alongside HMS *Danae* and *Dragon*. HMS *Hood*, meanwhile, was taken in hand while at Devonport between 5 and 26 November to undergo a minor refit before embarking on the cruise.

2

The Ships of the Squadron

The previous chapter has detailed how the ships that composed the Special Service Squadron were selected for inclusion in the cruise. It is the purpose of this chapter to briefly outline the history of each of the vessels which composed the squadron.

HMS *Hood*

HMS *Hood* was a product of the First World War. The only ship of her class, the *Hood* was to prove to be the final battlecruiser constructed for the Royal Navy. The contract for the construction of the *Hood* was awarded to the John Brown & Co. works at Clydebank which had been responsible for the construction of the battlecruisers HMS *Inflexible*, *Tiger*, and HMAS *Australia*, the battleship HMS *Barham*, and the liners RMS *Lusitania* and *Aquitania*.

The immediate origins of the *Hood* can be traced back to a note drafted by the then controller of the navy, Admiral Sir Frederick Tudor, to the director of naval construction, Sir Eustace Tennyson d'Eyncourt, in October 1915. In the note, Tudor requested a series of designs for an experimental battleship based on the *Queen Elizabeth*-class battleships, which incorporated the latest advances in underwater protection and sea keeping. Between November 1915 and January 1916, d'Eyncourt oversaw the evolution of five designs, the most promising of which had a greatly enlarged hull and beam. The studies made by d'Eyncourt were rejected by the commander-in-chief of the Royal Navy's Grand Fleet, Admiral Sir John Jellicoe, in a lengthy memorandum. As part of his rejection of d'Eyncourt's studies, Jellicoe pointed out that while the Grand Fleet had a marked superiority over the German High Seas Fleet, it did not have an answer to the Imperial German Navy's 13.8-inch gun *Mackensen*-class battlecruisers which were then under construction.[1]

In February 1916, six further designs were produced which were based on the earlier studies, highlighting an enlarged hull and beam in order to reduce draught and emphasising speed over protection. Of the six designs produced in February 1916, one was selected for further development which itself resulted in two

HMS *Hood* photographed during her speed trials, March 1920. (*Richard Toffolo*)

further designs being produced in March that year. The second of these designs, 'Design B', received approval from the Admiralty on 7 April 1916 and was upon which the ship that was to become HMS *Hood* was based.[2] The design approved by the Admiralty was named the *Admiral*-class battlecruiser and was to be a class of four vessels. Ultimately, the *Hood* would be the only vessel of the class to be constructed, the other three vessels being laid down but later scrapped.

The *Hood* was a large warship; indeed, at the time of her construction, she was the largest warship ever constructed for the Royal Navy and when launched would be the largest ship in the world.

It has often been written that the keel of the *Hood* was laid down as the battlecruisers of Admiral David Beatty's Battlecruiser Squadron sailed into action at Jutland. This is nothing more than a legend. Work did not begin on ship No. 460 as she was referred to, until 1 September 1916.[3] Lessons learned following the loss of the battlecruisers *Indefatigable*, *Queen Mary*, and *Invincible* during the Battle of Jutland were incorporated into the design of the *Hood*. Revised design plans were drawn up and submitted by d'Eyncourt in early July 1916, which were accepted by the Admiralty in early August. The main design changes concerned armour protection. Belt armour was increased from 8 to 12 inches, which was to be angled providing the equivalent of 15 inches of horizontal armour. Armour over the barbettes was increased while a 460-foot-long bulge packed with steel tubing was included which offered protection against torpedoes.[4] Debate on the ship's armour arrangement would, however, continue through to 1918.

HMS *Hood* was launched at 1.05 p.m. on 22 August 1918 by Lady Hood, the widow of Rear Admiral Horace Hood who had been killed aboard HMS

Invincible at Jutland. Having been launched, fitting-out work began, which was completed in December 1919.

The *Hood* had an overall length of 860 feet, 7 inches (262.3 metres), a maximum beam of 104 feet, 2 inches (31.8 metres), which was 95 feet (28.9 metres) at the waterline and a draught of 32 feet (9.8 metres). Her armament consisted of eight 15-inch guns in four twin turrets, a weapon which would be fitted and utilised aboard British capital ships between 1915 and 1959. The 15-inch guns fitted to HMS *Hood* were the same as those fitted to the *Queen Elizabeth*-class battleships. Where the two differed, however, were in the gun mounts. The *Queen Elizabeth*-class used the BL 15-inch Mk I which had been specifically designed for the class in order to counter the new generation of Imperial German Navy dreadnoughts under construction. HMS *Hood*, by contrast, had her Mk I guns housed in a unique mounting referred to as the Mk II which incorporated a number of design improvements which allowed the guns to be elevated to 30-degrees, included flash doors in the gun loading hoist and telescopic sights among other improvements.[5] It may be noted that the *Hood* was the only vessel to have Mk I guns fitted in the specifically designed Mk II housing. Capable of firing a salvo every thirty seconds, she could fire a shell weighing 1,920 pounds (870 kg) 17.4 miles (27.6 km).

As a secondary armament, the *Hood* was equipped with twelve 5.5-inch guns which were mounted along the upper deck and on the forward shelter deck. As a defence against aircraft, the ship was fitted with eight high-angle 4-inch anti-aircraft guns. In addition to her guns, the *Hood* was also equipped with two submerged torpedo tubes located below the waterline just forward of 'A' turret and four above water torpedo tubes, parallel with the main mast. The torpedo tubes were divided evenly to port and starboard.

Following being fitted out, the *Hood* was towed down the river Clyde on 9 January 1920 to Greenock from where she sailed to conduct her first trials off the Isle of Arran before heading to Rosyth for inspection work. Official sea trials began on 8 March off the Isle of Arran. During her sea trials, *Hood* attained a speed of 32.07 knots, giving her the distinction of not only being the largest ship in the word, but also the most powerful in the world by some margin. Following the trials, the ship returned to Rosyth where she was once more inspected before being commissioned into service on 29 March and became flagship of the Royal Navy's Battlecruiser Squadron on 18 May 1920. The final cost to the British government for the construction of the *Hood* was £6,025,000, the equivalent of £344,532,724.51 in 2023.

The end of 1920 saw the *Hood* embark on her first official voyage when she departed Portland accompanied by HMS *Tiger* and nine destroyers for a cruise of Scandinavia.[6] Exercises with the fleet and cruises to the Mediterranean followed in 1921. In July 1922, *Hood* was selected alongside HMS *Repulse* to represent the Royal Navy at the centennial celebrations of Brazilian Independence in Rio de Janeiro. The *Hood* and *Repulse* departed Devonport on 14 August and made their way south, arriving at Rio on 3 September. *En route*, the *Hood* crossed the equator for the first time. At Rio, a ceremonial march was held through the city ahead of sporting competitions in a foretaste of things to come.

Builder	John Brown & Company, Clydebank
Laid Down	1 September 1916
Launched	22 August 1918
Commissioned	29 March 1920
Length	860 feet, 7 inches (262.3 m)
Beam	104 feet, 2 inches (31.8 m)
Draught	32 feet (9.8 m)
Displacement (Deep Load)	47,430 tons
Speed	32.07 knots
Range	6,140 miles (9,870 km)
Main Armament	8 × BL 15-inch Mk I guns
Main Armament Range	17.14 miles (27.59 km)
Complement	1,433

HMS *Repulse*

In late 1914, the first sea lord, Admiral of the Fleet John 'Jackie' Fisher, commenced the construction of a huge fleet of specialised craft for his long-held plan for an invasion of the Baltic. The main vessels of this fleet were to be armed with heavy guns, be able to attain a high speed and possess as shallow draught.[7] The battlecruisers of the *Renown*-class were to be the first manifestation of this design theory. The requirements for the design reached the director of naval construction

HMS *Repulse* photographed in late 1916 or early 1917 following her post-trial alterations. The ship is yet to receive her searchlight towers on her aft funnel. (*NH 525, US Naval History and Heritage Command*)

on 14 December 1914. The proposed design was to have a speed of 32 knots and be armed with six 15-inch guns in three twin turrets. On 21 December 1914, the dimensions of the new vessels were decided upon, whereupon Fisher requested that modifications be made.

In the meantime, he wrote to Admiral Jellicoe and requested that the commander-in-chief of the Grand Fleet write back a casual letter pointing out the requirement for more battlecruisers. Jellicoe was happy to do so and Cabinet approval was forthcoming the following day whereupon a model was quickly produced to be inspected by Fisher. On 28 December, such was the pace at which Fisher worked, the director of naval construction was informed that the model was approved and that the design should be started at once.[8]

With the design approved, Fisher went out of his way to ensure that the ships were at sea in the shortest possible timeframe. Fifteen months was the time he insisted upon from the laying of the keel to the commissioning of the ships. To facilitate this incredible demand, it was decided that the machinery of HMS *Tiger* would be duplicated as far as possible with additional boilers being incorporated into the design.[9]

The contract for the construction of the second ship of the class, which was to be HMS *Repulse*, was awarded to John Brown & Co., Clydebank, on 29 December 1914. By 21 January 1915, enough information had been supplied to John Brown & Co. to allow the shipyard to construct the midships portion of the ship to the turn of the bilge, to prepare the main structural drawings, and to order the majority of the steel required for the hull. The keel of the ship was laid on 25 January.[10] A little less than a year later, on 8 January 1916, the *Repulse* was launched and fitting-out work commenced before the ship was completed and formally commissioned on 18 August 1916.

As completed, the *Repulse* had an overall length of 794 feet, 2 inches (242.1 metres), a beam of 90 feet, 1.75 inches (27.5 metres), possessed a draught of 27 feet (8.2 metres), and displaced 27,600 tons (32,740 tons at deep load). Capable of 31.5 knots, the ship was armed with six 15-inch guns in three twin turrets. Supplementing the main armament, the ship was equipped with a secondary armament of seventeen 4-inch guns in five triple and two single mounts and with two torpedo tubes, one to port and one to starboard. The ship's armour protection consisted of belt armour which varied between 3 and 6 inches in thickness and deck armour of between 1 and 2.5 inches.

Sea trials in the Atlantic led to the discovery that the ship's design was weak forward, with Atlantic rollers bending the deck forward and causing it to sink inwards, leading to additional pillars being added to strengthen the forward hull. The funnels of both the *Repulse* and her sister ship HMS *Renown* were altered post-construction. Both ships had originally been fitted with squat funnels in keeping with contemporary designs of the era, but this was found to create difficulties in which funnel smoke hampered fire control and made the bridge untenable at times. Both ships subsequently had their fore funnels raised by 6 feet to rectify these issues.[11]

It was the lack of armour protection which was the greatest cause of concern, particularly so soon after the Battle of Jutland. In October 1916, both the *Renown* and *Repulse* were condemned by Jellicoe who recommended that both ships be immediately sent for modifications. HMS *Repulse* returned to Rosyth, where between 10 November 1916 and 29 January 1917 she was fitted with an additional 500 tons of horizontal armour over the decks, magazines, and steering gear.[12] In late September 1917, *Repulse* underwent another minor refit which saw Carley rafts fitted along with a 12-foot rangefinder tower on the roof of the foretop. HMS *Repulse* became the first capital ship to be fitted with a flying off platform when an experimental one was fitted atop 'B' turret. This was followed by the fitting of another platform atop 'Y' turret in October. All of the changes that the *Repulse* and *Renown* underwent required frequent dockyard visits, and it was not long before the *Renown* and *Repulse* were re-christened *Refit* and *Repair* by the sailors of the Grand Fleet.[13]

During 1917, the Admiralty became increasingly concerned about German efforts in the North Sea to sweep paths through the British-laid minefields intended to restrict the actions of the High Seas Fleet. A preliminary raid conducted by light forces on 31 October destroyed ten light German vessels and prompted the Admiralty to launch a larger operation to destroy German minesweepers and their escorting light cruisers. Based on intelligence reports, the Admiralty decided on 17 November to allocate two light cruiser squadrons, the First Cruiser Squadron covered by the First Battlecruiser Squadron, and the battleships of the First Battle Squadron to the operation. The result was the Second Battle of Heligoland Bight.

The battle began around 7.30 a.m. when lookouts aboard HMS *Courageous* sighted German vessels. The German admiral in command, Hans Hermann Ludwig von Reuter, in command of a force comprised of four light cruisers and eight destroyers advanced towards the British while the minesweepers withdrew. The battle developed into a stern chase as the German forces withdrew to the south-east at high speed behind smokescreens under fire from the First Cruiser, First Light Cruiser and Sixth Light Cruiser Squadrons. HMS *Repulse* was detached from the First Battlecruiser Squadron to close the range and engage. Around 10 a.m., the *Repulse* briefly engaged the light cruiser *Königsberg* and scored a single hit which damaged all three of the ship's funnels, sparked a fire, and caused a reduction in speed to 17 knots. Shortly thereafter, the German battleships *Kaiser* and *Kaiserin* were sighted whereupon the British broke off the pursuit with the *Repulse* covering the withdrawal.[14] During the course of the battle, the *Repulse* fired forty-five 15-inch shells.

On 12 December 1917, the *Repulse* was involved in a collision with HMAS *Australia*, for which both ships required repairs.[15] Present at the surrender of the High Seas Fleet at Scapa Flow on 21 November 1918, the *Repulse* began a major refit at Portsmouth on 17 December.[16] The refit was intended to drastically improve the ship's armour protection, increasing the belt armour to 9 inches and deepening the torpedo bulges along the lines of those fitted to HMS *Ramillies*.

Three 30-foot rangefinders were also added along with eight torpedo tubes in twin mounts on the upper deck while the flying off platforms were removed. Recommissioned into service on 1 January 1921, during the following year, the *Repulse* accompanied HMS *Hood* to Rio de Janeiro to partake in the centenary celebrations of Brazilian independence.

Builder	John Brown & Company, Clydebank
Laid Down	25 January 1915
Launched	8 January 1916
Commissioned	18 August 1916
Length	794 feet, 2 inches (242.1 metres)
Beam	90 feet, 1.75 inches (27.5 metres)
Draught	27 feet (8.2 metres)
Displacement (Deep Load)	32,740 tons
Speed	31.5 knots
Range	4,200 miles (6,760 kilometres)
Main Armament	6 × BL 15-inch Mk I guns
Main Armament Range	13.48 miles (21.7 km)
Complement	1,222

HMS *Danae*

The lead ship of her class of light cruisers, HMS *Danae* was laid down on 11 December 1916 at the Armstrong Whitworth shipyard at Walker on Tyneside. Armed with 6-inch guns, the *Danae*-class was based on the preceding C-class cruisers but featured a hull which was lengthened by 20 feet to accommodate a sixth gun between the bridge and fore funnel, giving the ships of the class an 'A', 'B', 'P', 'Q', 'X', and 'Y' arrangement. In addition to this, the twin torpedo tubes of the C-class were replaced by triple mounts, providing the *Danae*-class with twelve torpedo tubes, the heaviest torpedo armament carried by cruisers anywhere in the world at the time.

Named after Danaë, an Argive princess and mother of Perseus in Greek mythology, HMS *Danae* was launched on 26 January 1918 and commissioned later that year on 22 July. Following being commissioned, the *Danae* was attached to the Harwich-based Fifth Light Cruiser Squadron. As part of the Fifth Light Cruiser Squadron, she took part in several patrols in the North Sea during the final months of the First World War. In October and November 1919, the ship saw service in the Baltic, where alongside HMS *Dragon* and *Dauntless*, she provided support to the forces of the Russian Republic, known as the Whites, during the Russian Civil War. In February 1920, HMS *Danae* was transferred to the First Light Cruiser Squadron of the Atlantic Fleet.

HMS *Danae* at sea, *circa* 1937.

Builder	Armstrong Whitworth, Wallsend
Laid Down	1 December 1916
Launched	26 January 1918
Length	445 feet (136 metres)
Beam	46 feet, 5 inches (14.2 metres)
Draught	14 feet, 5 inches (4.4 metres)
Displacement (Deep Load)	5,603 tons
Speed	29 knots
Range	7,700 miles (12,400 km)
Main Armament	6 × BL 6-inch 45 Calibre Mk XII guns
Main Armament Range	12.21 miles (19.66 km)
Complement	462

HMS *Dauntless*

Part of the original batch of three *Danae*-class cruisers ordered in September 1916 under the War Emergency Programme, HMS *Dauntless* was constructed by Palmers Shipbuilding and Iron Company in Jarrow on Tyneside. Laid down on 3 January 1917, the ship was launched on 10 April 1918. The ship was completed with a hanger to accommodate a floatplane under the bridge, the compass

HMS *Dauntless* photographed alongside at the Royal Naval Dockyard, Bermuda, in 1930.

platform being on top. The hanger would be removed in 1920. Commissioned into service on 22 November 1918, the ship missed out on seeing action in the First World War. In 1919, HMS *Dauntless* was assigned to operate in the Baltic against Bolshevik revolutionaries and in support of White forces in the Russian Civil War. Following service in the Baltic, *Dauntless* was attached to the West Indies Station before being assigned to the Atlantic Fleet as part of the First Light Cruiser Squadron.

Builder	Palmer Shipbuilding and Iron Company, Jarrow
Laid Down	3 January 1917
Launched	10 April 1918
Commissioned	22 November 1918
Length	471 feet (144 metres)
Beam	46 feet (14 metres)
Draught	14 feet, 5 inches (4.4 metres)
Displacement (Deep Load)	4,650 tons
Speed	29 knots
Range	2,300 miles (4,300 km)
Main Armament	6 × BL 6-inch 45 Calibre Mk XII guns
Main Armament Range	12.21 miles (19.66 km)
Complement	462

HMS *Dragon*

The third ship of the *Danae*-class ordered in September 1916, the contract for the construction of HMS *Dragon* was awarded to the Scotts Shipbuilding and Engineering Company, Greenock. The keel was laid down on 24 January 1917. Launched on 29 December 1917, it was not until 10 August 1918 that the ship was commissioned at Harwich dockyard. Like HMS *Dauntless*, *Dragon* was completed with a hanger to accommodate a floatplane beneath the bridge. Attached to the Fifth Light Cruiser Squadron, HMS *Dragon* saw service in the North Sea and on 9 November 1918 engaged German seaplanes off Heligoland Bight.

Following the cessation of hostilities, in August 1919, HMS *Dragon* escorted HMS *Renown* to Canada as the latter transported the prince of Wales on a royal tour. Between 13 and 17 August 1919, *Dragon* embarked the prince of Wales and took him to St John's, Newfoundland, and then to Halifax, where he re-embarked aboard the *Renown*.[17] Returning to Britain in September, *Dragon* formed part of a task force which provided assistance to Latvian and Estonian forces against Bolshevik and German *Freikorps* forces. While forming part of the British intervention forces, on 17 October, *Dragon* was hit by three shells from a shore battery which resulted in the deaths of nine crew members while five others sustained wounds as the ship operated against German forces attacking Riga.[18] From 1920, the ship operated as part of the First Light Cruiser Squadron attached to the Atlantic Fleet.

HMS *Dragon*. (*302356, Australian War Memorial*)

Builder	Scotts Shipbuilding and Engineering Company
Laid Down	24 January 1917
Launched	29 December 1917
Commissioned	16 August 1918
Length	445 feet (136 metres)
Beam	46 feet, 5 inches (14.2 metres)
Draught	14 feet, 5 inches (4.4 metres)
Displacement (Deep Load)	5,693 tons
Speed	29 knots
Range	2,300 miles (4,300 km)
Main Armament	6 × BL 6-inch 45 Calibre Mk XII guns
Main Armament Range	12.21 miles (19.66 km)
Complement	462

HMS *Delhi*

HMS *Delhi* was one of three *Danae*-class cruisers ordered in July 1917. Laid down at the Armstrong Whitworth yard in Elswick, Newcastle upon Tyne, on 29 October 1917, the ship was launched on 23 August 1918. The fitting-out work saw the cruiser provided with flying-off platforms aft for wheeled aircraft. The fitting-out work lasted into the following year with *Delhi* not being completed and commissioned until June 1919, too late to see action during the First World War.

HMS *Delhi* photographed in 1930 while at Vancouver during a tour of Canada. (*CVA 447-4206.2, Walter E. Frost, City of Vancouver Archives*)

Following the completion of her sea trials, HMS *Delhi* was attached to the First Light Cruiser Squadron as part of the Atlantic Fleet, during which time she was worked up. While part of the First Light Cruiser Squadron, *Delhi* was dispatched to the Baltic as part of the British interventionist forces engaged in the Russian Civil War. Following service in the Baltic, the *Delhi* returned to Britain.

Builder	Armstrong Whitworth, Newcastle upon Tyne
Laid Down	29 October 1917
Launched	23 August 1918
Commissioned	7 June 1919
Length	445 feet (136 metres)
Beam	46 feet, 6 inches (14.17 metres)
Draught	14 feet, 4 inches (4.4 metres)
Displacement (Deep Load)	4,927 tons
Speed	29 knots
Range	7,700 miles (12,400 km)
Main Armament	6 × BL 6-inch 45 Calibre Mk XII guns
Main Armament Range	12.21 miles (19.66 km)
Complement	469

HMS *Dunedin*

Ordered in July 1917, HMS *Dunedin* was laid down on 5 November 1917 at the Armstrong Whitworth works at Elswick. Launched on 19 November 1918, eight days following the armistice, she was christened *Dunedin*, a Scottish Gaelic name

HMS *Dunedin*.

The Ships of the Squadron 39

for the capital of Scotland anglicised as Edinburgh. The ship has so far been the only ship of the Royal Navy to be named *Dunedin*, while seven vessels have carried the name *Edinburgh*. Following being launched, HMS *Dunedin* was fitted out at Hawthorn, Leslie and Company at Hebburn on Tyneside before proceeding to Devonport Royal Dockyard, where she was commissioned on 13 September 1919.

Following working up, in October 1920, HMS *Dunedin* was dispatched alongside three other vessels to assure the protection of workers unloading munitions in the Free City of Danzig (modern day Gdańsk) intended for Polish separatist forces.

Builder	Armstrong Whitworth, Newcastle upon Tyne
Laid Down	5 November 1917
Launched	19 November 1918
Commissioned	13 September 1919
Length	445 feet (136 metres)
Beam	46 feet, 6 inches (14.17 metres)
Draught	46 feet, 6 inches (14.17 metres)
Displacement (Deep Load)	5,603 tons
Speed	29 knots
Range	2300 miles (4,300 km)
Main Armament	6 × BL 6-inch L/45 Mk XII
Main Armament Range	12.21 miles (19.66 km)
Complement	462

HMAS *Adelaide*

HMAS *Adelaide* was a modified version of the *Chatham* sub-class of Town-class light cruisers.[19] Armed with nine 6-inch guns, a 3-inch anti-aircraft gun, a 12-pounder 8-cwt field gun, two 21-inch torpedo tubes, and two depth charge chutes, the ship had an overall length of 462 feet, 6.5 inches (140.9 metres), a beam of 49 feet, 9.5 inches (15.17 metres), and a draught of 19.66 feet (5.9 metres).[20] Powered by Parsons turbines, *Adelaide* had a maximum speed of 25 knots.

Laid down at the Cockatoo Island Dockyard in Sydney on 20 November 1915, HMAS *Adelaide* was launched on 27 July 1918 by Lady Helen Munro Ferguson, the wife of Sir Munro Ferguson, the governor-general of Australia.[21] Following the launching of the hull, the fitting-out work and completion encountered severe delays due to the loss of important forgings for the turbines and other machinery parts which were lost as a result of enemy action. The lost forgings and equipment could not be constructed in Australia at the time and owing to wartime conditions, replacement parts could not be immediately dispatched, taking two years to reach Sydney. In addition to this, based on wartime experiences, it was decided to incorporate extensive modifications into the *Adelaide*, which further

HMAS *Adelaide*. (*Royal Australian Navy*)

delayed the ship's completion. Such was the length of time taken to fit out and complete the *Adelaide* that she was nicknamed 'HMAS *Long Delayed*'.[22] HMAS *Adelaide* was finally commissioned into service with the Royal Australian Navy on 5 August 1922.

Following being commissioned, *Adelaide* underwent a brief period of sea trials and working up off Jervis Bay. Declared operational, HMAS *Adelaide* spent the period from her commissioning until February 1924 operating on standard duties and conducting exercises throughout the Australian Station.[23] Between February and mid-April 1924, *Adelaide* was taken in hand for a brief refit before joining the Special Service Squadron.

Builder	Cockatoo Island Dockyard, Sydney
Laid Down	20 November 1915
Launched	27 July 1918
Commissioned	5 August 1922
Length	455 feet (138.8 metres)
Beam	49 feet (14.9 metres)
Draught	19 feet (5.7 metres)
Displacement (Deep Load)	5,560 tons
Speed	25 knots
Range	4,760 miles (7,670 km)
Main Armament	9 × 6-inch Mk XII guns
Main Armament Range	12.21 miles (19.66 km)
Complement	483

3

Admirals and Captains

It is the purpose of this chapter to provide an overview of the admirals and captains of the vessels that formed the Special Service Squadron.

Vice-Admiral Sir Frederick Field

Frederick Laurence Field was born in Killarney, County Kerry, on 18 April 1871. Privately educated, Field joined the Royal Navy as a cadet in 1884 at HMS *Britannia*.[1] Two years later, he was posted to the armoured frigate HMS *Minotaur* in the Channel Squadron as a midshipman. A transfer to the China Station followed in March 1888, in which Field saw service first aboard HMS *Imperieuse* and then the corvette HMS *Constance*. Promoted to sub-lieutenant in November 1890, Field was posted to the iron-clad HMS *Dreadnought* as part of the Mediterranean Fleet in April 1892, and a year later, he was promoted to lieutenant.[2] Following being promoted to lieutenant, Field saw service in the Training Squadron before attending the torpedo school at HMS *Vernon* in November 1895.

A period serving on the directing staff of the torpedo school HMS *Defiance* followed before Field was appointed as the torpedo officer aboard HMS *Barfleur* on the China Station in July 1898. While serving aboard HMS *Barfleur*, the Boxer Rebellion broke out. The Boxer Rebellion was an armed insurrection lasting from 1899 to 1901 initiated by the Militia United in Righteousness, who were more commonly known as the Boxers because many of their members had practiced Chinese martial arts which was referred to in the western world at the time as Chinese boxing. A number of factors combined to cause the insurrection; extreme weather, Western attempts at colonising China, and anti-imperialist sentiment fuelled the movement. Alongside this, in northern China, a major source of discontent was missionary activity. The result was the Boxer Rebellion, fought by the Boxers and Qing empire against the Eight Nation Alliance comprised of Great Britain and the British empire, the United States, Germany, France, Austria-Hungary, Italy, Japan, and Russia.[3] During the Boxer Rebellion, Field was mentioned in dispatches for leading a raiding party which landed at Tianjin tasked with repairing damaged trains under heavy fire. During this action, Field was wounded.

Promotion to commander followed on 26 June 1902. On that same date, Field was posted to command the torpedo boat *Jaseur* before in August that same year, he was posted to HMS *Albion* on the China Station. Promoted to captain at the end of 1907, Field was appointed the commanding officer of the torpedo school HMS *Defiance*, a position he held until 1910 when he was appointed to command HMS *Duncan* as flag captain to Admiral Thomas Martyn Jerram, the commander-in-chief, Mediterranean Fleet.

The outbreak of the First World War in August 1914 found Field as the commanding officer of HMS *Vernon* before he was appointed to HMS *King George V*, the flagship of the Grand Fleet's Second Battle Squadron, where he served once more as flag captain to Jerram. As captain of the *King George V*, he partook in the Battle of Jutland, during which we was applauded for 'the great skill with which he handled the *King George V*, as leader of the line [of battle], under very difficult conditions'.[4] Appointed a companion of the Order of the Bath on 15 September 1916, Field was appointed chief of staff to Vice-Admiral Sir Charles Madden, the admiral commanding the First Battle Squadron. Field held this position until June 1918 when he was appointed to the Admiralty as the director of torpedoes and mining.[5] On 26 October 1918, he was appointed as a naval aide-de-camp to King George V.

Promoted to rear admiral on 11 February 1919, Field became the third sea lord and controller of the navy in March 1920.[6] Awarded a knighthood in the 1923 New Year Honours, on 15 May 1923, he was appointed as the admiral commanding the Royal Navy's Battlecruiser Squadron, where he flew his flag in HMS *Hood*.[7] Given the acting rank of vice-admiral shortly before the beginning of the cruise, on 26 September 1924, shortly before the ships arrived back to Britain, Field would be confirmed in the rank.

Vice-Admiral Sir Frederick Field.

Rear Admiral Sir Hubert Brand

Hubert George Brand was born on 20 May 1870 into a distinguished family. His father, Henry Brand, 2nd Viscount Hampden, was the governor of New South Wales between November 1895 and March 1899 while his grandfather, Henry Brand, 1st Viscount Hampden, was speaker of the House of Commons from 1872 to 1884. Brand joined the Royal Navy in 1883. In November 1897, Brand, then a sub-lieutenant, was given his first command, the torpedo boat HMS *Contest*. Promoted to lieutenant on 30 June 1892, Brand relinquished command of HMS *Contest* when he was appointed as the commanding officer of HMS *Griffon*, an appointment he held for two years.

Promoted to commander in 1902 and given command of the destroyer *Success*, in August 1903, he was appointed a member of the fourth class of the Royal Victorian Order by King Edward VII. A series of destroyer commands followed until December 1904. During this period, while commanding officer of HMS *Cherwell*, the ship visited Kiel where valuable intelligence on German destroyer equipment and practices was obtained. From 1905, Brand spent three years aboard the battleship *Britannia*. Promoted to captain in December 1907, he was appointed to command the protected cruiser *Blenheim* and then the armoured cruiser *Good Hope* in February 1909, at which time he served as flag captain to Rear Admiral Frederick Hamilton, the admiral commanding, First Cruiser Squadron.

On 7 February 1911, Brand was appointed as the commanding officer of the scout cruiser HMS *Bellona* and as captain (D), Second Destroyer Flotilla. On 9 October 1912, Brand succeeded Captain Sir Douglas Brownrigg as the British naval attaché in Tokyo, a position he held until the beginning of December 1914. During the course of the First World War, Brand held a number of positions within

Rear Admiral Sir Hubert Brand. (*NPG x165468, National Portrait Gallery*)

the Admiralty and at sea. From February 1915 until June 1916, he served as the naval assistant to the second sea lord before being appointed as the chief of staff to the admiral commanding, Battlecruiser Fleet, Vice-Admiral Sir David Beatty. Brand's tenure as the chief of staff to the admiral commanding, Battlecruiser Fleet was brief as in December 1916, he was appointed captain of the fleet, Grand Fleet, a position he held until 6 March 1919 when he was appointed as the commanding officer of HMY *Victoria and Albert*.

On 12 February 1919, Brand was promoted to rear admiral and two months later, in recognition of his services during the First World War, was knighted. At the beginning of May, Brand was appointed as the rear admiral commanding HM yachts, a position he held until 15 April 1922, when he was appointed as the admiral commanding, First Light Cruiser Squadron.

Captain John Im Thurn

John Knowles Im Thurn was born on 7 March 1881 and joined the Royal Navy in January 1895. Promoted to lieutenant on 15 January 1902, in August that year, he was posted to the Mediterranean Fleet to serve aboard the torpedo boat depot ship HMS *Vulcan*. During the First World War, Im Thurn's service saw him predominated with wireless telegraph and signalling duties. Promoted to captain on 30 June 1918, following the signing of the armistice in November 1918, Im Thurn held several staff appointments, principally as assistant director of electrical torpedo and mining, a position he held until 1920, and then as director of the signal department.

Im Thurn would remain the director of the signal department until 1921, when he was appointed as the commanding officer of the light cruiser *Ceres* before being selected to command HMS *Hood* as Field's flag captain.[8]

Captain John Im Thurn. (*Steve Locks*)

Captain Henry Parker

Henry Wise Parker was born on 15 June 1875. Following enlisting in the Royal Navy, on 8 July 1896, Parker, then a sub-lieutenant, was given his first command when he was placed in command of the torpedo boat T.B. 66 for the annual manoeuvres of 1896.[9] Promoted to lieutenant, Parker was given command of the torpedo boat HMS *Haughty* for the annual manoeuvres of 1904 and in 1908 was promoted to commander. Promoted to captain on 30 June 1914, in January 1915, he was appointed as the commanding officer of the depot ship *Hecla*. Parker did not remain as the commanding officer of the *Hecla* for long as on 24 August 1915, he took up a new position as the commanding officer of the *Iron Duke*-class battleship HMS *Benbow*, the flagship of Admiral Sir Frederick Doveton Sturdee, the admiral commanding, Fourth Battle Squadron.[10]

Commanding the *Benbow*, Parker saw action during the Battle of Jutland, where the ship was stationed towards the centre of the British line.[11] In June 1916, Parker relinquished command of *Benbow* when he was appointed to HMS *Hercules*. Following the end of the war, in April 1919, Parker was appointed to the new position of captain of the fleet, Atlantic and Home Fleets, following the dispersal of the Grand Fleet on 7 April. With the dispersal of the Grand Fleet, the fleet in home waters was divided between the new Atlantic Fleet, which was comprised of the navy's most powerful units, and the Home Fleet, which consisted of ships with nucleus crews and other units in home ports. Parker held this position until 1 August 1921. In February 1922, Parker served at the Admiralty as the director of the operations division before being appointed as the commanding officer of HMS *Repulse* on 21 November 1923.

Captain Henry Parker. (*Steve Locks*)

Captain James Pipon

James Murray Pipon was born on 25 October 1882. His father, John Pipon (1849–1899), was also an officer in the Royal Navy. Pipon underwent entrance examinations in July 1897 and gained entrance to Britannia Royal Naval College in August of that same year. Promoted to lieutenant on 31 August 1904, in August 1912, he was promoted to lieutenant-commander. Appointed to the light cruiser HMS *Penelope* in late 1914, Pipon was promoted to commander the following year. Service aboard the light cruiser *Lowestoft* followed, where Pipon served as flag commander and undertook war staff duties before being promoted to captain on 31 August 1920. On 28 August 1922, he took command of HMS *Delhi*, his first command.

Captain Francis Austin

Francis Murray Austin was born on 10 September 1881. Having joined the Royal Navy, in May 1902, he was promoted to the rank of lieutenant. Until 1913, Austin served as the gunnery officer aboard the *Bellerophon*-class battleship HMS *Temeraire*. Promoted to commander on 31 December 1913, on 23 January 1918, he took command of the cruiser HMS *Leviathan*, during which time he also served as chief of staff to Commodore Gaunt. Austin's time as the commanding officer of the *Leviathan* was short as in May 1918, he took command of the cruiser *Astraea*. Austin would serve as the commanding officer of the *Astraea* until she was paid off on 1 July 1919 to be sold the following year and broken up. On 30 June 1919, Austin was promoted to captain and on 28 August 1923 took command of HMS *Danae*.

Captain Charles Round-Turner

Little is known about Charles Wolfran Round-Turner. Born on 6 April 1879, he qualified as a gunnery officer at HMS *Excellent*. Promoted to captain, his first command was HMS *Dauntless*, aboard which he served as commanding officer from 15 April 1922 until October 1924.

Captain Bernard Fairbairn

The eldest son of Reverend W. M. Fairbairn, Bernard William Murray Fairbairn was born on 18 April 1880. Following joining the Royal Navy, Fairbairn was promoted to the rank of lieutenant in July 1901 and to lieutenant-commander on 15 July 1909. On 9 January 1913, he was appointed to the armoured cruiser HMS *Cochrane*, then attached to the Second Cruiser Squadron, in the dual position of first officer and gunnery officer. Promoted to commander, Fairbairn departed the cruiser on 6 November 1915, when he was superseded as gunnery officer.

Above left: Captain James Pipon. (*Steve Locks*)

Above right: Captain Francis Austin. (*Steve Locks*)

Captain Charles Round-Turner. (*Steve Locks*)

Captain Bernard Fairbairn. (*Steve Locks*)

Following leaving HMS *Cochrane*, Fairbairn would find himself largely sidelined from the war for around two and a half years, during which time he was appointed to the Admiralty to provide gunnery expertise to Captain Morgan Singer, the director of naval ordnance. In late July 1918, Fairbairn took up a new appointment as the gunnery officer aboard HMS *Warspite*.

Fairbairn would see out the remainder of the war aboard *Warspite*. On 30 June 1919, he was promoted to captain and departed the ship on 11 July, having been superseded as gunnery officer. In the immediate post-war years, Fairbairn returned to the Admiralty, working with the Gunnery Division of which he served as deputy director from 10 January 1921 until 15 August 1922, when he was given his first sea-going command, HMS *Dragon*.

Captain Alister Beal

Alister Francis Beal was born on 21 March 1875. Upon passing out from HMS *Britannia* in July 1890, he was appointed to the armoured cruiser *Immortalité*, part of the Channel Squadron. An appointment to HMS *Warspite* on the Pacific Station followed. Beal would remain with *Warspite* until June 1893, when the ship was paid off. His evaluation from *Warspite*'s commanding officer, Captain Hedworth Lambton, described Beal as being of 'G[ood] physique, rather lazy, [but] improving'.[12] Promoted to lieutenant in December 1896, he was appointed to HMS *Volage*, as part of the Training Squadron. Promotion to commander was forthcoming in June 1908, whereupon Beal saw service as the commander aboard

HMS *Princess Royal* when she was commissioned at Devonport on 14 November 1912 under Captain Osmond de Beauvoir Brock.

Promoted to captain on 30 June 1915, Beal received his first sea-going command, the light cruiser *Lowestoft*, in January 1918. Beal's tenure as the commanding officer of the *Lowestoft* was brief for the following month, he was appointed as the commanding officer of the light cruiser *Weymouth*. Beal would remain in command of HMS *Weymouth* until the end of August 1921, when he was appointed to the Admiralty as the deputy director of the Operations Division. On 12 July 1923, he was appointed as the commanding officer of HMS *Dunedin* and at the same time was appointed as the commodore of the New Zealand Division.

Captain John Stevenson

John Bryan Stevenson was born on 7 August 1876 in Toxteth Park, Lancaster. Entering the Royal Navy, Stevenson passed out of HMS *Britannia* in July 1892, whereupon he was appointed to the battleship HMS *Camperdown* attached to the Mediterranean Fleet. Stevenson was aboard the *Camperdown* when on 22 June 1893, she collided with the flagship of the Mediterranean Fleet HMS *Victoria*, which sank with the loss of 358 members of her crew.[13]

Promoted to lieutenant on 14 March 1898, in January 1906, Stevenson was given his first command when he was appointed as the commanding officer of the destroyer HMS *Ferret*. Stevenson's time in command of the *Ferret* was brief and on 1 April that year, he relinquished command to Lieutenant Arthur Popham and took up command of another destroyer, HMS *Starfish*. His time in command of HMS *Starfish* was equally as brief for on 21 July, he was appointed as the commanding officer of the tender *Empress* (later renamed HMS *Herron*), a command he would hold until 10 January 1907. Stevenson's next appointment was to the *Duncan*-class pre-dreadnought HMS *Albemarle*, aboard which he served as the torpedo officer and then as the first officer. Promotion to the rank of commander followed on 31 December 1910.

In June 1912, Stevenson was loaned from the Royal Navy to the Australian government and Royal Australian Navy. Severing aboard the cruiser HMS *Encounter*, Stevenson contributed to good battle practice and saw his loan extended for a further two years, during which time the First World War had broken out. Appointed as the commanding officer of Flinders Naval Depot, a Royal Australian Navy training facility which in April 1921 was renamed HMS *Cerberus*, on 1 November 1916, he was given command of HMS *Encounter*.

Following relinquishing command of HMS *Encounter*, Stevenson was transferred to the Royal Australian Navy and promoted to the rank of captain. On 5 August 1922, he was appointed as the commanding officer of HMAS *Adelaide*.

4

'The "Floating Power" of Britain'

On the morning of 27 November 1923, at Devonport and Portsmouth, the *Hood* and *Repulse* along with HMS *Delhi*, *Dauntless*, and *Dunedin* weighed anchor. Shortly before the ships set sail, the final preparations for the cruise were made when known troublemakers were landed. The five ships slipped out of harbour without ceremony, their departure stirring scarcely a ripple upon the calm surface of English life. Shortly before the *Hood* weighed anchor, Field had received a message of farewell from King George V:

> On the eve of your departure on the Empire Cruise, I wish you, the officers and ships' companies of the Squadron, a happy, successful voyage and safe return. My thoughts and good wishes will always be with you.[1]

Similar messages of encouragement and farewell were received from the board of the Admiralty, Admiral Sir John de Robeck, the commander-in-chief of the Royal Navy's Atlantic Fleet, William Massey, the prime minister of New Zealand, and many others. While there was something of a muted atmosphere in Britain, for those who crewed the ships that comprised the squadron, the departure of the ships, by and large for most, was the beginning of an unforgettable adventure, one which would be the zenith of the peacetime navy. Leading Stoker William Stone was one who described the prospect of the cruise and the adventure that lay ahead as 'wonderful'.[2] Arthur Russell of HMS *Repulse* recorded his feelings at being part of the cruise in his diary following an announcement made by Captain Parker: '[H]e tells us that H.M. the King is very interested in this cruise (so am I)'.[3] Meanwhile, Wilfred Woolman noted the background excitement that existed prior to the departure of the squadron and recorded in his diary:

> For weeks past, the great cruise has been the one topic of conversation dominating all others. Again and again the itinerary has been gone over on maps and charts and now a globe is brought into the mess with the trip marked on by a white strip, adding a new zest to the journey...[4]

For others, such as Lieutenant Geoffrey Wells of HMS *Hood* who was leaving behind a new wife, it was a desperate wrench:

> We were casting off the wires and by 0730 hrs we were clear of No 6 wharf, Keyham Dockyard. As the engines started I felt a pang of realisation of the fact that I was here, Inez in London and that realisation only grew greater as we steamed passed Plymouth Hoe and turned seawards. Just to think of 10 months ahead, 30,000 odd miles steaming. I can't![5]

Out of Devonport, the ships made their way down the Devon coast out towards the Atlantic. HMS *Danae* and *Dragon* were detained at Sheerness and did not join the squadron until 8 a.m. on 28 November. From the mouth of the English Channel, the squadron headed for what would be their first port call on the voyage: Freetown, Sierra Leone.[6]

The weather was serene as the ships of the squadron sailed south; no storms in the Atlantic developed to vex the passage. Early on the morning of 3 December, Tenerife, one of the Canary Islands, appeared on the horizon. Four of the cruisers rode in echelon between *Hood* and the island cliffs which cut deeply into the sea as they proceeded south. The squadron altered course towards Gran Canaria, the *Hood*, *Repulse*, and the ships of the First Light Cruiser Squadron altering course in unison before passing between the islands.

The time following the departure of the ships from the British Isles was taken up with a range of activities. Men were drilled and exercises were conducted including collision quarters and action stations alongside sea boat exercises. When not engaged in an exercise or being drilled, parties of men could be found painting and cleaning the ships.[7] Tropical rig was adopted on board on 7 December before the squadron arrived at Freetown the following day.

While at anchor, launches and boats sailed between the ships. As stocks began to be replenished, Field departed the *Hood* to call upon the governor of Sierra Leone, Alexander Rushford Slater. The governor returned the call, after which leave was granted to members of the squadron. On 11 December, visitors were permitted aboard the *Hood* and *Repulse*. Lieutenant Charles Benstead recalled:

> We saw our ships invaded by Freetown negroes who gaped in open-mouthed astonishment at a ventilating fan; by the bearded Boer farmers from the South African veldt; by white-robed Mohammedans from Zanzibar who, at sunset, spread their prayer-mats upon the quarterdeck and reverently knelt to invoke the protection of Allah.[8]

Another lieutenant who served on board the *Hood* at the time described a 'white-robed dignified figure … who boarded us and, in amazement, rolling his eyes so violently that, losing his balance, he sat down—all were impressed'.[9]

While at Freetown, the men of the squadron had to contend with two separate itineraries: one for Europeans and one for members of the African community, while Field would admit to the Admiralty in a letter on 22 December 1923 that

Tropical rig was adopted on board the squadron's ships on 7 December. This photograph shows men aboard the *Hood* in tropical rig. (*Steve Locks*)

Replenishing stocks aboard HMS *Repulse*. (*Empire Photographic Publishing, Steve Locks*)

Visitors to the squadron's ships at Freetown gathered on a jetty. (*Steve Locks*)

A boat full of visitors arriving alongside HMS *Hood* at Freetown. (*Empire Photographic Publishing, Steve Locks*)

The quayside at Sierra Leone. Members of the squadron can be seen here walking among the local population. (*Empire Photographic Publishing, Steve Locks*)

the visit of the squadron tended to exacerbate local tensions.[10] 'White society lampooned the idea of Africans entertaining the visiting Jack Tars, insisting that they would provide "snake charmers, juju, fetish men, and secret occult societies".'[11] While at Freetown, Field encouraged the West African colonies, with their long maritime tradition, to create a branch of the Royal Navy Volunteer Reserve. The Colonial Office and Admiralty, however, demurred, with one government official citing the idea as 'impracticable'.[12]

The squadron weighed anchor and departed Freetown for Cape Town, South Africa, on 13 December. The squadron had been hospitably received, nevertheless, Freetown was not a place that the crews were reluctant to leave owing to the heavy air and stifling heat. The Special Service Squadron would spend nine days covering the 3,156 miles from Freetown to Cape Town. During the course of the journey, further exercises were conducted by the squadron, including a day and night searchlight exercise, action stations, and a number of gunnery exercises. Two days after departing Freetown, on 15 December, the squadron crossed the equator, an event which was celebrated in a time-honoured fashion known as the 'Crossing the Line' ceremony before King Neptune and his court. V. C. Scott O'Connor, a journalist who had been contracted by the Admiralty to produce a commemorative book on the cruise and sailed with the ships, recalled the ceremony as conducted aboard the *Hood*:

On December 15th we crossed the Line, and 950 men who had never crossed the Equator prepared to face the terrors of the bath! Thrones or chairs were placed upon a dais for Neptune and his Court at the end of the quarterdeck—with eight chairs below them for the Admiral and other distinguished persons. The rest of the deck was crowded with spectators. The Oceanic Court was seen approaching to the strains of music, the drum-major brandishing his staff at the head of the bandsmen whose cheeks were filled out with air, while the drummers beat a rataplan on their drums. The spectators made way; the Royal Marines delivered a salute with their customary smartness—but to-day with grins upon their faces. Neptune ascended his throne. His bears, well suited by their massive frames and hairy forms to inspire novices with terror, lay at his feet.

The Admiral then left his seat and marching up to the dais, saluted and went down upon his knees to receive the ribbon and the Order of the Bath. He then rose, saluted, and returned to his seat. One by one the other recipients of honours went up and returned with smiling faces, like schoolboys at an annual prize-giving. All round us were assembled, in the scantiest of clothing, the neophytes who were this day to be initiated; while those who still wore uniform, the captain of the *Hood* himself, the Admiral's political secretary, and other persons of rank, made a dash for their cabins, to shed their trappings and appear in bathing suits. An enormous bath, some 10 feet high, had been erected on the port side of the quarter-deck, with a steep ladder for those ascending to their ordeal, on one side, and another for those descending after its completion on the other. Every vantage-point, including the gun turrets and the gangways, was occupied by hilarious onlookers, including hundreds of those who were themselves to be initiated. Upon a wooden platform above the bath were now assembled the Chief Justice in his scarlet robes, the Neptune barber and physician, and other officials. As each neophyte ascended the ladder he was well beaten over the head with an inflated bladder, or baton, by the Neptunic police; seized and placed upon a stool and dosed by the physician with a very disagreeable pill, that to make sure it reached its goal was rammed into his mouth and was followed by a glass of medicine, which willy nilly he had to swallow, while an attendant held his nose! He was then rapidly passed on to another stool, to the ministrations of the court barber, his face lathered and 'shaved' with a wooden razor, until of a sudden the stool, most unexpectedly, tipped over and he found himself descending head-foremost, his feet flying in the air, along a soapy slide into the bath. Swift and sure was his descent into this Avernus, where he was seized by the grimy bears and ducked repeatedly until at last, completely out of breath and spluttering sea-water, he came to the end of his purgatory and was suffered to rise up on his feet, and make for the descending ladder, half-choked, but delighted to find himself free, while from behind him came the splash of his successor's arrival, to shouts of laughter from the assembled spectators.

Meanwhile Neptune still sat upon his throne, administering justice to all backsliders, shammers, conscientious objectors and other recalcitrant. These delinquents, arrested in secret haunts and caverns of the ship, were brought up in custody by the Oceanic police and their offences detailed. One who may have been shamming only to please the company, was produced from a bag carried on a pole, from which he rolled out at His Majesty's Feet, emerging with a smile; another it was reported 'had been found skulking in the Admiral's galley frying a kipper, in defiance of your Majesty's commands'.

'Have them rubbed into him' came the stentorian judgement, 'and especially the kipper!'

After this there were sliced oranges and champagne and similar polite attentions from the Admiral.

'Let those not interested look the other way', roared His Oceanic Majesty, gazing benevolently at the bubbly.

By 1 o'clock in the afternoon the Captain and 950 officers and men had been received into the fold, and as joyous and hearty a ceremony as it is possible to imagine came to an end, lightening people's hearts, making a break in the routine of the voyage, and increasing good-fellowship and comradeship all round.[13]

As the squadron approached Table Bay in the shadow of Table Mountain, it had sailed 6,057 miles. On the morning of 22 December, the ships of the First Light Cruiser Squadron led the *Repulse* followed by *Hood* into Table Bay, Cape Town. It was a morning of grey mists and thin rain behind which Table Mountain was invisible. The mist prevented five aircraft of the South African Air Service, which had flown into Cape Town from Pretoria for the special purpose of escorting the squadron into harbour, from getting airborne. Nevertheless, the arrival of the squadron was greeted by launches and tugs full of people dressed in raincoats which circled around the ships. The weather was also a source of disappointment for the men on board the ships who were mindful of the spectacle provided by some of the most powerful British warships sailing into port as Arthur Russell recorded in his diary:

King Neptune's bears pose for a photograph on board one of the squadron's ships during the 'Crossing the Line' activities.

Neptunic police on board one of the squadron's ships. (*Steve Locks*)

King Neptune and members of his court on board HMS *Delhi*. (*Steve Locks*)

King Neptune, members of his court, and Neptunic police aboard HMS *Hood*. (*Empire Photographic Publishing, Steve Locks*)

Right: Captain Pipon (left) and Rear Admiral Brand (right) following receiving the ribbon and Order of the Bath from King Neptune.

Below: 'Upon a wooden platform above the bath were now assembled the Chief Justice in his scarlet robes, the Neptune barber and physician, and other officials. As each neophyte ascended the ladder he was well beaten over the head with an inflated bladder, or baton, by the Neptunic police; seized and placed upon a stool and dosed by the physician with a very disagreeable pill, that to make sure it reached its goal was rammed into his mouth and was followed by a glass of medicine ... He was then rapidly passed on to ... the ministrations of the court barber, his face lathered and 'shaved' with a wooden razor'. (*Steve Locks*)

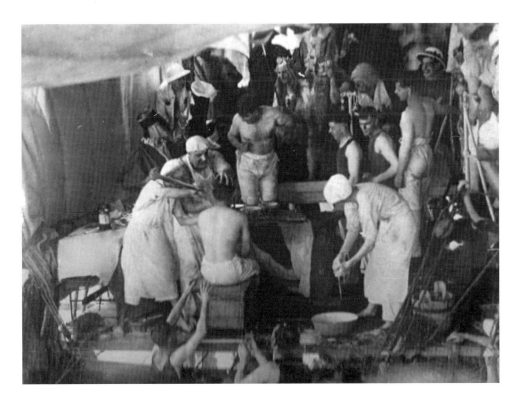

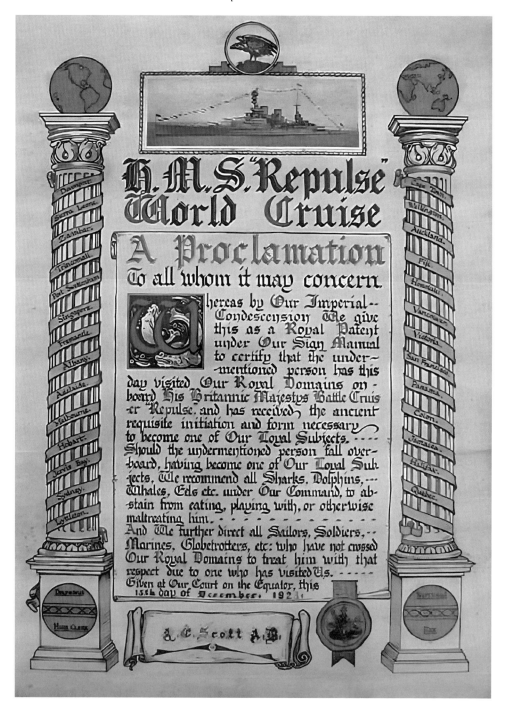

The certificate awarded to Albert Edward Scott of HMS *Repulse* following Crossing the Line and being initiated by Neptune and his court. (*Steve Locks*)

Great disappointment was felt by all through the existence of the bad weather—because nothing looks more inspiring and beautiful than to watch from the shore Britain's two largest warships and four [*sic*.] powerful cruisers slowly steaming into harbour, the decks of each ship lined with bluejackets and the bands playing a 'march'.[14]

Upon arriving in South Africa, the ships saluted a number of dignitaries before the officers of the ships landed in order to conduct a number of official functions ashore. In the town hall, a civic address of welcome was delivered by the mayor, Ryno J. Verster, on behalf of the council. Admirals Field and Brand sat in the din with the mayor and the councillors while members of state stood alongside. Before them, like an audience in a vast theatre, sat and stood the elite of Cape Town. Two illuminated copies of Verster's address, inscribed on vellum, were presented to each of the admirals. Both Field and Brand delivered an address in reply, winning the plaudits of the assembly, Field by his delivery of a message from King George V and Brand through his beaming smile and references to the days when as a midshipman he had been stationed on the Cape.

That evening, a banquet was held at the town hall at which 100 officers of the squadron were in attendance alongside many prominent officials. Among the dignitaries and officials in attendance were the acting governor-general of South Africa, Sir James Rose-Innes, the commander-in-chief Africa, Rear Admiral Sir Rudolph Bentinck, and the minister of agriculture, Sir Thomas Smartt, who was one of the founders of, and in 1912 became leader of, the Unionist Party. During the course of the banquet, speeches were made in which reference was made to the high appreciation to the services rendered by the Royal Navy to South Africa. Smartt, during his speech, stressed the duty of the people of South Africa to take their share in maintaining the Royal Navy to help police and protect the lines of communication and the open seas. Smartt's remarks were well received by the British press.

The Dutch press was noticeable in that it made no mention of the squadron's visit to South Africa. Nevertheless, the officers and men of the squadron met much personal kindness from the Dutch members of the population with many showing a considerable interest in naval defence problems. At a banquet held during the course of the squadron's visit, aimed at leaders of the Afrikaner community, Sir James Rose-Innes reminded his audience of the historical Dutch maritime tradition and used this to convey the message that for this reason all white South Africans should be interested in the navy. Despite these appeals, the Afrikaner community remained largely aloof from the squadron.

Privately some members of the squadron registered their frustration with the lack of interest from the Afrikaner community, which they blamed not on ethnic divisiveness but rather on a 'stubborn unwillingness to view the sea as a common preserve of all imperial subjects'.[15] Members of the South African Party had recognised the immense political sensitivity that surrounded the Special Service Squadron and its mission prior to its arrival in South Africa; Jan Smuts, the prime minister of South Africa, and an Afrikaner, had quietly declined to travel from Pretoria to Cape Town to greet the squadron. When Field offered to visit Pretoria for a meeting, Smuts quickly informed him that he had pre-existing holiday plans. Like many Afrikaners, Smuts ignored the squadron and its clarion call for a greater commitment to the British empire.

The *Hood* and *Repulse* were opened to the public on 23 and 24 December and again from 28 to 31 December, during which time approximately 50,000 people visited the ships and were entertained by the men of the squadron in spite of the inclement weather. Aboard the *Repulse*, a children's party was organised by Commander Francis Sandford, the ship's executive officer. Sandford has been described as 'a pay-master in the art of making young people happy' and the party that he organised aboard the battlecruiser was so great a success that it was repeated for those who had not been able to attend the first time around.[16] On Christmas Day, over 900 sailors and 300 Marines participated in a ceremonial march through Cape Town while the following day the squadron held a ball.

Three days after the squadron ball, on 29 December, the First Light Cruiser Squadron parted company with the *Hood* and *Repulse* and set out upon a voyage along the east coast of Africa and across the Indian Ocean. On 1 January, HMS *Delhi*, *Danae*, and *Dauntless* arrived at Durban. HMS *Dragon*, meanwhile, put into Simonstown for repairs.

Above left: Captain Parker (left) standing with Commander Sandford (right) on board HMS *Repulse*. (*Empire Photographic Publishing, Steve Locks*)

Above right: A children's party on board HMS *Repulse* while the squadron was at Cape Town. Commander Sandford, who organised the parties on board the battlecruiser, was described as 'a pay-master in the art of making young people happy'. (*Empire Photographic Publishing, Steve Locks*)

Above: A children's party aboard HMS *Repulse*. The first party organised aboard the battlecruiser was so great a success that it was repeated for those who had not been able to attend the first time around. (*Empire Photographic Publishing, Steve Locks*)

Right: (*Empire Photographic Publishing, Steve Locks*)

A civic address of welcome was delivered at the town hall followed by a lunch at the Durban Turf Club. That evening, the president of the Navy League of South Africa, Walter Greenacre, held a dinner for Brand and Captains Pipon, Austin, and Round-Turner, which was followed by a reception at the mayor's private residence. The Durban Light Infantry performed a concert for all ratings of the squadron and a series of entertainment and hospitality events followed.

Brand, eighteen officers, and 180 men visited Maritzburg as the guests of Sir George Plowman, the governor of Natal. Some 450 men marched through the streets of Durban, headed by the band of the Durban Light Infantry, and were guests at a war dance was performed by members of the Zulu nation. The First Light Cruiser Squadron returned the hospitality and entertainment. HMS *Delhi*, *Danae*, and *Dauntless* were all opened to the public and were visited by 15,000 people. Among those who visited HMS *Delhi* was Royal Chief Sidiya of the Zulus, who was profoundly impressed by the cruiser. Large numbers of women and children were entertained aboard HMS *Danae* when the ship was placed 'At Home', before a dance for 300 guests was held aboard the *Delhi* and *Dauntless* as the two ships lay alongside one another. 'At Home' events were one particularly important aspect of the cruise. 'At Home' events saw the ship's opened up to visitors in an official but less formal capacity allowing crewmen to interact more freely with visitors and to engender friendly relations.

A number of sporting events were also held. Crewmen from HMS *Danae* won a whaler race against members of the Royal Navy Volunteer Reserve while the squadron won five out of six boxing contests against the city. Each winner was presented with a silver cup bearing the arms of Natal. The squadron did not excel

Royal Chief Sidiya of the Zulus at Durban. When the royal chief visited HMS *Delhi*, he was profoundly impressed by the cruiser. (*Steve Locks*)

The quarterdeck of HMS *Danae* rigged ready for an 'At Home'. Large numbers of women and children were entertained aboard *Danae* when the ship was placed 'At Home', before a dance for 300 guests was held in *Delhi* and *Dauntless* as the two ships lay alongside one another. (*Empire Photographic Publishing, Steve Locks*)

Two men from the First Light Cruiser Squadron enjoying a rickshaw ride while at Durban. (*Empire Photographic Publishing, Steve Locks*)

at all of the sporting events, however. The Durban Light Infantry won a shooting contest with 682 points against the Royal Navy in second with 490 points and the Royal Marines in third with 475 points. The squadron also took on Durban at water polo, losing 4–1. Durban also beat the squadron at cricket. Athletics, swimming races, and golf rounded off the list of sporting events.

The activities of the First Light Cruiser Squadron were not confined to Durban. At the invitation of the government of Rhodesia, four officers and twenty ratings were invited to Livingston, the capital of northern Rhodesia.

On the morning of 5 January, the First Light Cruiser Squadron weighed anchor. Large numbers of people crowded the coastline to watch the squadron's departure. As the ships got underway, the bands of the cruisers struck up a musical farewell.

While the First Light Cruiser Squadron was at Durban, the *Hood* and *Repulse* had remained at Cape Town. The arrival of the Special Service Squadron at Cape Town engendered a desire for the spectacle to such an extent that every seaport on the South African littoral began to clamour for a visit by the squadron. In an effort to try and fulfil these desires and aspirations, Field decided to weigh anchor on 2 January 1924, a day earlier than had been intended whereupon a high-speed dash was made for Mossell Bay where anchor was dropped the following day. Of this decision, Arthur Russell recorded, 'each port holds an excited and enthusiastic population—the excitement being due to the fact that the Admiral has proposed to stay at each port for about 12 hours and allow the people to see the "floating power" of Britain'.[17]

A large number of people turned out to see the ships. Owing to the confines of time, it was not possible to open the *Hood* and *Repulse* up to the public with the result that many had to be satisfied with a boat trip around the battlecruisers. That evening, the two ships once again weighed anchor and proceeded to Port Elizabeth. Dense fog made it impossible for the ships to enter the bay without undue risk. After waiting offshore for several hours, with regret Field was forced to take the *Hood* and *Repulse* down the coast to Port Alfred where a display using the ships' searchlights had been planned. This too had to be abandoned owing to the dense fog.

Continuing further along the coast of South Africa, East London was reached on 5 January. Here the mayor, port captain, and principal military authorities were welcomed aboard the *Hood*. For the majority of men aboard the battlecruisers, the time in East London consisted of sea boat exercises, the mending of clothes, and the cleaning of the ships.

Durban was the next stop for the *Hood* and *Repulse* on 6 January. At Durban, the public were again prevented from being welcomed aboard the battlecruisers, the port authorities determining that harbour tugs and launches could not come alongside the *Hood* and *Repulse* safely owing to the continual swell. It may be noted, however, that a few people who made their own way out to the ships in small boats were welcomed aboard. From Durban, the battlecruisers proceeded to Zanzibar, a passage that was made in fine weather. As the *Hood* and *Repulse* sailed into Zanzibar, a long procession of small craft flying the Zanzibar Red

Ensign surrounded the ships to provide an escort. Also at anchor in the harbour was the yacht *Khalifa* of the sultan of Zanzibar, Sayyad Khalifa II bin Harub Al-Said, which was anchored at the head of a long line of native craft all of which were dressed in honour of the visit. Upon seeing this, Field deemed it desirable that *Hood* and *Repulse* should dress ship upon anchoring. As they proceeded into the harbour, the battlecruiser rendered a salute of twenty-one guns to the sultan before returning a reply of fifteen guns to the light cruiser USS *Concord* which was also in harbour.

Having anchored and with the ships dressed, Field, along with Captains Im Thurn and Parker and members of his personal staff, called upon the sultan whereupon a reception was held. Addresses were presented to Field by the Zanzibar Arab Association, the Khoja Ismaili Community, and the Zanzibar Chamber of Commerce, all of whom referenced the importance of the Royal Navy to the continued prosperity of the empire. For the majority of crewmembers, life continued more or less as usual with much cleaning and provisioning taking place. HMS *Hood* conducted a gunnery programme before members of the ship's company joined sailors from the *Repulse* for a ceremonial march. Some leave was also granted to crewmembers before the two battlecruisers departed on 17 January amid much fanfare which included a personal 'escort' by the sultan aboard the *Khalifa*.[18] Having been led out of harbour by the *Khalifa*, the *Hood* rendered the sultan another twenty-one-gun salute before slowly disappearing out of sight over the horizon. For the battlecruisers, the next stop was Trincomalee, Ceylon, across the Indian Ocean.

A native craft containing dancing Zanzibaris welcomes the *Hood* and *Repulse*. (*Empire Photographic Publishing, Steve Locks*)

The scene through a porthole of one of the battlecruisers while at Zanzibar.

Zanzibar Harbour viewed from either HMS *Hood* or *Repulse*. (*Empire Photographic Publishing, Steve Locks*)

Right: Captain Im Thurn, Sayyad Khalifa II bin Harub Al-Said, Admiral Field, and an unidentified officer aboard HMS *Hood*. (*Empire Photographic Publishing, Steve Locks*)

Below: The *Khalifa*, the state yacht of the sultan of Zanzibar, Sayyad Khalifa II bin Harub Al-Said, departing the *Hood*. (*Empire Photographic Publishing, Steve Locks*)

70   *Empire Cruise*

While the battlecruisers were at Zanzibar, on 12 January, Brand arrived at Mombasa, Kenya, with HMS *Delhi* and *Dauntless* while HMS *Danae* proceeded to Dar es-Salam. HMS *Dragon*, meanwhile, remained at Simonstown. While Field was doing his utmost to try and fulfil the many desires of the many seaports along the South African littoral which clamoured for a visit by the squadron, Brand split the First Light Cruiser Squadron to visit several ports; in Kenya, local officials protested to the Rear Admiral when only HMS *Delhi* and *Dauntless* arrived at Mombasa.[19] For his part, the president of the Chamber of Commerce delivered an impassioned speech in which he 'emphasised the importance of impressing the native mind with the size and power of the British Navy'.[20]

At Mombasa, HMS *Delhi* and *Dauntless* anchored in Kilindini, a stretch of blue water enclosed by low wooded hills. In his account of the events of the cruise, V. C. Scott O'Connor chronicled the events following the arrival of the *Delhi* and *Dauntless* and Mombasa.

> On arrival at Kilindini the Rear-Admiral called on Sir Robert Coryndon, Governor of Kenya and High Commissioner for Zanzibar. He was received on landing by the Senior Commissioner, the Resident Commissioner, and the Liwali of the coast, Sheikh Ali Bin Salim. A Guard of Honour of the King's African rifles presented arms. His Excellency the Governor soon after returned the Rear-Admiral's call on board the Flagship. These ceremonies are carried out according to the ritual of His Majesty's Ships, and are unsurpassed in their beauty and dignity. A Guard of Royal Marines is drawn up on the quarter-deck; the officer-in-command stands before them, his sword drawn, himself rather like a sword. The boatswain pipes His Excellency up the gangway; the band plays. When the visit is over, the trumpeter blows his trumpet, His Excellency salutes and descends the gangway to the sea, his red and white feathers fluttering in the full blaze of the African sun. A salute of 17 guns is fired in his honour. He is by this time on his way. At the sound of the guns he rises in his barge and stands at the salute until the last gun has fired.[21]

That night, a series of receptions were held before Brand held a dinner on the quarterdeck of the *Delhi* for the governor-general after which they attended a ball held at the Mombasa Club. There was to be no rest for at 11 p.m., Brand, Captain Round-Turner, his secretary and war staff officer left Kilianini aboard the governor's train bound for Nairobi. On the heels of Brand and his party, detachments drawn from the *Delhi* and *Dauntless* also journeyed to Nairobi. In his account of the cruise, O'Connor went on to detail some of the events that took place during the visit to Nairobi:

> The visit of the Rear-Admiral and of detachments from the Light Cruisers was characterised by much kindness and hospitality on the part of the inhabitants of Nairobi. Their enthusiasm and determination to do everything possible to make it a success was most remarkable. At a boxing competition, which was well staged in the open-air, the Rear-Admiral took the opportunity to thank His Excellency the

Governor of the Colony of Kenya for all they had done. He visited some of the best coffee plantations and was impressed ... He had the great pleasure of receiving a deputation of ex-Naval Officers of the Colony, and was presented by them with a silver cup for the First Light Cruiser Squadron, as a memento of its visit; and paid a visit to Lord Delamere ...

Seventeen officers and a hundred men were entertained in Nairobi. They were welcomed on arrival by the Colonial Secretary and a large number of inhabitants. Headed by the superb band of the King's African Rifles, they marched to their quarters at the New Stanley Hotel. Thirty motor-cars took them for tours through the country. Concerts, public dinners, and a Ngoma given by a thousand natives, were part of the entertainment provided for by our men. The officers of the detachment were badly beaten at cricket, golf and tennis. The cricket of Nairobi was practically up to County form. The men were rather more successful, and at boxing distinguished themselves, winning six out of seven bouts. The last bout was for the Middle-Weights Championship and belt of Kenya. Able-Seaman Hopper of HMS *Delhi* knocked his opponent out in the second round, and received a very handsome cup for his victory.

All these competitions were carried through in the most sporting manner and were enjoyed by all; and when on January 16th the Contingent marched to the station on its departure for Mombasa, again headed by the band of the K.A.R., it was acclaimed with the wildest enthusiasm ...

While these fortunate officers and men were being entertained in the salubrious climate of Nairobi ... the rest of the Squadron were making the best of their lot in the intense and stifling heat of Mombasa. They played football, they played cricket, they went to dances. Disastrously beaten at first at rugger, the arrival of *Dragon* enabled them to put a better team into the field and very nearly to secure victory. Five hundred people visited the ships, including thirty Arab Chieftains, and forty native chiefs from the interior of the country: people in full regalia and of the most picturesque appearance. Some of them who had never before set eyes upon a ship-of-war, had travelled eight hundred miles to pay their visit. *Dauntless* gave a concert, and the Rear-Admiral a dinner on board *Delhi*, followed by a reception, at which a hundred guests were present.[22]

At 11 a.m. on 17 January, the same day that the *Hood* and *Repulse* departed Zanzibar, the ships of the First Light Cruiser Squadron departed Mombasa and Dar es-Salam bound for Trincomalee.

Members of Kenyan tribes assembling prior to a Ngoma which was delivered to the men of the squadron at Nairobi. (*Empire Photographic Publishing, Steve Locks*)

(*Empire Photographic Publishing, Steve Locks*)

(*Empire Photographic Publishing, Steve Locks*)

Crowds gathered along the shoreline to bid farewell to HMS *Danae* at Dar es-Salaam. (*Empire Photographic Publishing, Steve Locks*)

5

'The Warmest Tribute in its Power'

The squadron's journey across the Indian Ocean from the coast of Africa to Ceylon took nine days. Travelling at an average speed of 14 knots, the ships arrived as a squadron at Trincomalee at 3 p.m. on 26 January. During the journey across the Indian Ocean, the *Delhi*, *Danae*, and *Dauntless* conducted a series of torpedo exercises.

At Trincomalee, there were to be no official functions, no events and ceremonies of state; instead, the protocols and events that had hitherto dominated the port calls gave way to intimate events; speeches gave way to quiet talk while banquets gave way to private parties. A garden party was held for the men of the squadron by the Mudaliyars and their families. Of the squadron's arrival in Ceylon, the *Times of Ceylon* wrote:

> Whenever the White Ensign is seen in distant ports, Englishmen at once feel that a part of England itself has as it were, been brought to them, for no stronger reminder of Home could be afforded than when a British man-o-war pays the distant ports of the Empire a visit.[1]

The lack of official functions did not mean that the men of the squadron sat idle. Shooting parties were arranged for officers while at the invitation of the Ceylon government, a party of eight officers and 125 men visited Kandy, the ancient capital of the island. It was during the visit to Kandy that the first tragedy struck the squadron. During the journey, one of the buses that had been laid on as transport overturned while making a sharp turn. Stoker Petty Officer George Wood of HMS *Repulse* was pinned under the bus and killed while four others sustained injuries.[2] A large number of wreaths were sent by the people of Kandy in expressions of sympathy for Wood's death. Wood was buried at Kandy, his funeral attended by the officers and men of the squadron.

The stay at Trincomalee was brief, lasting until 31 January. During the period that the squadron was at anchor, 2,000 people visited the ships. At 8 a.m., the squadron weighed anchor and began to glide out of harbour to resume the

During their journey across the Indian Ocean, HMS *Delhi*, *Danae*, and *Dauntless* conducted a series of torpedo exercises. (*Empire Photographic Publishing, Steve Locks*)

(*Empire Photographic Publishing, Steve Locks*)

HMS *Hood* during the squadron's time at Trincomalee, Ceylon. (*Author's Collection*)

Men of the Special Service Squadron with native hunters at Trincomalee. (*Empire Photographic Publishing, Steve Locks*)

cruise, bound for Malaya. As the squadron got underway, many vantage points, particularly on Elephant Ridge and Round Island Light, were lined by people bidding the squadron farewell.

The squadron sailed together until 3 February when it once more divided as Brand and the First Light Cruiser Squadron sailed to Penang, which was reached the following day, while Field and the battlecruisers proceeded to Port Swettenham, Kuala Lumpur.

At the time, the Malay Peninsula consisted of the Straits Settlements which were directly administered by the British, and the Malay States which were ruled over by the indigenous princes who were advised and assisted by British officers.

At Penang, Brand was visited aboard HMS *Delhi* by the rajah of Perlis and the regent of Kedah. Gun salutes of thirteen and fifteen guns respectively were rendered to both men before Brand returned their calls. The following day, Brand and his staff crossed to the mainland before driving to Taiping. While Brand continued his journey through Malaya by travelling to Kuala Kangsar, the residence of the sultan of Perak, eighteen officers and 200 ratings were entertained at Taiping. Meanwhile, eighteen officers and 100 ratings were entertained at Ipoh. The state of Kedah likewise played host to thirteen officers and twenty-five ratings while a further ten officers and twenty-five ratings were entertained at Sungei Potani.

To list all of the activities at which the men of the First Light Cruiser Squadron were entertained would simply take up too much space. Indeed, the lavish hospitalities that were laid on occupied twelve pages of print in a programme published by the Entertainment Committee for the visit to Penang. It is, nevertheless, possible to provide a cursory overview of some of the activities which included elephant rides, cock fights, buffalo fighting, Chinese banquets, dances, concerts, as well as visits to local tin mines and rubber plantations. The party of officers and ratings who visited Ipoh arrived at 11.27 and were given elephant rides, taken out to picnics in the jungle, and sent flying down a waterfall over the smooth rocks. Some 500 gallons of beer was provided by the hosts for the occasion which was duly consumed. This party of men departed the company of their hosts at 11.30 p.m.

So far as it was possible to do so, the First Light Cruiser Squadron returned the hospitalities that had been extended to it. Captain Ramsay entertained the regent of Kedah and the rajah of Perlis on board HMS *Dunedin* while squadron dances were held aboard the *Delhi* and *Danae*. The ships were opened to the public and received 7,716 visitors before an 'At Home' was held aboard HMS *Delhi*. Brand, meanwhile, entertained the principal officers and members of the legislative council over dinner. A number of games of football were played along with two games of cricket and several games of tennis and golf. A number of water sports were held on 7 February, which were the source of much amusement. This included a cutter race which was won by the team from HMS *Danae* by three lengths. A squadron boxing competition was also held at which a cup was presented to the ship which won the most points. From this, *Dauntless* emerged victorious. The winner of each final bout in the different weight categories also

The rajah of Perlis and the regent of Kedah with Rear Admiral Sir Hubert Brand. (*Empire Photographic Publishing, Steve Locks*)

Crewmen from the light cruisers enjoying picnics and elephant rides during a visit to Ipoh. (*Empire Photographic Publishing, Steve Locks*)

received a cup while another was awarded to the ship. As a mark of the good feelings engendered by the visit, the local populace requested that the cups won by the ships be retained *In Perpetuam* and that they should be so engraved. At the Turf and Polo Club of Penang, a gymkhana was organised at which all sailors in uniform were regarded as honorary members of the Turf Club.

On 9 February, the light cruisers weighed anchor to re-join the battlecruisers. Before they departed, a parting gift of 5,000 pineapples was received from the Chinese community of Kinta. Thus ended what was for the men, one of the most enjoyable visits of the cruise.

While the First Light Cruiser Squadron had been at Penang, the battlecruisers had dropped anchor at Port Swettenham, Kuala Lumpur. It may be noted that while Port Swettenham is part of the area defined as Kuala Lumpur, from where the *Hood* and *Repulse* dropped anchor to the Malay capital was 27 miles. The day following the arrival of the ships at Port Swettenham, Field held a dinner party on board the *Hood*. The lunch was attended by the sultans of Selangor and Pahang as well as the Yam Tuan Bésar of Negri Sembilan, each of whom was accompanied by their British advisor. In addition to these distinguished guests, the colonial secretary of the Straits Settlements, Sir Frederick James, was also in attendance. The waters of the Klang and Langat reverberated to the salutes rendered to each individual while the quarterdeck became iridescent with a multitude of colours from the official dress of the guests and the saffron folds of their state umbrellas.

The arrival of the sultan of Selangor out to HMS *Hood*. (*Empire Photographic Publishing, Steve Locks*)

Each day that they were at anchor, the *Hood* and *Repulse* were open to visitors both in the forenoon and afternoon so that no one who had travelled to see the ships up close would go away disappointed. Of the opening up of the battlecruisers to visitors while at Port Swettenham, Arthur Russell wrote, 'The ships are open to visitors in the forenoon from 9.30AM rather an unusual privilege—but really not too great a privilege for such a patriotic nation'.[3] In total, approximately 15,000 people would visit the ships during their visit to Port Swettenham, including a large number of Boy Scouts and children. One schoolboy who visited the *Hood* and *Repulse* while they were at Port Swettenham was S. M. Ghani from the Victoria Institution in Kuala Lumpur. In an essay published in the 1924 school magazine, he recounted his visit to the *Repulse*:

This was the day of which I can say that I had a thorough enjoyment. With two of my friends, I pushed along with a pressing crowd to the cruiser, H.M.S. *Repulse*. Though our boarding this cruiser must be confessed was a surprise to us, yet, nevertheless, it was profoundly welcome.

Our faces beaming with joy, we wandered aimlessly for some time. It was during these wanderings that we came across a Corporal B. Oakley who proved a very friendly and an indefatigable guide. If I am able to recount my visits to the various compartments of the cruiser, I owe it to the untiring efforts of his to gain admittance wherever possible. We proceeded to the turret where the twin 15-inch guns are installed. We had to wait for a mass of people to leave it before we could find room in it. A stout man explained to us about the guns.

The shells for them are stored some one or two decks below, so that in the case of the enemies' shells striking the turret, the fear of their own shells inflicting some extra harm is forestalled. Every movement is controlled by levers. First the breach is opened. Then with a rumbling noise, a carrier swiftly ascends carrying a shell from the storeroom below and stops in line with the yawning breach. With the application of another lever, the shell is thrust into the breach. The breach is locked and an electric wire-end is inserted into a small opening in the shutter, just large enough to admit it. The aim is taken from a place between the guns. The switching on of the current into this wire is equivalent to the pulling of the trigger in an ordinary gun, and with a loud report away dashes off the messenger of destruction.

We listened and watched these movements with silence and genuine interest. Of course, I must not be confounded to mean that we actually heard the report, for, although these actions were shown us, a shell was not admitted to enact its share of the performance.

As we were later going along the corridors some decks below, a sailor invited us to enter a sundering corridor. No sooner had we three reached the end of this, when, with a click an iron door closed on us. There was barely room for us and it was suffocating. I was conscious of a feeling of something formidable in all this. And, in spite of that, I knew I could not rely upon myself to do any Houdini stunt. Without further ado, I concluded that the same feeling had pervaded the hearts of my friends. Imagine our horror then! Cold beads of perspiration stood on our foreheads. Each was staring into the face of the other askance.

'Courage, friends!' I uttered, but the words, however, fell with a chill on my own heart. I knew that if such words were needed at all, I was the one needing them most. Suddenly the planks on which we were standing sank under us, and all of a sudden the movement ceased. The door was opened by a sailor and I stepped out taking in a deep breath. My two friends also left that Black Hole of Calcutta, perhaps Black Hole of H.M.S. *Repulse* would be a more appropriate term for it.

'What is this?' I inquired of the sailor.

'This is the stoke room', he replied. I turned round and looked at the Black Hole and discovered it to be an electric lift. Feeling ashamed to look at it again, I, with my friends, followed the other to the stoves, which contained angry flames, leaping furiously.

We got a glimpse of the beautifully furnished captain's compartments. An orderly stood guarding their entrance.

The bookshop was slightly smaller than the one in the H.M.S. *Hood*. Photographs recording the finishes of the athletic events in which the members of the cruiser had taken part in different climes, could also be seen hanging nearby.

Here also we visited the engine-room, but it was not so hot. To my enquiry, Mr. Oakley told me that the heat would radiate when the cruiser is on the move.

To us it was very interesting to see a telephone exchange on board. There was a man on duty with a book and we were told that always there was a man there.

While again going along the corridors we came across the torpedo compartment. The torpedoes were stored here just as they were stored in the H.M.S. *Hood*. There are 4 twin tubes above the water line and 2 below. Each torpedo costs £1,200.[4]

The social activities of the visit were concentrated in Kuala Lumpur. The distance from the anchorage at Port Swettenham to Kuala Lumpur was overcome in a variety of ways. The railway service between the two locations waivered all fairs for the duration of the visit for both the men of the squadron and residents. Cars were laid on while some of the local residents put up officers in their houses. During the course of the visit, Field and his staff were entertained by George Maxwell, the chief secretary at his official country residence, a country house that resembled a Tudor mansion. At the same time, a distinguished member of the Chinese community in the city, Choo Kia Peng, entertained thirty-five officers from the *Hood* and *Repulse* at his bungalow. For the wider majority of the squadron, the Selangor Club laid on a ball to which fifty officers were invited, 600 men were entertained at Chinese tin mines, 100 at the Petaling rubber estate and tin mine, while 300 men were shown around local limestone caves by members of the Ceylonese and Indian communities. In addition to these activities, numerous open-air cinemas were established and Malay dances held. In the town hall, concerts were arranged and more dances given.

Sporting competitions also formed part of the entertainment programme. Teams from both battlecruisers beat Selangor State at football. The team from the *Repulse* also beat a team fielded by the Chinese Community while the team from the *Hood* was beaten by the YMCA. Both battlecruisers were also significantly

Visitors aboard HMS *Hood* at Port Swettenham. (*Empire Photographic Publishing, Steve Locks*)

beaten at rugby by the Selangor Club. One of the local newspapers, the *Malay Mail* summed up the visit of the squadron and the festivities with the following words:

> Selangor rejoices in its present opportunity, to pay the warmest tribute in its power to the British Navy. The visit of the ships of the Empire Squadron is more than an occasion for a round of festivities and an orgy of sporting events. There is a deep significance in it which those here for their working life, and those whose permanent home it is, do genuinely appreciate. It furnishes an incentive for the development of that real affection for, and faithfulness to, the Empire, which remain the finest thing in the life of the people of Malaya.[5]

While Selangor may have rejoiced at the visit of the ships, there were not smiles all round from the men of the *Hood* as on 5 February the ship suffered its first tragedy of the cruise when Able Seaman Walter Benger died following contracting malaria. Wreaths were sent to the *Hood* and Benger was buried in Kuala Lumpur. A tombstone was erected for him by the government of the Federated Malay States.

Four days following the death of Benger, on 9 February, the *Hood* and *Repulse* departed Port Swettenham. Weighing anchor at 7.30 a.m., the two battlecruisers

HMS *Repulse* at sea off Malaya. (*044777, Australian War Memorial*)

set sail, passed the historic port of Malacca, and rendezvoused with the First Light Cruiser Squadron before proceeding as a squadron to Singapore. At 4.30 p.m. the following day, amid a heavy rain storm, the ships dropped anchor at Singapore. The ships of the Special Service Squadron were not the only vessels of the Royal Navy to be at Singapore for also at anchor were the cruisers *Hawkins* and *Carlisle*, and the minesweepers *Bluebell* and *Petersfield* under the command of Admiral Sir Arthur Leveson, the commander-in-chief, China. The heavy tropic air of the island resounded to the sound of guns as the *Hood* saluted Leveson's flag with a seventeen-gun salute. HMS *Hawkins* returned the salute with fifteen guns.

On 11 February, the squadron dressed ship in honour of the visit, an act which was conducted by almost every other ship at anchor. At 10 a.m., Field, Brand, Im Thurn, Parker, the captains of the cruisers, and their staffs landed and drove through the crowded streets which were decorated with flags and lined with soldiers to call on Sir Laurence Guillemard, the governor of the Straits Settlements. Guillemard returned Field's call to the sound of a thirteen-gun salute. Further salutes that were fired while at Singapore included a seventeen-gun salute for the sultan of Kelantan who was received on board the *Hood* with the Tungku Makhota, the eldest son of the sultan of Johore, while a fifteen-gun salute was fired for General Sir Neill Malcolm, the general officer commanding the troops in the Straits Settlements.[6]

That evening, an official dinner was held on board the *Hood* at which Leveson, Malcolm, Sir Frederick James, and other prominent representatives of the administration were entertained.

While at anchor at Singapore, searchlight exercises were conducted and lifeboats tested. The ships were also cleaned and leave granted before the Naval Brigade undertook a ceremonial march through the city on 15 February. Included in the ceremonial march were the field and machine guns sections of the Royal Marines. Wilfred Woolman was one of those who partook in the march through the streets of Singapore and later recorded:

> The march undoubtedly impressed the natives. In the early part of the war [the First World War], there was a mutiny among the Sikh regiment at the Tanglin barracks, Singapore, which was nipped in the bud by a party landed from HMS *Cadmus* and thus prevented what would have proved an ugly affair. This show of force today evidently brought back that incident vividly to the minds of the inhabitants and impressed them with the might of Britain's power.[7]

In this, Woolman demonstrates a keen awareness of the politics that lay behind the display and the cruise itself and that he believed that the event was an important success which reinforced British imperial power to the colony.

The message of Britain's imperial power was further reinforced by the *Straits Times*, which reported to its readers that the *Hood* could render colonial cities 'a blazing inferno' before going on to note that despite this, the purpose of the *Hood* and the Royal Navy's other capital ships was 'to guard our rights and liberties and the humblest man, no matter what his race or creed or colour, has a share in it, because it stands for justice and liberty to him against the whole world'.[8]

As at the other port calls so far on the cruise, an entertainment programme was laid on for the men of the squadron and local population. Dances and dinners were held while some of the ships were placed 'At Home'. Some 29,000 visitors were welcomed on board by the squadron during the course of its stay. Sporting activities also formed part of the entertainment programme. As elsewhere, the squadron met with mixed success but did distinguish itself at boxing, defeating the China Station 5-2.

On 17 February, the squadron departed Singapore. That morning, as preparations were underway to prepare for sea and to weigh anchor, aboard HMS *Delhi*, Marine Henry Layfield fell down an ammunition hoist and was killed. HMS *Dragon* was detailed to remain behind to conduct the funeral for Layfield while the other cruisers preceded the *Hood* and *Repulse* out of the anchorage. As the squadron got underway, small launches and sampans sailed about and between the ships of the squadron. As the ships proceeded out of harbour, men not on duty lined up on deck. The sound of bugles filled the air as the *Hood* passed HMS *Hawkins*. Bugles also resounded from various passing ships. Aboard *Hood* the band struck up a musical farewell while three cheers rang out for the China Station as signals were flashed between the two flagships. Having made it to the open sea, course was set for Fremantle, Australia.

6

'The Navy Means Everything'

The journey from Singapore to Fremantle was one of some 2,300 miles. The route taken by the squadron took it past the Spice Islands and Sumatra. Two days following its departure from Singapore, the squadron transited the Sunda Strait. As the squadron proceeded along at a stately 11 knots, the distant shapes of volcanos, most notably Krakatoa, became visible. With little else to do as the ships continued on their way, the crews were put to work cleaning the ships and conducting sea boat exercises before a gunnery concentration exercise was undertaken. An interlude on the journey was included when on 20 February, the squadron briefly dropped anchor at Christmas Island.

Out from Christmas Island, the squadron sailed in fine weather without exceptional incident. HMS *Dragon* engaged in exercises which entailed the dropping of depth charges on 19 February, while the following day, HMS *Danae* and *Dunedin* conducted sub-calibre throw-off firing exercises. On the 22nd, the *Hood*, *Repulse*, *Dragon*, and *Dauntless* carried out a high-angle firing exercise. The squadron then sailed through a low pressure weather system that brought with it large waves crashing against the hulls and along the decks.

The nights were generally cool while the days were hot. As the squadron approached Australia, gradually there was a change and a cleaner, drier feeling slowly began to replace the sticky heat as the equator was left behind.

As the squadron neared Australia, wireless messages of welcome began to be received. Aboard each of the ships, preparations for the arrival in Fremantle began to be made. Daily, during the late afternoon, the quarterdecks were transformed into stadiums and gymnasiums as the sailors and Marines who were to compete in the athletics and other sporting events in Australia began to conduct hard and intense training. Runners set off sprinting down the decks at the word of command while on the boat deck of the *Hood*, men sparred as each man was determined to show his mettle and, so far as in him lay, maintain the honour of his ship.

It was not only in sporting terms that preparations for the arrival in Australia were made. Gun turrets were repainted as the ships began to glow in the southern

Officers aboard one of the squadron's ships relax on deck as they transit the Sunda Strait. As the squadron proceeded through the strait at a stately 11 knots, the distant shapes of volcanoes became visible. The volcano in the background is Krakatoa. (*Empire Photographic Publishing*)

HMS *Danae* passing Krakatoa. (*Empire Photographic Publishing, Steve Locks*)

HMS *Dragon* engaged in the dropping of depth charges on 19 February 1924 as the Special Service Squadron sails from Christmas Island to Fremantle. (*Empire Photographic Publishing, Steve Locks*)

Daily, during the late afternoon, the quarterdecks were transformed into stadiums and gymnasiums as the sailors and marines who were to compete in the athletics and other sporting events in Australia began to conduct hard and intense training. Here men aboard the *Hood* can be seen playing hockey. (*Empire Photographic Publishing, Steve Locks*)

light, decks were scrubbed, and steel and brass fixtures were polished until they gleamed with fresh lustre.

On 27 February, the ninety-third day of the voyage, amid the cool morning air and blue water, with the sun shining like gold, the squadron entered Fremantle. Sailing vessels met the squadron and darted around and between the ships, carried briskly along in the breeze. Behind the sailing vessels came small launches and small cabin cruisers sailing in proud procession, the Australian flag and ensign flapping in the breeze. Majestically, the *Hood* moved up the harbour to her mooring followed by the *Repulse*, the two battlecruisers seeming to dwarf the surrounding world.

Thousands of people, including parents holding their babies on their shoulders or small children by the hand, gathered at the harbour and other suitable vantage points to watch the arrival of the ships. Once alongside, the gangways were laid across to the wharf where a densely packed crowd stood waiting to board the ships.

With the *Hood* secured alongside, the mayor of Fremantle, John Cooke, along with members of the House of Representatives and Legislative Assembly called on Field and officially welcomed the squadron. Following these formalities, Field and Im Thurn landed to be received by a Guard of Honour drawn up from the Australian Naval Volunteer Reserve. They were joined in inspecting the Guard of Honour by Rear Admiral Brand, Captain Parker of the *Repulse*, the captains of the cruisers, and members of their personal staffs before travelling to Perth, located 12 miles distant, to call upon Sir Francis Newdigate, the governor of Western Australia, Sir James Mitchell, the acting prime minister and minister of defence, and the mayor of Perth, J. T. Franklin.

HMS *Hood* entering Fremantle Harbour. To the right of the *Hood*, behind the pier, HMS *Repulse* can be seen on her approach to the harbour. (*111886PD, State Library of West Australia*)

HMS *Hood* entering Fremantle Harbour, 27 February 1924. (*State Library of West Australia, 042155PD*)

HMS *Hood* entering Fremantle Harbour. (*008835PD, State Library of Western Australia*)

Above: With the assistance of a tug, the *Hood* enters Fremantle Harbour. (*State Library of West Australia, 111889PD*)

Left: HMS *Hood* being turned into Victoria Quay, Fremantle. (*State Library of Western Australia, BA533/512*)

'The Navy Means Everything'

Crowds gather along the wharf to watch *Hood* berth at Victoria Quay. (*State Library of West Australia, 111890PD*)

(*008840PD, State Library of South Australia*)

HMS *Repulse* entering Fremantle Harbour. (*111891PD, State Library of South Australia*)

HMS *Repulse* proceeding into harbour, 27 February 1924. (*11893PD, State Library of South Australia*)

A boat full of sightseers sails past HMS *Repulse* as she secures alongside in Fremantle. (*111894PD, State Library of South Australia*)

HMS *Delhi* passing HMS *Repulse* in Fremantle Harbour. (*111892PD, State Library of South Australia*)

Crowds gather to watch *Hood* berth alongside in Fremantle. (*State Library of West Australia, 008838PD*)

HMS *Repulse* as she entered Fremantle Harbour, 27 February 1924. (*3452B/148, State Library of Western Australia*)

HMS *Hood* moving alongside the wharf at Fremantle. (*111887PD, State Library of WestAustralia*)

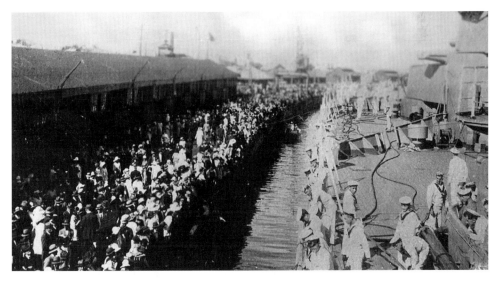

'Thousands of people including parents holding their babies on their shoulders or small children by the hand gathered at the harbour and other suitable vantage points to watch the arrival of the ships. Once alongside the gangways were laid across to the wharf where a densely packed crowd stood waiting to board the ships.' Crowds at Fremantle line the wharf as HMS *Hood* manoeuvres alongside. (*Empire Photographic Publishing, Steve Locks*)

Above: HMS *Delhi* sailing into Fremantle Harbour, 27 February 1924. (008837PD, *State Library of Western Australia*)

Left: HMS *Delhi* passing HMS *Hood* as the squadron enters Fremantle Harbour, 27 February 1924. (*State Library of West Australia*, 042154PD)

HMS *Delhi* berthing alongside Victoria Quay, Fremantle. (*BA533/524, State Library of Western Australia*)

HMS *Delhi* securing alongside Victoria Quay, Fremantle, in front of an extensive crowd of spectators who have turned out to see the squadron. (*008828PD, State Library of Western Australia*)

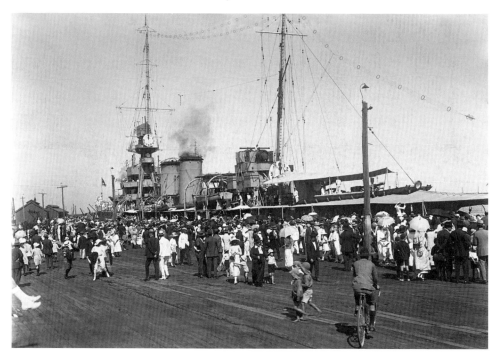

HMS *Delhi* berthing alongside Victoria Quay. (*008825PD, State Library of South Australia*)

The following day, a ceremonial march took place through Fremantle and then through Perth. A parliamentary lunch was held for the squadron on 29 February. As at Cape Town, speeches formed a key part of the lunch. Following once more delivering an address of welcome, Sir James Mitchell delivered an address in which he stated:

> To Australia as to Britain, the Navy means everything. Our trade communications lie across the seas. Whatever enemy comes to us will come across the seas. Our great settlements are around the coast. Without the dominant British Navy we could be utterly destroyed. Without the Navy the Empire would not exist, and without the Empire the world would lose its greatest guarantee of peace; the weak nations of the earth their greatest protector.[1]

Field followed Mitchell's address, in which he summed up his impressions of Western Australia:

> My foremost impression was of the unbounded loyalty of the people and their firm conviction of the need for an adequate Navy. Nothing could have exceeded the warmth of our reception, or the enthusiasm with which any reference to His Majesty the King or to the Royal Navy was greeted. Everywhere I found the strongest feeling in the State that everything should be done to increase the white population, as the only sound means of ensuring the development and prosperity of the country.[2]

A guard of honour drawn up on the quayside. (*111900PD, State Library of West Australia*)

Vice-Admiral Field and Rear Admiral Sir Hubert Brand landing from the *Hood* at 10.15 a.m. on 27 February 1924. (*State Library of West Australia, 008830PD*)

Vice-Admiral Field disembarking from the *Hood*. (*111902PD, State Library of West Australia*)

Field inspecting a guard of honour on 27 February 1924. (*State Library of West Australia, 008839PD*)

Field inspecting a guard of honour. (*111901PD, State Library of West Australia*)

Field and Brand on the quayside following their inspection. (*State Library of West Australia, 008829PD*)

102　　　　　　　　　　　　*Empire Cruise*

Officers of the squadron departing Victoria Pier before travelling to Perth. From left to right: Captain Parker, Rear Admiral Brand, Captain Im Thurn, and Vice-Admiral Field. (*111903PD, State Library of South Australia*)

Field inspecting a guard of honour at Government House, Perth. (*State Library of West Australia, 008832PD*)

Governor Sir Francis Newdegate with officers of the Special Service Squadron, 27 February 1924. (*008827PD, State Library of South Australia*)

Field and other officers of the Special Service Squadron departing the residence of the governor of Victoria. (*008826PD, State Library of South Australia*)

Officers of the squadron stand in front of a car while Field and Brand are in discussion with a representative of the government of Victoria. (*111909PD, State Library of South Australia*)

Rear Admiral Brand and Captain Parker departing an official function through a crowd of well-wishers at Fremantle. (*111907PD, State Library of West Australia*)

While the squadron officers were entertained at Perth, a small party of petty officers, as guests of McCallum Smith, a member of the West Australian parliament, were taken out into the Australian bush to Lake Preston. While *en route* to Lake Preston, the party stopped at Pinjarra, one of the first settlements in Western Australia. Through the centre of Pinjarra ran the long, wide high street, covered in red, sun-baked dust. Lining either side of the street were situated bungalows with iron roofs, verandas, and bay windows. The Murray River meandered around the settlement, a long wooden bridge straddling the river, connecting the two banks.

All the while, people had continued to visit the ships. In all, some 100,000 people (including 14,000 children) would visit the squadron while it was at anchor.

Men of the Special Service Squadron assembling by Fremantle railway station prior to their march through the city. (*111918PD, State Library of South Australia*)

Men from the Naval Brigade marching through Fremantle. (*111916PD, State Library of South Australia*)

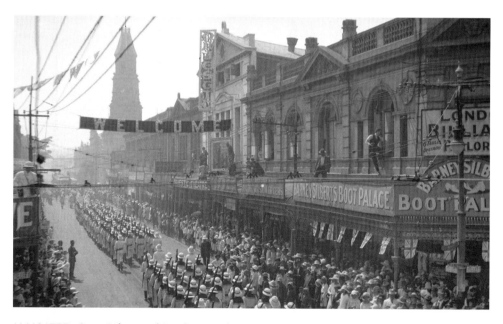
(*111917PD, State Library of South Australia*)

'The Navy Means Everything' 107

(111915PD, State Library of South Australia)

(111911PD, State Library of West Australia)

Members of the Special Service Squadron by Fremantle railway station at the end of their march through the city. HMS *Hood* and *Delhi* can be seen at the top of the photograph. (*111921PD, State Library of South Australia*)

Men of the Special Service Squadron parading through the streets of Perth. (*025972PD, State Library of South Australia*)

The view on the starboard side forward along the boat deck of HMS *Hood* taken while at Fremantle. In front of the *Hood* are the light cruisers HMS *Delhi* and HMS *Danae*. (008627PD, *State Library of Western Australia*)

Officers of the Special Service Squadron on an excursion to Lake Preston. (*BA1271/24, State Library of South Australia*)

Victoria Quay as viewed from the Hood. (*008625PD, State Library of West Australia*)

Right: Visitors on the quayside at Fremantle viewing the squadron's ships. (*Empire Photographic Publishing, Steve Locks*)

Below: Visitors on the quayside beside HMS *Delhi*. Immediately behind HMS *Delhi*, the *Hood* can be seen. (3542B/158, State Library of South Australia)

Some of the visitors to the squadron at Fremantle. (*Empire Photographic Publishing, Steve Locks*)

A crowd of visitors trying to board HMS *Hood* while the ship is alongside at Fremantle. (*111898PD, State Library of South Australia*)

Members of the public stream aboard the *Hood* while at anchor in Fremantle, 27 February 1924. (*State Library of West Australia, 008864PD*)

Visitors to HMS *Hood* while the ship is alongside at Fremantle. (*Empire Photographic Publishing, Steve Locks*)

A group of smiling visitors aboard HMS *Repulse*. (*Empire Photographic Publishing, Steve Locks*)

Children departing HMS *Repulse* at Fremantle. (*Empire Photographic Publishing, Steve Locks*)

'The Navy Means Everything' 115

HMS *Hood* alongside at Fremantle. (*BA1410/2/46, State Library of West Australia*)

(*BA1410/2/47, State Library of West Australia*)

HMS *Repulse* docked alongside the North Wharf, Fremantle. (*BA1934/56*, *State Library of Western Australia*)

HMS *Repulse* alongside at Fremantle. Note the visitors on the ship and on the gangway. (*BA1410/2/48*, *State Library of West Australia*)

'The Navy Means Everything' 117

Right: (BA1410/2/49, State Library of West Australia)

Below: HMS *Delhi* alongside at Fremantle. (BA1410/2/51, State Library of West Australia)

HMS *Danae* alongside at Fremantle. (*BA1410/2/54, State Library of West Australia*)

HMS *Dauntless* at Fremantle. (*BA1410/2/52, State Library of West Australia*)

Sailors line the deck of the *Hood* as the ship prepares to sail from Fremantle. (*State Library of West Australia, 111923PD*)

Hood preparing to sail, 1 March 1924. (*State Library of West Australia, 111924PD*)

Above: Hood preparing to depart Fremantle for Albany, 1 March 1924. (*State Library of West Australia, 111925PD*)

Left: Coloured paper streamers extended out to HMS *Hood* prior to her departure from Fremantle. (*Empire Photographic Publishing, Steve Locks*)

(*Empire Photographic Publishing, Steve Locks*)

HMS *Repulse* photographed as she departed Fremantle. (*BA1410/2/50, State Library of West Australia*)

HMS *Delhi* leaving the wharf at Fremantle. Ahead of HMS *Delhi* another vessel of the First Light Cruiser Squadron can be seen proceeding out of the harbour. (*111927PD, State Library of South Australia*)

On 1 March, the squadron's time at Fremantle drew to a close and it weighed anchor, setting sail for Albany, which was reached the following day. As she departed Fremantle, the *Hood* did so with an Australian ambassador on board in the form of Joey the wallaby, a mascot gifted to the ship by the Australian Imperial Band Committee.

Joey the wallaby was not the only animal gifted to the *Hood* during the course of the cruise. Indeed, the battlecruiser became a 'veritable Noah's Ark', acquiring a number of different animals.[3] During the visit to Calgary, a black beaver was gifted to Field which subsequently made its home on the boat deck. While in the tropics, some members of the ship's company elected to sleep on the deck and received something of a surprise when they awoke to find a beaver curled up beside them. Other animals that were gifted to the *Hood* during the cruise of the Special Service Squadron included a ring-tailed possum, a pair of cockatoos, numerous parrots, a kiwi, and a squirrel. Most of these animals would be offloaded to zoos following the return of the squadron to Devonport at the end of the cruise. The exception to this was Joey, who would remain aboard the *Hood* until 1926 before he too was donated to a zoo.[4]

In accordance with a request that had been received from the governor, the squadron sailed close to Bunbury to give the people ashore an opportunity to see the ships. While complying with this request, Brand took his light cruisers to within 2.5 miles of the shore where they conducted a brief series of manoeuvres before continuing on their way. Several small craft ventured out to cheer the squadron as it sailed past. Following the passage, the mayor of Bunbury would send a

Joey the wallaby held by one of the *Hood*'s crewmen while at anchor in Fremantle. Joey was presented to the crew of the *Hood* as a mascot by the Australian Imperial Band Committee, Fremantle. (*008831PD, State Library of Western Australia*)

telegram to Field in which he stated how much the spectacle was appreciated by the thousands of inhabitants and visitors who had gathered to gain a glimpse of the squadron as it sailed past.

At Albany, a large number of officers and men were taken into the interior by members of the local population where they were shown Mount Barker and Denmark. The squadron only remained at Albany for a handful of days. The departure of the squadron was marred by more than the usual tinge of sadness, however. As the ships were on the point of sailing, a signal reached Field from the naval secretary and first lord of the Admiralty notifying him of the death of Lady Norah Brand, the wife of Rear Admiral Brand. The signal also contained the request that he break the news to Brand, something which Field did immediately. This news cast a gloom over the squadron as Brand was respected by officers and sailors alike. Notwithstanding this great personal tragedy, Brand continued upon the task and duty that he had assumed on the day of the squadron's departure from England.

Departing Albany, the squadron sailed to Adelaide where it received a rapturous welcome. As the ships groped their way up the St Vincent Gulf to where they were to anchor, a message of welcome was received from Sir Henry Barwell, the premier of South Australia:

Genuine, whole-hearted, and spontaneous will be the welcome extended by South Australians to the Squadron which is now approaching our shores. The mere fact that these ships-of-war—real fighting units of first-class efficiency—are even within south Australian waters will be causing a thrill of satisfaction throughout the State.

The Squadron, representing as it does that unity, strength and purpose for which the Royal Navy stands, must inspire us one and all with a keen sense of national pride and security. The Navy, and the Merchant Service which is protected by the Navy, are the binding force that holds together the edifice of the Empire—an edifice which without them would very soon crumble to pieces.[5]

A message of welcome was also received from the governor of South Australia, General Sir Tom Bridges, which was no less explicit in its praise for the navy:

From the day the first Governor, Captain Hindmarsh, R.N., stepped ashore at Glenelg, from H.M.S. *Buffalo*, in 1836, the existence and prosperity of thus State have been dependant on the freedom of her maritime communications. That the Seven Seas have been kept clear for Britishers ever since the Battle of Trafalgar, and that we have been able, unmolested, to build up and to consolidate our great British Empire, is the work of the Silent Service which we welcome to-day. Let us foster those great Blue-Water traditions that our people of to-day and to-morrow may be found worthy of the great heritage bequeathed to them.[6]

HMS *Hood* and *Repulse* off Adelaide. (*Ref: 1-2-062598-F, Alexander Turnbull Library, Wellington, New Zealand*)

'The Navy Means Everything'

As the squadron approached, thousands of people gathered at Glenelg, 6.5 miles from Adelaide, to glimpse the ships as they sailed by on their approach to Adelaide. Acute disappointment was forthcoming, however, when it was learned that the squadron would not be able to enter the harbour, prompting the ships to anchor outside. Despite this, the *Adelaide Advertiser* wrote that the ships provided 'a glorious and impressive spectacle':

> The Marines and other sections of the Procession all turning to the salute as they passed, evoked bursts of cheering. The huge crowds remained steady and gazed with wonderful appreciation at the units of the British Navy, and gloried in the thoughts of the great traditions associated with Britain's supremacy at sea.

In addition to cheering crowds who gathered to gaze upon the squadron, flags and banners bearing the words 'South Australia welcomes the Sons of the Sea' were hung along all of the principal streets.

Perfect weather prevailed during the squadron's time at Adelaide. Some 69,510 people visited the ships, including thousands of children, 1,000 members of the Navy League, and 500 Boy Scouts. Here, as elsewhere throughout the cruise, hospitalities were lavished upon the men of the squadron. Picnics and sporting events were laid on at Belair National Park, dances were laid on for 1,200 liberty men, while excursions to places of beauty and interest were organised by the

HMS *Hood* off Glenelg, Adelaide. (*PRG 280/1/40/166, Searcy Collection, State Library of South Australia*)

Hood off Glenelg. (*B 41019/297, State Library of South Australia*)

Flags and banners on Grenfell Street, Adelaide. A multitude of flags and banners were hung along all of the principal streets to welcome the squadron. (*Empire Photographic Publishing, Steve Locks*)

HMS *Danae* alongside at Adelaide. Astern the *Danae* are HMS *Delhi* and *Dunedin*. (*Empire Photographic Publishing, Steve Locks*)

Tourist Bureau. Theatres and cinemas were made free to all men in uniform, free transport was laid on, and tea was provided by the YMCA. A party of men from the squadron were taken to Willunga, a town located to the south of Adelaide where a parade was held and sporting events on the recreation ground.

As a guest of Sir Tom Bridges, Field stayed for a few days at Government House, from where he was able to see something of the surrounding countryside.

On the morning of 15 March, the squadron weighed anchor and departed Adelaide for Melbourne. From Adelaide, the squadron passed close to Rosetta Head, Robe, and Port MacDonnell, where large crowds had gathered to watch the ships pass by. As at Bunbury, a message subsequently reached Field informing him of how grateful the local population were for the opportunity he had given them to see the squadron as it sailed past.

The First Light Cruiser Squadron detached from the battlecruisers during 16 March and proceeded into Port Melbourne while behind them, the *Hood* and *Repulse* stopped briefly at Port Philip Heads in order to embark pilots. When asked by a reporter why the cruisers had not stopped and taken pilots on board, Field gave his answer as thus: 'The Light Cruisers did what is customary in the

Men of the squadron in one of the streets of Willunga ahead of a parade through the town. (*GN03722, History Trust of South Australia*)

Men of the squadron parading through Willunga. (*GN03717, History Trust of South Australia*)

Men from HMS *Hood* at Willunga recreation grounds. (*GN03723, History Trust of South Australia*)

Navy. It trains its officers to go anywhere at any time, and so it teaches them pilotage'.[7]

The approach to Melbourne presented certain challenges to vessels the size of the battlecruisers owing to the strong tidal currents and the shallow channel depth. The *Hood* and *Repulse* made their approach to Melbourne during the early morning on 17 March; visibility was hazy and the leading markers at the entrance to the bay were hard to distinguish. Despite the haze, the weather was glorious and innumerable small craft ventured out to greet the squadron. In addition to the small craft, a large number of steam ships carrying members of the commonwealth and state governments and others crowded with sightseers accompanied the squadron to their berths. It was not just steam ships which were crowded with sightseers, every vantage point, pier and wharf was also packed with thousands of enthusiastic, cheering and waving spectators. According to Lieutenant Charles Benstead the population of Melbourne 'lined every foot of deck space, climbed every ladder, adorned every excrescence upon which a man could stand and suspend itself in monkey-fashion where foothold was denied' to gain a look at the ships.[8] Alf Batchelder, meanwhile, recalled:

> It was ... glorious weather. Every road and pathway was thick and families were making a day of it, taking out all the children and hampers and bottles of beer. The bay was dotted with sailing boats. Everyone who had anything that would float ... was out there on the water ... I believe the papers said there were 500,000 people wanting to see the ships ... It was a wonderful sight.... The mist out at sea and then

HMS *Hood* seen from the *Repulse*.

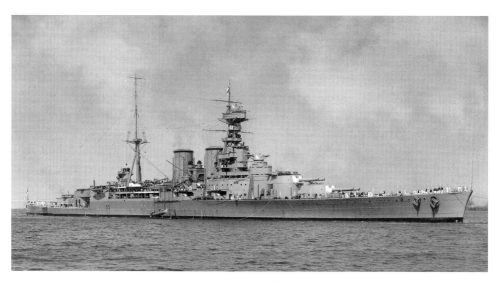

HMS *Hood* on 17 March 1924 while *en route* to Melbourne. The gleaming brass on the ship's guns and the whiteness of the scrubbed deck are clearly evident. (*Author's Collection*)

HMS *Hood* entering Melbourne. (*Author's Collection*)

a few minutes later the *Hood* herself, with the white cloud seeming to peel away from her as she came into the bridge sunlight of Port Philip ...⁹

In the sky above, aircraft of the Royal Australian Air Force roared overhead, providing an aerial escort.

Having berthed and secured alongside, Field inspected a Guard of Honour before he, Brand, and their captains along with their staffs departed the quayside to call upon the governor-general of the Commonwealth, Lord Forster of Lepe, the governor of Victoria, George Rous the earl of Stradbroke, as well as the prime minister, the premier of Victoria, the minister of defence, and the lord mayor of Melbourne. The fact that Melbourne was the seat of government for Australia and the capital of the state of Victoria duplicated the official ceremonies and intensified the hospitalities.¹⁰ Cheering crowds lined the streets which had been decorated in honour of the squadron's visit as Field, Brand, and the other men of their party drove through Melbourne.

The entertainment programme began almost immediately. A dinner was held by Lord Forster for the flag officers and captains which was followed by a ball at St Kilda town hall for the flag officers, captains, and officers of the squadron. Meanwhile, Lady Helena Stradbroke, the wife of the governor of Victoria, held a dance for the squadron's petty officer while the management of the Tivoli Theatre extended an invitation to 250 men of the squadron.

The day of the squadron's arrival in Melbourne, the city's leading newspaper, *The Argus*, carried a story on the arrival of the squadron:

Field inspecting a guard of honour at Melbourne. (*Empire Photographic Publishing, Steve Locks*)

> It is permissible for Australians to feel pride in their identity with the Empire and to share the prestige which its naval supremacy has conferred ... the British Navy, the symbol of the Empire's achievement for past centuries, will surely inspire Australian imagination and kindle the will to do great deeds in the future.[11]

The *Sun News Pictorial*, meanwhile, described how the squadron represented an 'ideal' and mused that without British sea power 'there could be no independent British-descended nation in this part of the world'.[12] It must be remembered that the cruise of the Special Service Squadron was not merely a good-will cruise but that it was also a politically motivated one. In contrast to *The Argus* and the *Sun News Pictorial*, the nationalist and anti-imperialist *Sydney Bulletin* warned its readers that while the squadron was touring Australia at the time there was no guarantee that such a squadron would be employed in the defence of British interests in the Pacific and with that, Australia, if the need arose. The *Sydney Bulletin* also pointed out that the arrival of the squadron in Australian waters had coincided with the scuttling of HMAS *Australia*, the Royal Australian Navy's sole battlecruiser, which was scuttled in accordance with the provisions of the Washington Naval Treaty, and that this sacrificial act could only be interpreted as a loss of national self-sufficiency.[13] The nationalist voice of the *Sydney Bulletin* and others like it also engaged in soul-searching of what British sea power meant for the future of Australia and its future identity. Lamenting that it was importing culture from the United States, the *Sydney Bulletin* stated:

Australia will have to decide shortly whether its orientation is to be west or east: whether it is to remain the easily recognisable British community it was when the World War began or become a nation of synthetic and second class Yanks, joined to the republic on the other side of the North Pacific by a tie compounded of Ford cars, Hollywood art, vaudeville and music comedy stars and dollars.[14]

The paper went on to conclude that the future of Australia lay in increased cooperation with Britain, the 'Mother Country', and that any financial burdens would be met 'when the Australian is brought to understand that the safety of his country lies in an approximation to the cultural and naval traditions of Britain: if we are once effectively Yankeefied they will never be made'.[15] Similarly, the Victorian branch of the Australian Navy League echoed the conclusion drawn by the *Sydney Bulletin*, insisting that 'we must all realise that should the Empire collapse, Australia goes under with the rest, as she is absolutely powerless to protect her'. It was only through cooperation with the Royal Navy, the League declared, 'that she can hope to retain her identity and remain as she is at present'.[16]

On 18 March 1,500 officers and men from the squadron took part in a march through the city. Ahead of the march, Field landed at St Kilda, where he was met by a demonstration of children gathered at the end of the pier, each of whom had been provided with a flag that they waved as they cheered the admiral as he walked down their lines. Shortly thereafter, Field was joined by Brand, members of their respective staffs and the captains of the ships whereupon they drove through streets packed full of enthusiastic, cheering crowds to the saluting base at the Federal Parliament House. Gathered at the foot of the building's stairs were the governor-general dressed in the uniform of the commander-in-chief of the Australian armed forces, the governor of Victoria who proudly displayed the medals he had won during the fighting in France during the First World War, and a number of military officers.

People swarmed in from across the city to watch the march. So many people attempted to make their way into the city to watch the event that the additional transport services that had been laid on by the railway and tramway authorities were hopelessly overwhelmed. As the men marched from the ships, their standards fluttering and bayonets glistening, the great throngs that had gathered responded with a great continuous roar of cheering.

During the course of 18 March, approximately 80,000 people visited the ships of the squadron. By the time the squadron departed Melbourne on 25 March, 486,467 people had visited the ships. During the time that the *Hood* was anchored alongside Prince's Pier, her crewmen welcomed aboard some 200,000 visitors. It has been estimated that a similar number of would-be visitors were turned away.[17] Lieutenant Geoffrey Wells noted:

Enormous crowds besieged us. Numbers unprecedented percolated into every place in the ship. Women fainted on the gangways which almost gave way beneath the

Left: On 18 March, 1,500 officers and men from the squadron took part in a march through Melbourne. 'People swarmed in from across the city to watch the march. So many people attempted to make their way into the city to watch the event that the additional transport services that had been laid on by the railways and tramways were hopelessly overwhelmed. As the men marched from the ships, their standards fluttering and bayonets glistening, the great throngs that had gathered responded with a great continuous roar of cheering'. (*Empire Photographic Publishing, Steve Locks*)

Below: Men of the squadron marching down Bourke Street, Melbourne. (*Empire Photographic Publishing, Steve Locks*)

'The Navy Means Everything'   135

Above left: HMS *Hood* alongside Prince's Pier, Melbourne. (*Empire Photographic Publishing, Steve Locks*)

Above right: HMS *Repulse* photographed while alongside at Port Philip, Melbourne. (*H2017.214/8, State Library Victoria*)

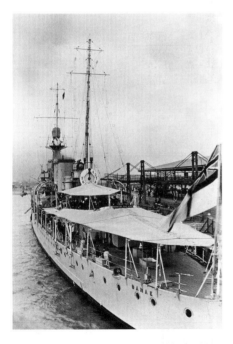 

Above left: HMS *Danae* photographed from astern while alongside at Port Philip, Melbourne. (*H2017.214/7, State Library Victoria*)

Above right: 'B' turret of HMS *Hood* is trained to port while the ship is alongside at Melbourne. HMS *Delhi* is the light cruiser in front of the *Hood*. The mast of HMS *Repulse* can be seen on the left of the photograph. (*H2017.214/6, State Library Victoria*)

weight. To get ashore became a feat of no mean skill and elbows. The *Repulse* also suffered. The little boys of the crowd fared best, they would squeeze where their sisters could not and could deal more rapidly with the ladders.[18]

It was through these crowds that Signal Boatswain Alfred Punshon had to be carried on a stretcher from the *Hood* following suffering a heart attack. According to V. C. Scott O'Connor, 'His heart had failed, though none of us had suspected this when he played the part of Neptune so jovially in the ceremonies of Crossing the Line But he took no part in our festivities at Melbourne'.[19]

The people of Melbourne combined not only to entertain the officers and men of the squadron, but also lavished their private hospitality on the squadron. Hundreds of the squadron's sailors were received into the homes of Melbourne's citizens. At the same time, those who did not reside in the city but who had travelled to the city for the occasion took suites of rooms in the city's hotels which they then placed at the disposal of the squadron.

While 18 March was a day of furious activity and events, back in Britain, Prime Minister Ramsey MacDonald, under whose leadership the Labour Party had taken power in January 1924, announced to the House of Commons that his government was suspending construction on the naval base in Singapore in the interests of international peace and austerity. The announcement by MacDonald caused Australasian societies to erupt with warnings of the perceived menace of Japan. Of this decision, the pro-empire *Sydney Morning Herald* wrote, 'the unpleasant fact that Australia and New Zealand have now to face is that they will have to rely more on themselves than they have ever done in the past'.[20] Following the announcement, Field met with Stanley Bruce, the prime minister of the Australian Commonwealth. Following his meeting with Bruce, Field notified the Admiralty:

> It cannot be fully realised in England with what consternation this decision has been received in Australia and I should be failing in my duty if I did not record the impression to me that this decision has been generally received in Australia with genuine feelings of Alarm.[21]

Meanwhile, for the squadron, the activities continued. On 19 March, the squadron fielded a football team to take on Victoria at the Melbourne Cricket Club's Albert Ground. Ahead of the game, *The Sporting Globe* reported, 'Soccer is the most popular game with the fleet. There can be no doubt about that. All the officers and men keenly debate the game, notwithstanding that it is solely the ratings that play'.[22] The game finished 2-2.

The following day, the Melbourne Cricket Club was the site of a cricket match between a team fielded by the squadron and a team drawn from the Australian Army, Navy and Air Force. In an unusual sporting display, the Australian team gave the men of the squadron two hours to bat. Despite this, they could only muster 113 runs against the Australian 211. Of this defeat to the Australian

Visitors attempting to rush the barriers to board the squadron's ships at Melbourne. (*Empire Photographic Publishing, Steve Locks*)

A snapshot of the large crowd that waited to board HMS *Hood* at Melbourne. (*Empire Photographic Publishing, Steve Locks*)

Left: Crowds of visitors aboard HMS *Hood* and *Delhi*, while docked at Prince's Pier, Melbourne. Approximately 80,000 people visited the squadron's ships on 18 March. By the time the squadron departed Melbourne on 25 March, 486,467 people had visited the ships. (*Ronald Alfred Cheers, Museums Victoria*)

Below: Crowds of visitors on the quayside and forecastle of HMS *Hood*. In front of HMS *Hood* is HMS *Delhi*. (*Empire Photographic Publishing, Steve Locks*)

'The Navy Means Everything' 139

Some of the 80,000 people who visited the squadron on 18 March. (*Empire Photographic Publishing, Steve Locks*)

Above left: Taken on the forecastle looking aft, visitors can be seen crowding every available space of HMS *Hood* and climbing the ship's superstructure. (*Empire Photographic Publishing, Steve Locks*)

Above right: Visitors to HMS *Hood* crowd the quayside and the superstructure of the battlecruiser.

Visitors on HMS *Hood*. Note the group of visitors atop 'A' turret and the forward rangefinder. (*H2017.214/12, State Library Victoria*)

Above left: Visitors on the forecastle of HMS *Hood*. Note the visitors standing atop the forward turrets and the superstructure. (*H2017.214/13, State Library Victoria*)

Above right: Taken while she was alongside at Melbourne, visitors can be seen beneath one of the canvas awnings erected over the deck aboard HMS *Hood*. Note 'X' turret which has been traversed to port. (*H2017.214/10, State Library Victoria*)

Taken from aboard HMS *Delhi*, HMS *Hood* (left) and HMS *Repulse* (right) are seen while alongside at Melbourne. (*Empire Photographic Publishing, Steve Locks*)

Visitors to the squadron on and beside HMS *Delhi*. (*H207.214.9, State Library Victoria*)

military, the newspaper *The Argus* remarked, 'It was apparent by their lack of judgement in the field that the visitors were very short of practice, but nevertheless they played keenly to the end'.[23] According to Lieutenant Charles Ransome of the *Repulse*, cricket was 'sadly in need of stimulation as far as the British Navy is concerned ... deck cricket is little practiced and the opportunity to gain proficiency is limited'.[24] Another game of cricket was held on the 22nd, which the Special Service Squadron also lost.

On 23 March, a massed band concert was held at the lord mayor's Fund for Metropolitan Hospitals and Charities. In anticipation of large crowds, additional trams and trains were laid on by the transport authorities. Massed bands from the *Hood*, *Repulse*, and *Delhi* were all scheduled to perform at the event. It had originally been intended that the squadron bands would march to the Melbourne Cricket Club where the event was being held but the idea was unpractical. Like the preceding days, 23 March was a day of glorious sunshine and large crowds of visitors flocked to Port Melbourne to tour the ships of the squadron. Such was the density of the crowds that mounted police had to clear the way for the bands who were then transported to the cricket club.

On 25 March, the squadron weighed anchor and left Melbourne. At 6 a.m. on that dull autumn morning, the officers and men aboard the *Hood* and the other ships of the squadron held masses of coloured paper streamers which were stretched over to the crowd that had gathered on Prince's Pier to bid them farewell. The streamers were a 'frail link with the friends they were leaving behind'.[25] One by one, the streamers snapped as tugs guided the ships away from the pier.

As *Hood* moved away from the pier, she did so without Signal Boatswain Punshon, who died that day. Aged forty-six when he died, Punshon was buried in the Independent Section of Melbourne General Cemetery. The following day, a memorial service was held for him aboard the battlecruiser:

> The ... day was one of the most perfect imaginable. A memorial service for him took place on the quarter-deck, attended by the Vice-Admiral, the officers and all those who were not on duty; for in the Navy men stand by each other. Eleven trumpeters on a gun-turret, standing erect in a line against the sky, sounded the Last Post; followed after a brief interval by the Réveillé. The flag fluttered at half-mast; and the Padre read the solemn and inspiring words of our burial service. That was the end of poor Punshon; in the words of the Vice-Admiral, 'one of the best and most loyal Warrant Officers he had ever known'.[26]

From Port Melbourne, the *Hood* and *Repulse* made for Mornington to conduct a day of speed trials in Port Philip Bay before proceeding to Hobart, Tasmania, which was reached on 27 March. Grey curtains of rain surrounded the squadron as it secured at the wharf. Despite the rain, a modest crowd of people gathered on the pier carrying umbrellas and wearing raincoats.

The welcome received by the squadron during the visit to Tasmania was in stark contrast to the welcome received in mainland Australia. Despite the crowds

'The Navy Means Everything' 143

Crowds gathering on the quayside to watch the squadron's departure from Melbourne. (*Empire Photographic Publishing, Steve Locks*)

Crowds beginning to gather on the pier beside HMS *Danae* to bid the cruiser and her sailors farewell on the day of the squadron's departure from Melbourne. (*Empire Photographic Publishing*)

Women on the quayside holding and throwing streamers to the men on the ships. (*Empire Photographic Publishing, Steve Locks*)

A 'frail link with the friends they were leaving behind': a mass of coloured paper streamers which stretched from the quayside to the men on the ships. This photograph shows the streamers extended out to HMS *Delhi* at Melbourne. (*Empire Photographic Publishing, Steve Locks*)

HMS *Delhi* shortly before her departure. (*Empire Photographic Publishing, Steve Locks*)

Taken from HMS *Danae*, HMS *Delhi* is seen moving away from Prince's Pier, Melbourne. (*Empire Photographic Publishing, Steve Locks*)

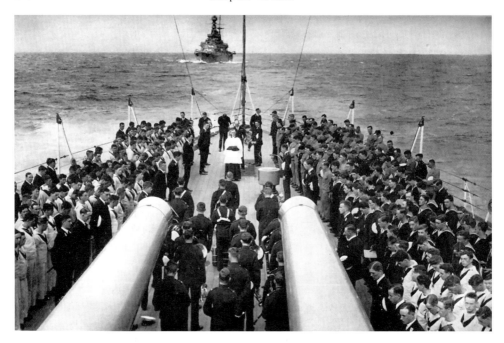

The memorial service held on the quarterdeck of HMS *Hood* for Signal Boatswain Alfred Punshon. (*Steve Locks*)

HMS *Repulse* photographed while conducting speed trials in Port Philip Bay. (*Empire Photographic Publishing, Steve Locks*)

of people who gathered on the pier amid the rain, the visit to Hobart 'was the most unenthusiastic visit recorded by sailors during the entire cruise and more surprising because it had a predominantly white populace'.[27] Wilfred Woolman recalled that '[t]here was no display of bunting, such as we have seen at all our other ports of call, and only a few flags here and there'.[28] Fredrick Bushell also commented on the reception given to the squadron at Hobart and of the atmosphere, noting, 'There were comparatively few people at the dock to see us come alongside and it seems very quiet after our last two ports'.[29]

The squadron's time at Hobart was to be brief, scheduled to last only until 3 April. For Frederick Bushell, things did not appear to improve when he went ashore on 28 March. Bushell 'did not get a very good impression of Hobart ... there seemed to be absolutely nothing to do at all'.[30] Wilfred Woolman, meanwhile, recorded:

> No cars were provided for us—we had to find our own way and walk through the muddy streets in our uniforms. The people we passed showed not the slightest interest. After Melbourne, it was so noticeable. It was the coolest reception we have had so far. Perhaps we have been spoilt and expect to be made a fuss of everywhere we go, but there was not a vestige of enthusiasm displayed anywhere...[31]

The impressions formed by Bushell and Woolman were not exclusive. The subdued welcome when compared to that received by the squadron at ports on the Australian mainland was blamed by *The Argus* and the Tasmanian *Daily Telegraph* on 'unpropitious and hazy weather'.[32]

For the men who were landed, two expeditions were organised: one to the north-west coast and one to Launceston. Both expeditions provided those who took part with the opportunity to see something of the interior of the island. The expedition to the north-west coast included visits to five towns at each of which an official reception was held. Commander John Vivian of the Royal Navy and Major Gerald Hickson of the Royal Marines, both of whom served aboard the *Hood*, served as the senior officers of the parties and delivered speeches which were greatly appreciated and well received. Meanwhile, Captain Parker of the *Repulse* along with Captain (E) Mark Rundle, the squadron engineering officer, made a visit to the centre of the island to look at the island's hydro-electric plant.

The photographs taken of the squadron while it was in Tasmania provide a mixed image of the reception provided to the squadron; in some, comparatively few people can be seen while in others, the piers can be clearly seen to be full of crowds.

While Bushell and Woolman may have been vexed by a lack of opportunities ashore, one standout point is a frustration at not being made a fuss of. As Simon Smith has written, 'their previous success undoubtedly increased their awareness of this, [and] it is likely that this also affected their own sense of pride and made for an uncomfortable time'.[33] Whatever the thoughts of the men of the squadron

Above: The Special Service Squadron arriving off Hobart. (*B 41019/242, State Library of South Australia*)

Left: HMS *Hood* at anchor in Hobart. (*B 41019/243, State Library of South Australia*)

'The Navy Means Everything' 149

Above left: Hood alongside Ocean Pier, Hobart. (*B 41019/232, State Library of South Australia*)

Above right: Hood at anchor at Hobart. (*B 41019/227, State Library of South Australia*)

Hood alongside at Hobart. (*B 41019/230, State Library of South Australia*)

Hobart Harbour. HMS *Hood* can be seen just to the left of centre. (*Empire Photographic Publishing, Steve Locks*)

Hood alongside the wharf at Hobart. (*B 41019/233, State Library of South Australia*)

A crowd of people gather on Ocean Pier to tour the Special Service Squadron's ships. (B 41019/255, State Library of South Australia)

Visitors boarding the *Hood* at Hobart. (B 41019/253, *State Library of South Australia*)

Above: 'At Home' status aboard the *Hood* while the ship is at anchor at Hobart. (B41019/248, State Library of South Australia)

Left: *Hood* amidships during the visit of the Special Service Squadron to Hobart. (B1019/247, State Library of South Australia)

Cleaning work being undertaken on the *Hood* while at Hobart. (*B1019/244, State Library of South Australia*)

HMS *Hood* pictured while at Hobart, Tasmania, between 27 March and 3 April 1924. (*Author's Collection*)

and in particular Frederick Bushell and Wilfred Woolman, it would appear that the visit of the squadron did good and achieved its aim of helping to cement imperial unity as later that year, a memorial tablet was installed at a signal station in Hobart to mark the visit of the squadron, leaving an indelible mark on the town. Had the visit not been a success or been unpopular, such a tablet to commemorate the visit would likely not have been erected.

The squadron departed Hobart on 3 April in perfect weather to return to Australia. The weather did not hold and the following day heavy seas were encountered. A distress signal was picked up from a Japanese merchant vessel, the *Honolulu Maru*, which reported that she was making little headway in the gale and that the strong wind had caused some of the cargo on her decks to become loose and move around leaving the ship in danger of capsizing. HMS *Dauntless*, at the head of the squadron, increased speed to 23 knots and set a course for the *Honolulu Maru* in order to render assistance. In her wake, HMS *Dragon* followed and stood by until the danger had passed.

The battlecruisers with HMS *Delhi*, *Danae*, and *Dunedin*, meanwhile, continued on their way and dropped anchor at Twofold Bay that same day. The heavy swell in the bay prevented the large crowds that had gathered on the cliffs from visiting the ships. Despite the swell, two members of the Shire Council did make the journey out to the *Hood*, where they were welcomed aboard to present

Crowds gather to bid farewell to the squadron on the day of its departure from Hobart. (*Empire Photographic Publishing, Steve Locks*)

'The Navy Means Everything' 155

HMS *Delhi* departing Hobart. (*Empire Photographic Publishing, Steve Locks*)

The *Honolulu Maru* viewed from HMS *Dragon* as she stood by to render assistance to the merchant vessel. (*Empire Photographic Publishing, Steve Locks*)

Field with an address of welcome. The crowds that had gathered were not to be left disappointed, however, for prior to dropping anchor, the *Delhi*, *Danae*, and *Dunedin* conducted a series of manoeuvres to the pleasure of the crowd. The following day, the *Hood*, *Repulse*, *Delhi*, *Dunedin*, and *Danae* weighed anchor and sailed up the coast to Jervis Bay, where they dropped anchor. A few hours after them, listing heavily, the *Honolulu Maru* entered Jervis Bay escorted by HMS *Dragon*.

Jervis Bay was an important stopping point for the squadron as situated on the perpendicular cliffs at Captain's Point overlooking the ocean is HMAS *Creswell*, the Royal Australian Naval College. At the college cadets were drilled, trained, and moulded into the future commanding officers of the Royal Australian Navy. Three days were spent at Jervis Bay before the squadron set a course for Sydney.

The squadron passed through Sydney Heads on the morning of 9 April. In brilliant sunshine, the squadron was escorted into Sydney Harbour by aircraft of the Royal Australian Air Force to the euphoria of the 500,000 people who packed the shoreline and decks of innumerable small craft to witness the arrival of the squadron. 'The scene of animation and enthusiasm, ashore and afloat', wrote Field of the welcome received by the squadron, 'surpassed anything in our previous experience, and left upon our minds an impression that none of us will ever forget'.[34]

Soon after the squadron had glided into the harbour and dropped anchor, the Naval Brigade landed and marched through the city. Following the march through the city by the Naval Brigade, a civic reception was held at Parliament House attended by Stanley Bruce and other principal ministers of state. There followed a full hospitality programme. Admiral Sir Dudley de Chair, the governor of New South Wales, held an official dinner for the flag officers and captains of the squadron. Meanwhile, 500 petty officers and other ranks were entertained at a ball at the town hall; 240 petty officers and men attended a supper and dance held by ex-servicewomen. Sixty officers were entertained at a dance at the Rose Bay Golf Club while a dinner and theatre party was held for chief petty officers and petty officers by the Overseas League.

The events continued the following day. Admiral de Chair along with Rear Admiral Albert Addison, the admiral commanding the Australian fleet, the premier of New South Wales, and the lord mayor, called on Field. The *Hood* was placed 'At Home', playing host to 1,500 guests. A banquet was held by the government for the flag officers, captains, and thirty officers while launches, cars, and buses ferried large numbers of crewmen into the interior of the country as well as to the beach resorts in the vicinity of the city. A picnic for petty officers and men from the *Hood* and *Repulse* was organised by the Soldiers and Sailors' Mothers, Wives, and Widows Association. Amid these activities, boxing competitions were held which saw the squadron win two bouts but lose six. The vast array of hospitality events continued throughout the time that the squadron was at anchor.

HMAS *Creswell*, the Royal Australian Naval College. Due to it being home to the college, Jervis Bay was an important stopping point for the squadron. (*Empire Photographic Publishing, Steve Locks*)

Two visitors stand between the forward 15-inch guns of the *Hood* while the ship is at anchor in Jervis Bay. (*IE1706475, State Library of New South Wales*)

Onlookers watch the arrival of the Special Service Squadron in Sydney. (*00035269, Samuel J. Hood Studio Collection, Australian National Maritime Museum*)

HMS *Repulse* followed by the First Light Cruiser Squadron's ships near Sydney Heads. (*00035274, Samuel J. Hood Studio Collection, Australian National Maritime Museum*)

HMS *Hood* (top) and HMS *Repulse* (bottom) entering Sydney Harbour. (*00035271, Samuel J. Hood Studio Collection, Australian National Maritime Museum*)

HMS *Hood* photographed as she sails into Sydney. (*Christopher Hancock*)

HMS *Hood* entering Sydney Harbour. (*00035273, Samuel J. Hood Studio Collection, Australian National Maritime Museum*)

Crowds on the shoreline watching the arrival of the squadron into Sydney Harbour. HMS *Hood* is in the background. (*Empire Photographic Publishing, Steve Locks*)

'The Navy Means Everything'

HMS *Hood* making her way into Sydney Harbour. (*00035270, Samuel J. Hood Studio Collection, Australian National Maritime Museum*)

HMS *Hood* near Fort Denison as she enters Sydney Harbour, 9 April 1924. (*00035272, Samuel J. Hood Studio Collection, Australian National Maritime Museum*)

162 *Empire Cruise*

(00035275, *Samuel J. Hood Studio Collection, Australian National Maritime Museum*)

HMS *Repulse* entering Sydney Harbour. (00035276, *Samuel J. Hood Studio Collection, Australian National Maritime Museum*)

Hood (left) and *Repulse* (centre) entering Sydney Harbour, 9 April 1924. (*SRV16083, City of Sydney Archives*)

Hood's arrival in Sydney viewed from Kurraba Point. Above the stern of the *Hood*, the Royal Australian Navy light cruiser HMAS *Adelaide* can be seen. (*00035279, Samuel J. Hood Studio Collection, Australian National Maritime Museum*)

HMAS *Adelaide* at anchor in Sydney Harbour on 9 April 1924. Between the third and fourth funnel of the *Adelaide*, the mast of HMS *Hood* can be made out as she enters the harbour. (*300079, Australian War Memorial*)

HMS *Delhi* moving up Sydney Harbour, 9 April 1924. (*P00250.011, Australian War Memorial*)

Boats surround the squadron as it enters Sydney Harbour. Half a million people packed the shoreline and decks of innumerable small craft to witness the arrival of the squadron. 'The scene of animation and enthusiasm, ashore and afloat,' wrote Field of the welcome received by the squadron, 'surpassed anything in our previous experience.' (*Empire Photographic Publishing, Steve Locks*)

Taken from one of the small craft that surrounded the squadron and welcomed it into harbour, this photograph shows the *Hood* entering Sydney Harbour and some of the small boats and craft that surrounded the battlecruiser. (*P00250.13, Australian War Memorial*)

Taken overlooking the quarterdeck of the *Hood*, men can be seen lined up on deck as the ship enters Sydney Harbour. Some of the boats and small craft that surrounded the squadron as it entered the harbour can also be seen. HMS *Repulse* follows behind the flagship. (*Empire Photographic Publishing, Steve Locks*)

Hood entering Sydney Harbour. (*Author's Collection*)

Puffs of smoke are emitted from the saluting guns of the *Hood* as the ship renders a salute upon her arrival in Sydney Harbour, 9 April 1924. (*IE1165795, Mitchell Library, State Library of New South Wales*)

A close-up of *Hood*'s aft section while she lies at anchor in Sydney Harbour. Note how on the railings the crew have begun hanging letters spelling 'HOOD' but have yet to hang the 'H'. (*City of Sydney Archives 90460, Graeme Andrews 'Working Harbour' Collection*)

HMS *Hood* in Sydney Harbour, 9 April 1924. (*00035277, Samuel J. Hood Studio Collection, Australian National Maritime Museum*)

HMS *Repulse* surrounded by small craft as she enters Sydney Harbour, 9 April 1924. (*392635, Victor Everson, State Library of New South Wales*)

'Soon after the Squadron had glided into the harbour and dropped anchor the Naval Brigade landed and marched through the city.' Royal Marines, officers, and sailors from the ships disembarking from a ferry at Wharf 9 at Woolloomooloo, Sydney prior to assembling to march through the streets of Sydney, 9 April 1924. (*00035282, Samuel J. Hood Studio Collection, Australian National Maritime Museum*)

Men from the Special Service Squadron disembarking at Woolloomooloo. (*00035280, Samuel J. Hood Studio Collection, Australian National Maritime Museum*)

(00035281, Samuel J. Hood Studio Collection, Australian National Maritime Museum)

Men drawn from the squadron assembling and waiting near Woolloomooloo prior to marching through the streets of Sydney. (00035283, Samuel J. Hood Studio Collection, Australian National Maritime Museum)

'The Navy Means Everything'   171

Members of the Royal Marines Band Service near Woolloomooloo prior to marching through the streets of Sydney. (*00035286, Samuel J. Hood Studio Collection, Australian National Maritime Museum*)

Members of the Royal Marines Band Service near Woolloomooloo. (*00035287, Samuel J. Hood Studio Collection, Australian National Maritime Museum*)

Members of the Naval Brigade marching through the streets of Sydney. (00035284, *Samuel J. Hood Studio Collection, Australian National Maritime Museum*)

(00035285, *Samuel J Hood Studio Collection, Australian National Maritime Museum*)

'The Navy Means Everything'

HMS *Hood* alongside the wharf in Sydney. (*ANMS0047[050]*, *Henry Stewart Collection, Australian National Maritime Museum*)

The cruisers HMS *Dragon* (left) and HMS *Dunedin* (right) at anchor off Garden Island, Sydney, 9 April 1924. Between the two cruisers is a tanker, the *British Beacon*. This photograph was taken by Frederick Wilkinson, one of many spectators to the squadron's arrival who ventured out on one of the many boats that swarmed around the ships. (*00037701, Frederick Garner Wilkinson, Australian National Maritime Museum*)

Taken from HMS *Hood*, the Sydney ferry *Kuttabul* packed with sightseers and visitors to the Special Service Squadron's ships. In the background, HMS *Repulse* can be seen. (*A-00075997, Graeme Andrews Working Harbour Collection, City of Sydney Archives*)

The ferry *Lady Carrington* carrying visitors past HMS *Repulse* as she lies at anchor in Sydney Harbour. (*81813, Graeme Andrews Working Harbour Collection, City of Sydney Archives*)

During the time that the squadron was at anchor, the ships were visited by 156,000 people. On the night of 11 April, the harbour and the city were lit up by the searchlights of the squadron and elements of the Royal Australian Navy, while a Venetian carnival took place on the water.

It was at a dinner held as part of the hospitality and entertainment programmes that the cruise began to achieve some of its aims. During the speeches made at the banquet held by the national government and the government of New South Wales, Sir George Fuller, the premier of New South Wales, proclaimed that 'It was the Royal Navy that discovered for us this magnificent land ... our feelings are those of gratitude, affection and admiration'.[35] Speaking as a man of business Sir William Brunton, the lord mayor stated:

> We feel that such visits should be made more often; So that the people of Great Britain may know more of Australia, of its potentialities, of our great need of population—British population—and of the wonderful opportunities that await our kinsmen who come here determined to make good.[36]

Stanley Bruce brought the high sentiments to a crescendo:

> It is not enough to express gratitude ... It is necessary to show it by our actions. For reasons of good sportsmanship and of sound practical common sense, Australia says unhesitatingly to-day, as she has ever said in the past, that she is determined to remain an integral part of the British Empire, and to shoulder her fair share of the burden of our common defence.

Bruce proceeded to announce the intention of the Australian government to immediately lay down two heavy cruisers before going on to deplore the decision of the British government to abandon plans for the construction of a naval base at Singapore.

No less patriotic, the leader of the Labour Party, Matthew Charlton, in his speech stated:

> If England were in danger, Australia would not only provide for her own defence, but would provide for the defence of the Empire. She was not unmindful of her debt to the Mother Country and would not be behindhand, if the necessity arose, in standing shoulder to shoulder with her.[37]

All of the speeches indicated a desire for peace to be maintained and indicated that reliance on the League of Nations was not the best way for peace to be maintained, rather, the consensus was that peace would be best maintained through the continued strength of the empire. On this subject, Stanley Bruce stated:

> Reduce the relative strength of the British Empire and you strike a fatal blow at the world's peace. With a strong Empire we can use our influence on the cause of peace; without it our voice will cease to be listened to in the Councils of the Nations.

Hood in Sydney Harbour between 9 and 20 April 1924. (*City of Sydney Archives 092503, Graeme Andrews 'Working Harbour' Collection*)

Hood at anchor while in Sydney Harbour. Note that 'X' turret has been traversed to starboard. (*City of Sydney Archives 092504, Graeme Andrews 'Working Harbour' Collection*)

Women and children sit on the deck of the *Hood* around the anchor cables while the ship is in Sydney. (*Author's Collection*)

HMS *Repulse* at anchor in Sydney. (*IE1685887, State Library of New South Wales*)

HMS *Repulse* surrounded by small craft while at anchor in Sydney. (00035278, Samuel J. Hood Studio Collection, Australian National Maritime Museum)

HMS *Dauntless* moored alongside buoy No. 12 while alongside in Sydney, 11 April 1924. (00037682, Frederick Garner Wilkinson, Australian National Maritime Museum)

I say unhesitatingly, that to reduce the defensive power of the British Empire and to substitute for that strength, reliance on the League, is to do a great disservice to the cause of peace, and is to lay the foundations of another world-cataclysm, beside which the tragedy through which we have passed will fade into insignificance.[38]

On 12 April, the battlecruiser *Australia* was towed out into the Pacific and sunk in accordance with the Washington Naval Treaty. Prior to being towed out to sea the ship had been gutted. Pieces of scrap metal lay on her decks, paint blistered, the once scrupulously clean quarterdeck was splintered, while the ship's brass elements had been removed. On one of the *Australia*'s gun shields, the words 'God help our Navy!' had been chalked. Many thousands ventured out to watch the end of the *Australia*. The day the *Australia* was sunk the First Light Cruiser Squadron weighed anchor and departed Sydney for Brisbane. *En route* to Brisbane the light cruiser squadron passed the *Australia*. Brand divided his ships so that they passed either side of the battlecruiser while ensigns were lowered and a twenty-one-gun salute was fired from the *Delhi* which also flew the Australian flag from her foremast as a tribute.

HMS *Hood* and *Repulse*, meanwhile, remained at Sydney where they were joined by the newly refitted Town-class light cruiser HMAS *Adelaide*, which was detached to join the squadron along with ten midshipmen from the naval college at Jervis Bay.[39] On 14 April, a musical revue of 'The Cheer Oh Girls' was held aboard the *Hood* before the battlecruisers and *Adelaide* departed Sydney on 20 April.

HMAS *Australia* while being towed out prior to her sinking. (*Empire Photographic Publishing, Steve Locks*)

HMAS *Australia* sinking after being scuttled off Sydney. (*Allan C. Green, State Library of Victoria*)

'The Navy Means Everything' 181

HMS *Repulse* anchored in Athol Bight, Sydney, photographed on 13 April 1924 from astern. (*00037697, Frederick Garner Wilkinson, Australian National Maritime Museum*)

HMS *Hood* at anchor while in Sydney. (*IE1165795, Mitchell Library, State Library of New South Wales*)

182   Empire Cruise

(IE1165795, Mitchell Library, State Library of New South Wales)

(IE1165795, Mitchell Library, State Library of New South Wales)

Above: (IE1165795, Mitchell Library, State Library of New South Wales)

Right: (IE1165795, Mitchell Library, State Library of New South Wales)

7

'We Only Did Our Duty'

Having paid their respects to HMAS *Australia*, the ships of the First Light Cruiser Squadron proceeded to Brisbane where they dropped anchor in the Brisbane River, in the centre of the city on 14 April. At Brisbane, the ceremonies which had been conducted at every major stop were once more conducted while Brand made official calls and had them returned in kind. Following these formalities, Brand, his staff, and his captains were entertained at a public dinner.

At the dinner, the table was uniquely set, arranged in the shape of the state of Queensland with the railways outlined on the tablecloth and samples of various products from the state placed according to their district. The governor of Queensland, Matthew Nathan, toasted to the health of the squadron before each of the guests was presented with a walking stick cut from a Queensland tree.

The following day, the Naval Brigade comprised of 850 officers and men marched through the city to the pleasure of enthusiastic crowds who had gathered and presented the men with a warm welcome. A sporting carnival followed at which exhibitions of boomerang and spear throwing were provided. In return the Royal Marines held a bayonet display. During the boxing competition, the squadron won ten bouts and lost seven. A rugby team fielded by Brisbane beat the First Light Cruiser Squadron 28-8 before the squadron beat Queensland 8-0 at hockey. Queensland also won the rifle shooting competition, scoring 1,794 points against the squadron's 1,262. The activities were not confined to sporting events. Brand and members of his staff travelled to Tamrookum, 50 miles outside of Brisbane, to visit a cattle station while the ships were opened to the public. During the week that the squadron was at anchor, HMS *Delhi*, *Danae*, *Dauntless*, and *Dunedin* were visited by 128,750 individuals.

One incident befell the First Light Cruiser Squadron that served to detract from the pleasure of the visit when on 18 April Able Seaman William Harrhy from HMS *Dauntless* fell overboard and drowned. Harrhy's body was recovered two days later, and a funeral service held with full military honours was conducted on 21 April.

'We Only Did Our Duty'

One of the First Light Cruiser Squadron's ships arriving on the Brisbane River during the squadron's arrival to Brisbane, 14 April 1924. The original caption of the photograph states that the ship is 'probably' HMS *Dunedin*. The admiral's flag from the foremast indicates the ship as being HMS *Delhi*. (*92352, John Oxley Library, State Library of Queensland*)

HMS *Dunedin* turning into Gardens Reach on the Brisbane River, 14 April 1924. (*130439, John Oxley Library, State Library of Queensland*)

HMS *Danae* and HMS *Delhi* alongside at Brisbane. (65328, *John Oxley Library, State Library of Queensland*)

HMS *Danae* and *Delhi* alongside at Brisbane. (108328, *John Oxley library, State Library of Queensland*)

HMS *Delhi* alongside at Brisbane. (168686, John Oxley Library, State Library of Queensland)

HMS *Dauntless* and HMS *Dragon* alongside at Brisbane. (168687, John Oxley Library, State Library of Queensland)

HMS *Dunedin* alongside at Brisbane. (*Empire Photographic Publishing, Steve Locks*)

Aboriginal chiefs being presented to Rear Admiral Brand in Brisbane. (*Empire Photographic Publishing, Steve Locks*)

'We Only Did Our Duty'

Right: Four crewmen pose on the forecastle of HMS *Dragon* while the ship is at anchor in Brisbane. (*85423, John Oxley Library, State Library of Queensland*)

Below: The headstone of Able Seaman William Harrhy who fell overboard from HMS *Dauntless* and drowned in the Brisbane River.

A week following their arrival at Brisbane, the ships of the First Light Cruiser Squadron, minus HMS *Dragon*, weighed anchor and departed the city. HMS *Dragon* was to remain behind to assist in the commemorations of Anzac Day. Henry Foster, 1st Baron Foster, the governor-general of Australia, travelled to Brisbane from Sydney for the occasion. He was received by a naval guard that fired three volleys at the ceremony unveiling the Stone of Remembrance and Cross of Sacrifice. Following this, Captain Fairbairn laid a wreath at the Stone of Remembrance on behalf of the officers and men of the Special Service Squadron. Following the ceremony, the governor-general laid the foundation stone of the Anzac Club before a special service was held in St John's Cathedral, at which the civil, naval, and military authorities were in attendance along with Fairbairn and a representation of officers and men from *Dragon*. At the conclusion of the service in St John's Cathedral, a march-past of ex-servicemen took place, which was headed by a ceremonial company of eleven officers and 150 men from HMS *Dragon*. The day's events were rounded off with an address from Vice-Admiral Field received via wireless, which was read by Captain Fairbairn, eliciting the enthusiasm of those present. Foster then delivered an address in which he spoke of the satisfaction that had been given to the people of Queensland by the presence of HMS *Dragon* on Anzac Day. The following day, 26 April, *Dragon* weighed anchor and departed Brisbane in the presence of cheering crowds. By the time the cruiser weighed anchor, she had been visited by 43,323 people.

Having left Brisbane, the bulk of the First Light Cruiser Squadron had returned to Sydney where Anzac Day was observed. In Sydney, a memorial service was held at the town hall at which 300 representatives of the squadron drawn from the cruisers were in attendance. On 26 April, the cruisers departed Sydney for New Zealand. As the ships slipped their moorings and got underway, the ship's bands played. The sea became rough almost immediately after passing through Sydney Heads. Scarcely had the squadron passed through the heads then HMS *Dunedin* and *Dauntless* detached and took up a course for Dunedin while *Delhi* and *Danae*, to be joined by HMS *Dragon*, steered for Christchurch.

The departure of the First Light Cruiser Squadron from Sydney marked the end of the Special Service Squadron's visit to Australia. At this point, it is worth briefly noting here that during the first six months of the cruise, a total of 151 individuals deserted from the ships of the squadron. Of these, 141 set up a new life in Australia.

While the First Light Cruiser Squadron had been at Brisbane the *Hood*, *Repulse* and *Adelaide* had departed Sydney and crossed the Tasman Sea to Wellington, New Zealand, where they dropped anchor on the morning of 24 April. At Wellington, the battlecruisers and *Adelaide* joined HMS *Chatham*, the flagship of the New Zealand Division. To the great delight and honour of the squadron, the governor-general of New Zealand, Admiral of the Fleet John Jellicoe, 1st Earl Jellicoe, who had commanded the Grand Fleet at the Battle of Jutland before being appointed first sea lord from November 1916 to December 1917, travelled to Wellington from Auckland to welcome the squadron.

'We Only Did Our Duty'

Crowds at Brisbane gathered on the wharf to bid farewell to HMS *Dragon*. The ship had remained in Brisbane following the departure of the other ships of the First Light Cruiser Squadron to participate in the Anzac Day commemorations in the city. (*85422, John Oxley Library, State Library of Queensland*)

Streamers extend out to HMS *Dragon* from the quayside as she prepares to leave Brisbane. (*Empire Photographic Publishing, Steve Locks*)

A wave washes over the quarterdeck of HMS *Hood* as she sails to New Zealand, accompanied by HMS *Repulse* and HMAS *Adelaide*. Between Australia and New Zealand, the ships sailed through rough weather. (*Empire Photographic Publishing, Steve Locks*)

HMS *Hood* proceeding through Wellington Harbour to her berth. (*0.040899, Museum of New Zealand*)

Above: HMS *Hood* entering Wellington Harbour, 24 April 1924. (*William Hall Raine, Ref: 1/2-100604-G, Alexander Turnbull Library, Wellington, New Zealand*)

Right: Admiral of the Fleet John Jellicoe, 1st Earl Jellicoe, who was governor-general of New Zealand, boarding HMS *Hood* while the ship is alongside at Wellington. To the great delight and honour of the squadron, Jellicoe, who had led the Grand Fleet at Jutland in 1916, travelled to Wellington from Auckland to welcome the squadron. (*Empire Photographic Publishing, Steve Locks*)

194   *Empire Cruise*

The *Hood*, *Repulse*, and *Adelaide* observed Anzac Day while in Wellington. At the request of the government of New Zealand, Field took part in a memorial service held at the cenotaph. A message was received from King George V, which was read to those assembled at the service by Jellicoe: 'The thoughts of the Queen and myself are with my people of New Zealand on this solemn day when they commemorate the glorious achievements of their beloved dead'.[1] Continuing, Jellicoe added his own words:

> I am sure that I am voicing the feelings of the people of New Zealand, when I say how greatly they appreciate the presence in our midst of Vice-Admiral Sir Frederick Field, the officers and men of the British Squadron, and of the Royal Australian Navy. The former represent the Navy which worked and fought with the men of the New Zealand Expeditionary Force on the Gallipoli Peninsula, and in that close comradeship were imbued with great admiration for their qualities; the latter stand for the other and larger part of that Anzac force which with the 29th Division achieved the impossible nine years ago. On that day the men of New Zealand commenced to build up a glorious record—a record on which such names as Gallipoli, Palestine, the Somme, Messines, Passchendaele, Beaumont Hamel, Bapaume, and Le Quesny stand out in bold relief for ever in history; the record not only of a magnificent fighting spirit, but of a discipline and chivalry which brought them equal honour.[2]

To this address, Field responded with his own brief address, in which he stated, 'I beg you, to regard this day not as one of mourning, but rather of thanksgiving that were are of the same flesh and blood as the heroes we now honour, and also as a day of earnest resolve to emulate their great examples'.[3] The address delivered by Field was read in twelve of the principal schools in Wellington by selected senior officers from the squadron.

The arrival of the squadron at Wellington coincided with a general railway strike across New Zealand. The railway strike served to considerably disorganise the entertainment programme that had been planned for the officers and men as well as the arrangements that had been made for transporting visitors to Wellington to see the ships. The strike would be brought to an end on 30 April subject to a commission of inquiry being set up to look into and address the grievances of the strikers. While disrupting the entertainment programme, the railway strike did not prevent a wide variety of events from taking place:

> There was a Navy League ball at the Town Hall; excursions in the neighbourhood of the city; concerts and dances for the men, and naval sports and athletic competitions. At soccer, rugger, hockey, and golf, the honours lay with Wellington; at cricket, *Hood*, *Repulse* and *Adelaide* won. A two-mile cutter race between *Hood* and *Chatham* was won by *Chatham*. [For her victory *Chatham* was awarded the Frobisher cup].
>
> *Repulse*, as usual distinguished herself by a children's party, and by a pantomime given by her Officers at the Opera House.

The public were entertained on His Majesty's ships; at a Squadron 'At Home', at which 900 guests were present; at a ball in *Hood*, at which there were 700 guests; at a Ship's Company 'At Home' in *Repulse*, and at the Vice-Admiral's official dinner in *Hood* to which the Governor-General, the Prime Minister and other distinguished persons were invited. In addition 153,872 visitors were shown over *Hood*, *Repulse* and *Adelaide* including 12,000 school children.[4]

A parade service was held at St Paul's Cathedral on 27 April at which the chaplain of the *Hood* officiated. The following day saw a naval brigade landed to march through the streets of Wellington, an event that was watched by thousands of citizens. Jellicoe, accompanied by Prime Minister William Massey and members of the government, took the salute rendered by the brigade.

On 8 May, the battlecruisers and *Adelaide*, accompanied by *Chatham*, departed Wellington to sail to Auckland. At the invitation of Field, Jellicoe joined the *Hood* for the journey and hoisted his flag beside that of Field. *En route* to Auckland, the ships made a brief stop at Napier.

In the meantime, HMS *Delhi*, *Danae*, and *Dragon* had sailed to Lyttleton, the seaport of Christchurch from where the crews were treated to the sight of the Southern Alps. Some 24,000 people visited the cruisers during their stay, including thousands of children. Following a few days at Christchurch, the three cruisers weighed anchor and proceeded to Napier where they rendezvoused with the *Hood*,

HMS *Hood* in Wellington Harbour. Note the crewmembers milling around her decks. (*Ref: PAColl-6304-11, Alexander Turnbull Library, Wellington, New Zealand*)

Above: HMS *Hood* at anchor in Wellington Harbour. (*Ref: PAColl-6304-12, Alexander Turnbull Library, Wellington, New Zealand*)

Left: Taken while alongside in Wellington, this photograph provides a detailed illustration of the area around the *Hood*'s conning tower, bridge, and foremast. (*Ref: PAColl-6304-13, Alexander Turnbull Library, Wellington, New Zealand*)

Hood alongside in Wellington. (*Ref: 1/2-062599-F, Alexander Turnbull Library, Wellington, New Zealand*)

Taken from the bow looking aft, this photograph was taken while *Hood* was in Wellington. The ship's main armament is clearly evident in all its imposing glory with the guns of 'A' turret elevated slightly to starboard and 'B' turret in the forward position. (*James Hutchings Kinnear, Ref: 1-2-015263-F, Alexander Turnbull Library, Wellington, New Zealand*)

A boat full of visitors arriving alongside HMS *Repulse* in Wellington. (*Empire Photographic Publishing, Steve Locks*)

Above left: (*Empire Photographic Publishing, Steve Locks*)

Above right: A smiling young boy on the slide erected on board the *Repulse* for the children's party held while at anchor in Wellington. (*Empire Photographic Publishing, Steve Locks*)

Members of the squadron engaging in sport while in Wellington. (*Empire Photographic Publishing, Steve Locks*)

HMS *Repulse* alongside in Napier. (*1/4-016960-G, Leslie Hinge, Alexander Turnbull Library*)

Left: Admiral Field (left) and Admiral of the Fleet John Jellicoe (right), governor-general of New Zealand, on the bridge of HMS *Hood*. At the invitation of Field, Jellicoe joined the *Hood* for the journey from Wellington to Auckland. (*Empire Photographic Publishing*)

Below: HMS *Delhi*, *Danae*, and *Dragon* alongside at Lyttleton during the visit to Christchurch. During their stay alongside, the cruisers were visited by 24,000 individuals. (*Empire Photographic Publishing*)

Repulse, and *Adelaide*. The cruisers of Brand's command rendered Jellicoe's flag a salute of nineteen guns before *Adelaide* joined the First Light Cruiser Squadron.

HMS *Dunedin* and *Dauntless*, in the meantime, had visited Dunedin and Bluff. The officers and men of the two cruisers were warmly received by the local populace who extended great hospitality to the ships which was rewarded in kind. Following their time at Dunedin and Bluff, the *Dauntless* and *Dunedin* proceeded directly to Auckland.

For those at Napier, the stay was brief, lasting twenty-four hours. Proceeding to sea, the battlecruisers and First Light Cruiser Squadron continued on their way to Auckland. By this point of the cruise, exhaustion was beginning to set in among members of the squadron's ships as the daily work of running the ships and the relentless entertainment programme began to wear the men out. One such sailor was Midshipman George Blundell, who recounted:

> I was running a picket boat, which meant solid work from 6 a.m. to 2 a.m. or midnight. And on my day off it meant entertaining visitors or being entertained ashore. The shore entertainment was a terrible duty. The official dances were a nightmare at which one had to stay until about 1 a.m. Sometimes I could hardly stand up, having had little sleep for several days. The job of laundering and keeping our clothes spotlessly clean was also a nightmare.[5]

In an effort to ease the burden on the crew of the *Hood*, Jellicoe volunteered to take the middle watch (lasting from midnight to 4 a.m.) on the bridge during the squadron's journey to Auckland.[6]

While men like George Blundell were beginning to feel fatigue, others aboard the ships faced continuous dress and supply worries. Mark Penfield was Field's valet and looked after thirty suits for the admiral. Able Seaman William Collier was a tailor and stitched together 300 new uniforms for the men aboard the *Hood*. Meanwhile victualing officers had to make advance arrangements to ensure that the ships remained operational and could provide for the crews. The victualing officers aboard the *Hood*, for example, had to ensure that the ship acquired enough stores to provide daily 1,400 pounds of bread, 1,000 pounds of meat, 1,500 pounds of potatoes, and 130 pounds of butter.[7]

The squadron arrived at Auckland amid fine weather and to enthusiastic scenes, reminiscent of Sydney, albeit on a smaller scale. Hundreds of small craft provided an escort into harbour, and all available vantage points were occupied by thousands of cheering spectators. With *Hood* secured alongside, Jellicoe hauled down his flag and departed the battlecruiser to return to Government House where he received the formal calls of Field, Brand, and the commanding officers of the ships.

As at the other stops on the cruise, large crowds of enthusiastic visitors gathered to tour the ships. The ships were opened to visitors on five mornings and four afternoons. On the first afternoon that the ships were open to the public, the crowd of 35,000 rushed the dock gates, sweeping aside the police who were on

Jellicoe leaving the squadron at Auckland. With *Hood* having secured alongside, Jellicoe hauled down his flag and departed the battlecruiser to return to Government House, where he received the formal calls of Field, Brand, and the commanding officers of the squadron's ships. (*Empire Photographic Publishing, Steve Locks*)

hand to control the crowd. The wharf gates were immediately closed to prevent more visitors as the crowds ran on to the wharf and charged the gangways of the *Hood*. Mounted police were called in to disperse the crowd and regain order while members of the ship's fire brigade stood by with levelled hoses ready to turn them on to the masses if the situation deteriorated. Lieutenant Charles Benstead went on to recall that 'The crowd, without displaying the slightest resentment at this curious expression of our appreciation, laughed loud and long at a speech made by our No. 1, which was meant to be a serious rebuke, and went back'.[8] Similar incidents were not repeated, and large numbers of people were welcomed aboard the ships; HMS *Hood* alone received 78,240 visitors.

A naval brigade was landed ahead of a march through the streets which was followed by a series of hospitalities, including an empire ball hosted by the Navy League and Victoria League, the Governor-General's Ball, a civic reception at Auckland town hall given to the flag officers as well as the commanding officers of the *Hood* and *Delhi*. A citizens 'At Home' was held (which was attended by Field, Brand, the ship's captains, and 100 officers), a ship's company 'At Home' aboard the *Repulse*, a squadron 'At Home' aboard the *Hood* at which there were 900 guests, and a children's party held aboard the *Repulse*. For the men of the squadron, there was also the opportunity to see something of New Zealand as recounted by V. C. Scott O'Connor:

HMS *Repulse* alongside at Auckland. (*Author's Collection*)

HMS *Hood* alongside at Auckland. (*IE1165795, Mitchell Library, State Library of New South Wales*)

HMS *Hood* photographed alongside Princes Wharf, Auckland, on 13 May 1924. (*2010.132.61, Auckland Harbour Board, NZ Museums*)

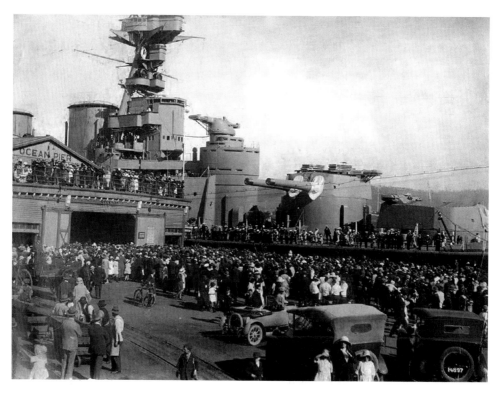

HMS *Hood* alongside Ocean Pier, Auckland. Note that 'B' turret has been trained to starboard. (*Author's Collection*)

The islands of New Zealand are of great beauty and interest, full of lovely places and of strange and wonderful things, such as volcanoes, and geysers and hot springs and lakes of hot water in the midst of snow; and abundant opportunities were given by the Government of New Zealand, in the most generous way, to our officers and men to travel in the interior to see these wonders for themselves. Interesting trips were made to Rotorua by the Rear-Admiral, 40 officers and 600 men, as the guests of the Government. There they were welcomed by the Maori population who are of the Ohinemutu tribe of the Arawas, who asked that the next warship built in Great Britain might be named after the tribe. The Maoris, who live upon happy terms with the white population, made an impression upon all by their fine physique and their courteous and dignified manners. The Rear-Admiral was accompanied by the Under Secretary of State for Internal Affairs, Mr. Hislop, who presented the principal Chiefs and notables, and made all the arrangements for two remarkable trips.[9]

The last official function of the visit to Auckland was an official dinner held aboard the *Hood* by Field. To the dinner Jellicoe was invited along with his wife, Lady Jellicoe, and their daughter Lucy. It marked the only occasion during the cruise when a lady was permitted to dine in the admiral's quarters and partook in such a party.[10] The dinner has been referred to as a personal tribute to Jellicoe and the atmosphere of the event was more akin to a family gathering than an official engagement. During the course of the dinner, Field, an expert conjuror, amused the guests by performing tricks.

As had occurred elsewhere during the cruise, the press spoke of a deep-seated feeling of affection for Britain and helped to contribute to the success of the voyage in its messages of welcome to the ships while also making the great questions of imperial policy that lay at the heart of the pageant understood. The *Evening Post* spoke in bold terms, telling its readership:

> New Zealand knows perfectly well that she owes her prosperity and her independence, and whatever she has and is, to the protection that has come to her without covenant or condition from the British Navy. Her full co-operation is required before she can qualify for the full measure of Imperial partnership regarding which all the Dominions have talked so much since the Armistice and have done so little.[11]

The *Herald* was no less explicit with its words:

> The Prime Minister has well said that the development of the Dominion's part in Empire defence is an inevitable duty. The alternative to that is becoming increasingly unthinkable in this country. Hitherto what we have done has been done cheerfully, but in itself it has been far from enough. In this a common experience has been shared by all the Overseas territories of the Empire. Whatever their varying designations, they have been 'dependencies', their growth, their prosperity, their very existence as units of the British Commonwealth being secured by a Royal Navy to which they have contributed very meagrely. They have never been asked to buy

Left: Brand led a party of forty officers and 600 men on a trip to Rotorua as the guests of the New Zealand government where they were welcomed by members of the Maori population. Here Brand was photographed rubbing noses with a Maori lady in a traditional greeting. (*Empire Photographic Publishing, Steve Locks*)

Below: The visit to the Rotorua was organised by Under Secretary of State for Internal Affairs Hislop, 'who presented the principal Chiefs and notables' to Brand. Brand is seen here shaking hands with one such 'notable' (Mr Harris) following a presentation. (*Empire Photographic Publishing, Steve Locks*)

the Navy's protection; it has been proudly given. Even in recent years no suggested arrangement of full payment for services rendered has been put to them. It could not be. Any such stipulation would have left them either bankrupt or defenceless. But a stalwart sense of honour has prompted them to lessen, at least a little, the gap between contributions and benefits. That feeling persists. It is the counterpart of the enthusiasm which has greeted the Squadron. Huzzas are not a substitute for help; they are an earnest of it.[12]

Herbert Massey made an announcement on the determination of the government to spend one million pounds each year on naval defence while Field offered advice and opinions on Dominion naval policy which was well received.

While in New Zealand, HMS *Dunedin* departed the Special Service Squadron as she was officially handed over to the New Zealand Division in place of HMS *Chatham*, which was to sail for Britain in order to undergo a refit.

The evening of 17 May had been fixed for the departure of the squadron. During the course of the day a storm broke over Auckland which severely reduced visibility. So poor was the visibility that taking the squadron to sea in such conditions in peacetime was judged to be an unjustifiable risk. Overnight, visibility improved and the ships of the squadron slipped their moorings at dawn the following day. As the squadron departed Auckland, and with that New Zealand, warm hearted messages of farewell were received from Jellicoe and Massey. To Field, Jellicoe signalled:

You leave behind you ineffaceable memories. These are intensified by the exemplary behaviour of the men on leave. They have shown to New Zealand an example of the conduct of British Naval personnel, of which I, as a brother-officer, am exceedingly proud and which must be most gratifying to you.[13]

Massey, meanwhile, signalled to the squadron, 'It was a pleasure to us to do what we could for our gallant kinsmen from the Motherland. We only did our Duty'.[14]

8

'We Surrender Our City Unto You'

Having departed Auckland, the Special Service Squadron set a course for Suva, Fiji. For some, as the squadron embarked on this latest part of the tour, the cruise was becoming a bore. One such individual for whom this was the case was Geoffrey Wells of the *Hood*, who noted:

> It is very noticeable that now passed New Zealand everyone seems to be getting bored with the cruise. I certainly am. Going round the world is alright. In fact being paid to go round and under such circumstances as this is great but one needs a fortnight's holiday at home in the middle of it. Everything moves at such pace.[1]

The squadron approached Suva at 2 p.m. on 21 May where the spirits of the crews would be revived by draughts of kava and the women of Western Samoa where the squadron briefly dropped anchor on 29 May. As the squadron approached Fiji on 21 May, the islands rose up from the horizon as mountains cut into the cloudy sky. With caution, the ships worked their way through the open channel between the coral reefs to enter Suva Harbour. As the ships entered the harbour, house boats, cabin cruisers with waving individuals, and native craft ventured out to greet the ships.

Shortly after the squadron had dropped anchor, crewmen began to disembark ahead of a ceremony at which Fijian warriors, dressed in traditional clothing, gathered on a green plain and danced while kava was thrust upon the sailors.

Moving on from Suva the following day, the squadron visited the island of Beqa, whose inhabitants had cultivated the art of walking on fire. At low tide, the squadron threaded its way through the coral reef that surrounds the island. In the harbour, the squadron was confronted on the shoreline by a line of huts with high thatched roofs, a line of palm trees that stood drunkenly swaying in the breeze, and a gathering of inhabitants beneath a banner bearing the word 'Welcome'.

Representatives of the squadron were landed, transported ashore from the ships aboard the yacht of the governor of Fiji. They were led into one of the huts in which there were seats for the admirals, captains, and the governor while the

Boats full of people travelling out to the squadron's ships while it is at anchor at Samoa, 29 May. In the background, two cruisers can be seen. (*Empire Photographic Publishing, Steve Locks*)

Fijian warriors in traditional clothing providing a demonstration to the men of the squadron. (*Empire Photographic Publishing, Steve Locks*)

The squadron photographed while at anchor at Fiji. HMS *Repulse* is just to the right of the centre of the photograph. HMS *Hood* is on the extreme right. The First Light Cruiser Squadron's ships are on the left of the photograph. (*Empire Photographic Publishing, Steve Locks*)

Beqan chiefs and notables from the island sat on the floor. The ceremony was the same as that which had occurred at Suva with kava offered and drank. Following this reception, a move slightly inland over one of the surrounding hills followed whereupon a traditional ceremony around a fire pit over which fire-walkers wandered was conducted. Admirals Field and Brand were invited by some of the Beqan to accompany them over the hot stones, an act of hospitality which was respectfully declined. The party from the squadron returned to the shore where the women of Beqa were assembled along with tribal warriors who performed a traditional dance. In return, the squadron conducted a ceremonial march through the streets of Suva and that night lit up the palm trees and hills with searchlights.

On 2 May, the squadron departed Suva. At 10 a.m., the squadron got underway with the *Repulse* leading *Hood*; behind the *Hood*, the light cruisers followed in a long, curving line. Having navigated the passageway of deep water between the coral reefs which was clearly defined to port and starboard by the white breakers of the pacific, once in open water the *Repulse* drew back and relinquished guide of the squadron to the *Hood*. During the course of the day, the squadron crossed the International Date Line, spending the best part of two days on 27 May. From Fiji, the squadron set a course for Honolulu, Hawaii. The passage from Fiji to Hawaii was to take seven days with the squadron making a brief stop at Western Samoa *en route* at the request of the government of New Zealand in light of recent unrest in the mandate.

At 10 a.m. on 29 May, the squadron arrived off the long mountainous island of Upolu, Western Samoa. The islanders ventured out to welcome the squadron, some in long boats reminiscent of canoes, the rowers all dressed alike in white jackets and pink waist coats. Amid the canoes were launches full of people. One of those who journeyed out to meet the squadron was the administrator of Western Samoa, Major General Spafford Richardson, who journeyed out to the *Hood* where he was received with the customary honours on the quarterdeck of the battlecruiser by Field. Richardson inspected *Hood*'s Royal Marines who

Field and other representatives of the squadron watching a Meke display at Fiji. (*Empire Photographic Publishing, Steve Locks*)

were drawn up in a Guard of Honour before being taken inside to the admiral's quarters whereupon the people who had ventured out to the ships in canoes and launches were welcomed on to the quarterdeck. Among the visitors were island chieftains, protestant missionaries, a Roman Catholic bishop, and many women. The men of the ships, acting as a sort of envoy from Britain, showed the visitors around the ships and explained in a mixture of plain and technical language the workings of the ships. The visits were completed by midday. Richardson was escorted to the gangway where the *Hood*'s band were struck up before a gun salute was fired. The many other visitors were escorted from the ships to their boats which began to make for the shore as the propellers of the *Hood* and the other ships of the squadron began to rotate and churn a white froth as they got underway. As the ships began to move away, cries of farewell rang out. The stay at Western Samoa was very brief, no opportunity was provided for men to be landed. From where anchor was dropped the white houses of Apia and Vailima, where the writer Robert Louis Stevenson lived during the final years of his life, could be seen.

Following the visit of the squadron to Western Samoa, Field would inform the Admiralty, 'I am sure that the visit of the squadron to a territory which was so recently in German occupation created a very deep impression on the native mind'.[2]

During the journey to Hawaii from Fiji, the equator was crossed for the fourth time. Following the brief stop at Western Samoa, HMAS *Adelaide*, which was not with the squadron when the equator was first crossed in the Atlantic, conducted the traditional 'Crossing the Line' ceremony. On 3 June, the birthday of King George V was celebrated. To mark the occasion the squadron was dressed with masthead flags from 8 a.m. until sunset while a message conveying best wishes was sent by Field on behalf of the squadron. A message was in turn received from the king, which stated, 'It is gratifying to receive on my birthday the loyal congratulations of the officers and ships' companies of the Special Service Squadron; the cruise of which I have been following with much interest. I heartily thank you and them for the good wishes contained in your telegram'.[3] The birthday of Queen Mary, eight days earlier, had been observed in the same manner.

During the passage to Hawaii, the opportunity was taken to conduct a number of exercises. Smoke screen trials were conducted by the *Repulse* on 28 May which were followed by inclination exercises on 30 May. All of the ships of the squadron partook in a sub-calibre concentration firing on 2 June. The 4th saw the *Hood* and *Repulse* conduct a high-angle shoot while the First Light Cruiser Squadron conducted a full calibre throw-off shoot using the *Repulse* as the target. The following day, the *Hood*, *Repulse*, and *Adelaide* undertook divisional torpedo practice against the light cruisers before *Adelaide* conducted her own sub-calibre shoot.

The United States, at the time, was in the Prohibition era. From leaving Western Samoa, there was a gradual suspension of alcohol aboard the ships so that they became 'dry' in deference to the Prohibition laws of the United States, an act of courtesy that was appreciated by the American authorities. A few days before the squadron arrived in Honolulu, a diagram was fixed to the noticeboard in the *Hood*, drawn up by Engineer Captain Frank Goodwin, illustrating the gradual suspension of alcohol aboard the ship so that it was dry by the time anchor was dropped in Honolulu.

The squadron arrived offshore Hawaii at 6 a.m. on 6 June. Flights of aircraft including seaplanes from the US Navy and Army Air Corps flew out to meet the ships and escort the squadron in to anchor. In Honolulu, for the first time since departing England 190 days earlier, the squadron dropped anchor and secured alongside in a 'foreign' port.

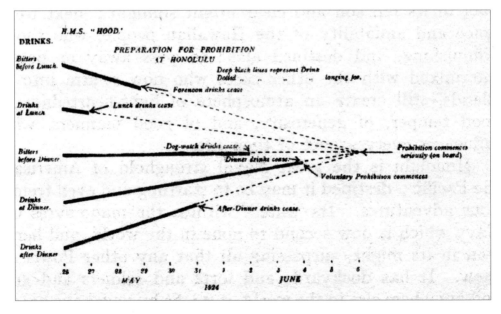

The diagram drawn up by Engineer Captain Frank Goodwin, which was fixed to the noticeboard aboard HMS *Hood* showing the suspension of alcohol as the ships became 'dry' in deference to the prohibition laws of the United States. (*Empire Photographic Publishing, Steve Locks*)

Shortly after securing alongside, young women from local schools and organisations were welcomed on board, laden with oranges and lei, alongside cameramen and reporters. The *Honolulu Star* later reported that Field 'received a new decoration on the deck of H.M.S. *Hood* to add to those he had already won by distinguished service to his country, in the form of a *Lei* presented by Miss Berenice Ahi representing the Hawaii Tourist Bureau'.[4] Having received his first lei, Field was led out into the commander's lobby at the entrance to his quarters where he stood while numerous leis were thrown over him.

Of the time spent at Hawaii, Field later commented:

The Naval, Military and Civil Authorities vied with one another in doing everything possible to make our stay enjoyable, and I must confess that I was considerably gratified by the extraordinary warmth of our welcome. The enthusiasm and hospitality became even more overwhelming as the visit progressed, and not a single incident occurred to mar the success of our stay. The people genially gave me the impression of being imbued with the most friendly feelings towards Great Britain, and I am happy to think our visit did something to strengthen these feelings.

I was most favourably impressed by the smart bearing and appearance of the Officers and men of the Naval and Military forces at Honolulu; and when I returned General [Charles] Summerall's call I was received by a Guard of Honour numbering 800 men who were undoubtedly a very fine type of soldier.[5]

With the formal calls made and returned, an entertainment programme followed. As has been the case elsewhere throughout, the list of hospitalities that was received by the squadron is too long to quote, therefore only the major keystone or unique events have been noted here. Governor Wallace Farrington held a ball at which Field, Brand, and the squadron captains and sixty officers were in attendance. On another occasion, Major-General Charles P. Summerall, the Commander of the Hawaiian Department hosted a dinner for the admirals, captains, and a number of officers from across the squadron. In return, a dance was held aboard the *Hood* at which Governor Farrington and 1,100 other guests were present. It has been written that '*Hood* surpassed herself on this occasion, and this was perhaps the finest and most successful of all the balls given during the cruise'.[6] During the course of the dance, toasts were made to King George V and President Calvin Coolidge with water.

The weather was perfect during the squadron's time at Hawaii. Tents were erected on the forecastles and quarterdecks and along a portion of the quayside whereupon supper was served outside. Sport also formed part of the entertainment programme. While at Hawaii, the squadron cricket team was embarrassed when it was beaten at cricket by an American baseball team.[7] While alongside, the squadron was visited by 47,175 people.

During the evening of 11 June, the night before the squadron set sail, Field held a dinner aboard the *Hood* for forty-five guests including Vice-Admiral John D. McDonald, the commandant of the Fourteenth Naval District. The following

HMS *Hood* (foreground) and *Repulse* (background) anchored alongside at Honolulu, 11 June 1924. Three vessels of the First Light Cruiser Squadron can be seen at anchor between the two battlecruisers, their bows pointing towards the shore. (*23939173, National Archives Washington D.C.*)

The Special Service Squadron at anchor at Honolulu. HMS *Repulse* is on the left of the photograph. Three vessels of the First Light Cruiser Squadron are in the centre of the photograph with HMS *Hood* on the right in the foreground. (*23939175, National Archives Washington D.C.*)

HMS *Delhi* and HMS *Dauntless* at Honolulu. (*Empire Photographic Publishing, Steve Locks*)

HMS *Hood* docked at Honolulu, Hawaii, on 11 June 1924. (*NH 58635, US Naval History and Heritage Command*)

HMS *Hood* seen from an overflying aircraft, anchored alongside at Honolulu at 8.13 a.m. on 11 June 1924. (*23939181, National Archives Washington D.C.*)

morning, the men of the squadron manned the rails laden with garlands that they had been presented with in the presence of large and enthusiastic crowds which had assembled to witness the squadron's departure. Of the squadron's departure, the *Honolulu Times* recorded:

> The excellent behaviour of the British sailors ashore has been widely remarked. They gave a fine example of discipline and good conduct. They fraternized informally and freely with American sailors, soldiers and civilians.
>
> The British Squadron is circling the Globe on a mission of friendship as well of Naval development. In this port it succeeded 100 per cent. As an advertisement of the British Navy it certainly made good, from its genial and able Commanding Officer to the newest Midshipman and the youngest sailor.[8]

Seaplanes and aircraft provided an escort to the squadron long after the shores of Hawaii had faded from view behind a veil of rain which blotted out the horizon behind the ships. Setting a course for Canada, as the squadron sailed north it became colder and grey prompting the men to be more brisk at carrying out their work; they doubled along as much out of choice as by command.

Sailors wave farewell to the gathered crowds as the squadron departs Honolulu. (*Empire Photographic Publishing, Steve Locks*)

Officers aboard one of the battlecruisers, likely HMS *Hood*, look on as the ship moves away from the quayside at Honolulu. (*Empire Photographic Publishing, Steve Locks*)

HMS *Hood* off Honolulu, 12 June 1924. (*NH 60409, US Naval History and Heritage Command*)

HMS *Hood* viewed from an American aircraft following the squadron's departure from Honolulu, 12 June 1924. (*NH 60404, US Naval History and Heritage Command*)

HMS *Repulse* photographed off the coast of Oahu, Hawaii, 12 June 1924. The photograph was taken from an aircraft from the Pearl Harbor Naval Air Station. (*NH 57164, US Naval History and Heritage Command*)

HMS *Repulse* photographed by one of the aircraft that escorted the squadron from Hawaii on 12 June 1924. Note the crewmen drawn up along the forecastle. (*NH 55609, US Naval History and Heritage Command*)

Another view of HMS *Repulse* taken on 12 June 1924. Note the flying-off platforms for aircraft atop 'B' and 'X' turrets. (*NH 55608, US Naval History and Heritage Command*)

HMS *Delhi* off Oahu, 12 June 1924. Another ship of the First Light Cruise Squadron can be seen in the distance astern. (*NH 60818, US Naval History and Heritage Command*)

An US seaplane escorting the Special Service Squadron as it departs Hawaii. In the background is one of the First Light Cruiser Squadron's ships. (*Empire Photographic Publishing, Steve Locks*)

During the course of the journey to Canada, further exercises, notably star-shell practices, were conducted. The sharp crack of the 6-inch guns split the night as the star shells headed skyward and burst whereupon the light fell from behind the banks of cloud to light up the waves below and the hulls of the ships.

Approaching Victoria, Canada, on the morning of 21 June, at 7 a.m., the squadron was met by HMCS *Patrician* which carried the senior officer to Esquimalt, who were accompanied by Commander Adrian St Vincent Keyes, the officer in charge of arrangements for the official organisation of entertainment. Both men were welcomed aboard the *Hood* while pilots and mail were embarked by the ships of the squadron. With pilots embarked, the *Hood*, *Repulse*, and *Adelaide* proceeded to Victoria while HMS *Delhi*, *Danae*, *Dragon*, and *Dauntless* made their way to Esquimalt across the water.

As the squadron approached the Canadian shore, the grey clouds of the morning broke leaving the sun to dominate the sky. During the approach up the Salish Sea, *Repulse*, which had led the squadron following the embarkation of pilots, stood aside to allow the *Hood* to pass and lead the squadron into anchor while the light cruisers slipped away to their anchorage at Esquimalt. In the Salish Sea, a boat full of well-wishers had greeted the squadron and followed the ships as they made their approaches to their respective anchorages. As the *Hood*, *Repulse*, and *Adelaide* approached Victoria, launches and motorboats came out of the harbour and began to circle the ships. Ashore, people crowded the piers and atop the lighthouse to watch the squadron's arrival, the air all the while thick with their cheers.

Taken from HMS *Hood*, the *Repulse* can be seen leading the First Light Cruiser Squadron as the Special Service Squadron turns to enter the approaches to Victoria and Esquimalt. (*Empire Photographic Publishing, Steve Locks*)

HMS *Dragon* coming alongside at Esquimalt. (*Empire Photographic Publishing, Steve Locks*)

'We Surrender Our City Unto You'

Having berthed alongside, the mayor of Victoria, Reginald Hayward, was welcomed aboard the *Hood* to call on Field. He was accompanied by the mayors of the inland towns of Vancouver Island. Aboard the *Hood*, Hayward delivered an address inspired by great sentiment:

> On behalf of the citizens of Victoria, it is with a feeling of deep pleasure and justifiable pride that we bid you and those under your command a hearty welcome. Our people have ever taken an intense interest in the fortunes and exploits of the British Navy. Its course during the Great War, when it proved the determining factor in the victory of the Allied Nations, was followed by Victorians with eagerness, but always with indomitable confidence that it would be, as His Majesty expressed it, the sure shield of Britain and the Empire. You come to us with the message from the Motherland that Britain's strength on the seas and her realisation of the responsibilities of sea power have not been dimmed, and that her sea-might is ready, as in the past, to be placed at the disposal of the Empire. This city rejoices in your strength and in your humanity.[9]

The squadron was to spend four days at Victoria. As usual, hospitalities were lavished upon the squadron which included a dinner hosted by the Dominion government; a dinner for flag officers and captains which was followed by a ball at Government House attended by seventy-six officers hosted by the lieutenant-governor of British Columbia, Walter Nichol; and a citizen's ball at the Canadian Pacific Railway Hotel. Some 1,500 petty officers were invited to a succession of dances while 700 men from across the squadron were taken on tours.

One of the hospitality events, a lunch hosted by the local Navy League branch on 21 June, sparked an incident that placed the cruise at the centre of Canadian political battles. During the course of the lunch, Field was pressed by a journalist for his views on the future of Canadian naval policy. For his part, Field stated that he would 'reply from the standpoint of, say, a Canadian wheat farmer', and went on to explain that in a time of war enemy ships could blockade grain shipments and thus wreck regional economies.[10] In this context, Field linked the lessons of sea power to local economic circumstances, a rhetorical device that had been used throughout the cruise. His words were published in the *Daily Colonist* the following day and elicited a quick response from nationalists in the Canadian parliament. On 1 July, the Liberal MP Andrew McMaster who was a staunch supporter of disarmament and the League of Nations questioned the Canadian government on whether or not they had invited Field to offer the view that he put forward. McMaster went on to request that the government request that the Admiral avoid comments 'on matters of purely Canadian national policy'. Another Canadian politician was more forthright and blunt informing the government that they should 'tell him to mind his own business'.[11]

Debates ensued in the national press that adopted a partisan tone and linguistic divide which otherwise characterised Canadian politics.

On 22 June, Coronation Day, the *Hood* and *Repulse* were decorated with bright coloured flags that trailed in the air from the masts and fluttered in the breeze.

All throughout the day people arrived in their thousands to visit the ships. It may be noted that it was not merely Canadians and individuals of British birth who visited the ships. The visitors included a number of Indians, Chinese, Japanese, and Native Americans. During the four days alongside, a total of 52,000 people would visit the *Hood*, *Repulse*, and *Adelaide*.

The sunset ceremony closed the naval day and there have been many descriptions written of the event. The ceremony conducted on 22 June has been described as being 'more beautiful than usual' by V. C. Scott O'Connor and it worth quoting here at length:

> The Olympic Mountains that had looked down upon us from their silver solitudes up in the heavens, creatures remote and aloof in their far-off beauty, became flushed with a rosy pink; small gold clouds hung over the tops of the Canadian fir trees; and as the sun neared the horizon, the trumpeters who herald his departure, the drums beat at the close of day, assembled for the ceremony of his passing. There they stood stiffly at attention, waiting for the word of command. At each of the flags, the Jack at the fore, the White Ensign aft, on each ship two seamen stood waiting for the signal to haul down the Flag.
>
> Along the quarter-deck to port and starboard stood other seamen, holding in their hands the lateral chords. An officer of the Royal Marines stood at attention, a telescope under his arm. All waited in silence for the signal. And then of a sudden it was given, and the whole line of flags came fluttering down to the surface of the quarter-deck; the bugles sounded the Last Post, the White Ensign slowly descended, as if the proud Flag were reluctant to give way to the shadows of night.

HMS *Hood* (left) and *Repulse* (right) photographed while moored at Government Docks, Victoria. (*Empire Photographic Publishing, Steve Locks*)

HMS *Hood* photographed during the ship's visit to Victoria. The ship is decorated from stem to stern in flags indicating that this photograph was likely taken on 22 June, Coronation Day. (*2011-024-583, Irvine Family, Saanich Archives*)

The First Light Cruiser Squadron's ships photographed at anchor while at Esquimalt. The ships are decorated in flags indicating that this photograph was likely taken on Coronation Day. (*Empire Photographic Publishing, Steve Locks*)

Far up at the top of each tall mast, a seaman retreated step by step down the hundred runs of a ladder, making his departure with the same calm and unhurried deliberations.

At last it was over. The snows of the Olympics withdrew into their invisible monotones in a grey sky; the band struck up, its drum-beats throbbing in the clear Canadian air, and one more day closed in the life of the Empire.[12]

On 23 June, a naval brigade from the battlecruisers and *Adelaide* marched through the city to the enthusiastic cheers of the gathered crowd.

On 25 June, the *Hood*, *Repulse*, and *Adelaide* weighed anchor and proceeded to Vancouver where they arrived later that same day. The First Light Cruiser Squadron, meanwhile, remained alongside at Esquimalt. Tens of thousands of people gathered along the shores of Burrard Inlet to cheer the ships as they arrived. Meanwhile, the battlecruisers and *Adelaide* were escorted and followed into harbour by hundreds of small craft that had ventured out to greet the squadron. The arrival of the squadron was described in the *Morning Sun*, which told its readership of the intense excitement that existed from the moment the first individuals saw the *Hood* approaching leading the *Repulse* followed by HMAS *Adelaide*, which, as a light cruiser of the Royal Australian Navy, carried with her a message of empire co-operation in naval defence.

At Brockton Point, an escort of aircraft dropped twenty-one bombs in a royal salute, followed by a shower of rockets that burst, giving birth to flags which slowly descended attached to parachutes. Having secured alongside, Field landed and was presented with an address by the mayor, William Owen, in which he spoke of the abiding influence of Drake, Grenville, Blake, Collingwood, Nelson, and Commander George Vancouver, after whom the island and city are both named.[13]

Taken to the Canadian Club, Field, at the public request of the chairman, delivered the speech that he had made at Victoria, which was broadcast live across Canada. The following day, Field responded to a number of questions which were put to him by the *Vancouver Sun*. Two of the questions that were put to Field were: 'Should Overseas Dominions directly or indirectly contribute [to the cost of naval defence and the security of the Empire] and why?' and 'What percentage of the total cost should they contribute and why?' Having answered a previous question by stating that Britain must continue to carry the burden of empire security and defence, stating that naval defence cost thirty shillings per head per annum and that any weight the Dominions could shoulder would ease the burden on Britain, Field stated:

The Empire must be regarded as a whole, for it any one of its component parts is isolated, it will affect the trade and supplies of all the others. The prosperity and existence of a sea-empire rest upon its sea-communications. It must keep open its trade routes in the event of war. This is every bit as important to the Overseas Dominions as it is to the Mother Country. Money contributed to Naval defence by

'We Surrender Our City Unto You' 227

Crowds gather at Brockon Point to watch the arrival of the Special Service Squadron in Vancouver. (*Stuart Thomson, CVA 99-1210, City of Vancouver Archives*)

HMS *Hood* entering Burrard Inlet Harbour. (*W. J. Moore, Bo N88.4, City of Vancouver Archives*)

HMS *Hood* as she sails through the Burrard Inlet into Vancouver Harbour. (*CVA 289-003.053, City of Vancouver Archives*)

HMS *Repulse* entering the Burrard Inlet to Vancouver Harbour. (*CVA 289-003.052, City of Vancouver Archives*)

HMS *Repulse* in the Burrard Inlet as she sails into Vancouver Harbour. Note the crewmen assembled on deck manning the rails. (*Bo N88.3, City of Vancouver Archives*)

(Bo N88.2, City of Vancouver Archives)

HMAS *Adelaide* entering the Burrard Inlet to Vancouver Harbour, 25 June 1924. (CVA 289-003.054, William Orson Banfield, City of Vancouver Archives)

HMAS *Adelaide* in the Burrard inlet approaching Vancouver. (*Bo N119.2, City of Vancouver Archives*)

(*Bo N119.1, City of Vancouver Archives*)

HMS *Repulse* during her passage up Burrard Inlet to Vancouver, 25 June 1924. This photograph was taken at Stanley Park. Note the cottage on the edge of the park by the water. (*AM1052 P-145, City of Vancouver Archives*)

HMAS *Adelaide* in Vancouver Harbour. (*CVA 152-9.02, City of Vancouver Archives*)

HMS *Hood* sailing into Vancouver Harbour. (*Stuart Thomson, CVA 99-1204, City of Vancouver Archives*)

Stern quarter view of the *Hood* as she enters Vancouver Harbour. (*Stuart Thomson, CVA 99-1205, City of Vancouver Archives*)

HMS *Repulse* entering Vancouver Harbour. (*CVA 447-8, Walter E. Frost, City of Vancouver Archives*)

'We Surrender Our City Unto You' 233

(CVA 447-2625, Walter E. Frost, City of Vancouver Archives)

Photographed from astern, HMS *Repulse* proceeds into Vancouver Harbour. (CVA 447-2625.4, Walter E. Frost, City of Vancouver Archives)

(CVA 447-2625.1, Walter E. Frost, City of Vancouver Archives)

HMS *Hood* entering Vancouver. (*City of Vancouver Archives, CVA 447-2304, Walter Edwin Frost*)

(*City of Vancouver Archives, CVA 447-2304.1, Walter Edwin Frost*)

(*City of Vancouver Archives, CVA 447-2304.2, Walter Edwin Frost*)

(City of Vancouver Archives, CVA 447-2304.4, Walter Edwin Frost)

(City of Vancouver Archives, CVA 447-2304.3, Walter Edwin Frost)

Photographed from astern, HMS *Repulse* is seen shortly before she dropped anchor in Vancouver Harbour, 25 June 1924. (*Bo P99, Stuart Thomson, City of Vancouver Archives*)

Mayor William R. Owen presents an illuminated address to and welcomes Admiral Field, Captain Im Thurn (*Hood*), and Captain Henry Parker (*Repulse*) to Vancouver. (*Port P728.2, City of Vancouver Archives*)

'We Surrender Our City Unto You' 237

Mayor Owen delivering his welcome to the squadron. During his welcome speech, Mayor Owen spoke of the abiding influence of Drake, Grenville, Blake, Collingwood, Nelson, and Commander George Vancouver after whom the island and city are both named. (*CVA 99-1210.2, Stuart Thomson, City of Vancouver Archives*)

(*CVA 99-1210.3, Stuart Thomson, City of Vancouver Archives*)

Field delivering a few words in response to Mayor Owen's welcome. (*CVA 99-1210.4, Stuart Thomson, City of Vancouver Archives*)

Brand shaking hands with an officer of the Canadian army following the speech of welcome delivered by Mayor Owen. (*CVA 99-1210.5, Stuart Thomson, City of Vancouver Archives*)

Right: Dignitaries on the dockside with a bison's head waiting to board HMS *Hood*, 25 June 1924. (*CVA 99-1211.1, Stuart Thomson, City of Vancouver Archives*)

Below: Mayor Owen delivering an address and presenting Field with a bison's head aboard HMS *Hood* following the squadron's arrival in Vancouver, 25 June 1924. (*CVA-1211.2, Stuart Thomson, City of Vancouver Archives*)

240　　　　　　　　　　　　　*Empire Cruise*

(CVA 99-1211.3, Stuart Thomson, City of Vancouver Archives)

(CVA 99-1212.1, Stuart Thomson, City of Vancouver Archives)

'We Surrender Our City Unto You' 241

(CVA 99-1212.2, Stuart Thomson, City of Vancouver Archives)

(CVA 99-1212.3, Stuart Thomson, City of Vancouver Archives)

the Dominions is expended solely on ships which are their own property and under their own control, and only in the event of war would these ships be placed under the sole control of the Admiralty.

To the question regarding the percentage of the total cost the Dominions should contribute, Field replied, 'This is a matter entirely for Dominion Governments to decide and must depend on their capacity, having regard to such factors as National wealth, population, and volume of sea-borne trade.'[14]

On 30 June, a ceremonial march was held through the streets of Vancouver. School children had not been able to watch the arrival of the squadron, as such Field requested that as many children as possible be allowed to watch the march. The Naval Brigade was enthusiastically cheered along the entire route at the end of which there were thousands of children. The following day, 1 July, was Dominion Day, a national holiday throughout Canada. While large numbers of people visited the ships, crew members partook in naval and military sports as well as in athletic competitions. HMS *Repulse* lost the boxing competition 5 bouts to 1, the *Hood* meanwhile triumphed at tug-of-war, her sailors receiving a cup for their efforts. The flagship was, however, defeated 3-4 at football by the Royal Canadian Mounted Police. A squadron officers' dance and ship's companies' 'At Home' were held aboard the *Hood* while the *Repulse* once more delighted children with a party.

A steam launch from HMS *Hood* carrying civilians out to visit the battlecruiser in Vancouver Harbour. (*CVA 152-9.10, City of Vancouver Archives*)

Shore parties from HMS *Hood*, *Repulse*, and HMAS *Adelaide* parade on Burrard Street during the ceremonial march held on 30 June. (*City of Vancouver Archives, CVA 99-1201, Stuart Thomson*)

Men from HMS *Hood*, *Repulse*, and HMAS *Adelaide* turning on to Cordova Street watched on by a cheering crowd. (*CVA 99-1200.10, Stuart Thomson, City of Vancouver Archives*)

Officers and crewmen from the *Hood*, *Repulse*, and *Adelaide* parading down Hastings Street, Vancouver. (*City of Vancouver Archives, Bo P540*)

Admiral Field saluting the men of the squadron as they march past the saluting base during the parade through Vancouver. (*CVA 99-1200.13, Stuart Thomson, City of Vancouver Archives*)

'We Surrender Our City Unto You' 245

A steam picket boat from HMS *Hood* underway in Vancouver Harbour. (*CVA 152-9.11, City of Vancouver Archives*)

HMS *Hood* while at anchor in Vancouver Harbour. Note the boats alongside ferrying visitors out to the ship and the crowded forecastle. (*City of Vancouver Archives, CVA 152-9.09*)

Signalmen aboard the *Hood* showing a group of children a semaphore signal device. (*City of Vancouver Archives, CVA 99-1203, Stuart Thomson*)

A sailor aboard HMS *Hood* showing a device to a group of onlookers during a tour of the battlecruiser. (*CVA 99-1201.1, Stuart Thomson, City of Vancouver Archives*)

HMS *Hood* photographed while at anchor in Vancouver. Note the visitors on her decks. (*City of Vancouver Archives, CVA 447-10, Walter Edwin Frost*)

HMS *Hood* at anchor in Vancouver Harbour. (*CVA 289-003.060, William Orson Banfield, City of Vancouver Archives*)

HMS *Repulse* at anchor in Vancouver Harbour. (*CVA 289-003.056, William Orson Banfield, City of Vancouver Archives*)

HMS *Repulse* at Vancouver. (CVA 447-2625.2, Walter E. Frost, City of Vancouver Archives)

(CVA 447-2625.3, Walter E. Frost, City of Vancouver Archives)

Visitors to the *Hood* mill around the foredeck while the ship iss anchored in Vancouver. (*City of Vancouver Archives*, CVA 289-003.062)

A crowd of visitors swamp *Hood*'s forecastle. (*CVA 289-003.059, William Orson Banfield, City of Vancouver Archives*)

Visitors on the deck of HMS *Hood*. (CVA 289-003.061, William Orson Banfield, City of Vancouver Archives)

Above left: A sailor aboard HMS *Hood* with Joey the wallaby on deck while in Vancouver, 25 June 1924. (CVA 99-1213, Stuart Thomson, City of Vancouver Archives)

Above right: Crewmen aboard HMS *Hood* with Joey the wallaby. (CVA 99-1213.1, Stuart Thomson, City of Vancouver Archives)

Above: A group of sailors playing cards beneath one of the main battery turrets of HMS *Hood* while the ship is at anchor in Vancouver. (*CVA 99-1212.4, Stuart Thomson, City of Vancouver Archives*)

Right: A Ferris wheel erected on board HMS *Repulse* for a children's party while alongside in Vancouver. (*Empire Photographic Publishing, Steve Locks*)

While these activities were taking place, twenty officers and 200 men under Captain Parker of the *Repulse* were invited on a trip into the heart of the Canadian Rockies and into the great wheat plains that lay beyond by the Canadian government. The men travelled by train, which made brief stops at towns including Banff and Calgary along the way, where as much freedom as possible was given to the men. At each town, the men of the squadron were given a spontaneous welcome and many of the men expressed regret that they could not continue on to Winnipeg and the eastern towns.

The squadron weighed anchor and departed Vancouver and Esquimalt respectively on 5 July. Out in the eastern Pacific, the squadron set a course south, down the western seaboard of North America to San Francisco.

At 2 p.m. on 7 July, hours before San Francisco was reached, it became clear that the squadron could expect a hearty welcome when a flotilla of destroyers carrying navigating officers and members of the press dispatched by Admiral Samuel S. Robinson, the commander-in-chief of the US Pacific Fleet, rendezvoused with the squadron.

While at Victoria, twenty officers and 200 men under Captain Parker of the *Repulse* were invited on a trip into the heart of the Canadian Rockies. The men travelled by train, which made brief stops at towns along the way. This photograph was taken at Strathcona Lodge Station, British Columbia. (*Empire Photographic Publishing, Steve Locks*)

'We Surrender Our City Unto You'   253

Above: Officers and men gather around the front of a train for a photograph at Banff during the visit into the Canadian Rockies and beyond. (*Empire Photographic Publishing, Steve Locks*)

Right: Fraser Canyon in the Canadian Rockies, one of the places visited by the party led by Captain Parker. (*Empire Photographic Publishing, Steve Locks*)

(*Empire Photographic Publishing, Steve Locks*)

The Canadian Rockies. (*Empire Photographic Publishing, Steve Locks*)

HMS *Delhi* leading HMS *Dauntless* out of Esquimalt, 5 July 1924. (*Empire Photographic Publishing, Steve Locks*)

The entrance to San Francisco Harbour. (*Empire Photographic Publishing, Steve Locks*)

256   *Empire Cruise*

The squadron passed beneath the Golden Gate Bridge at 4 p.m. As the squadron approached, tens of thousands of people lined every vantage point along the shore while above, flights of aircraft provided an escort. Aboard one of the escorting aircraft was Brigadier-General William 'Billy' Mitchell, the deputy director of the air service. The apostle of air power, Mitchell advocated for increased investment in air power believing that air power would prove vital in future wars. In November 1918, Mitchell had been quoted as saying:

> The day has passed when armies on the ground or navies on the sea can be the arbiter of a nation's destiny in war. The main power of defense and the power of initiative against an enemy has passed to the air.[15]

Mitchell's views brought him into direct conflict with the navy. Mitchell argued particularly for the ability of bombers to sink battleships and other naval vessels and organised a series of demonstrations in which aircraft conducted a series of bombing runs against stationary ships to test and prove his idea. Learning of a plan to use an aircraft to drop a symbolic floral key to 'unlock the Golden Gate' on to the quarterdeck of HMS *Hood*, Mitchell took over the controls of the aircraft himself intent on making a further demonstration of the vulnerability of capital ships to air attack. Mitchell's efforts resulted in the key unceremoniously dropping into the bay as the guns of Fort Scott thundered out in welcome.[16] The anticipation prior to, and the arrival of the squadron was recalled by Phyllis Marquiss-Munro, the president of the San Francisco Women's Press Club in an article published in *The Wasp* on 19 July 1924:

> San Francisco awoke through a golden veil of mist to a city of fluttering flags. Overnight, the somber streets had been transformed into a pageant of red, white and blue, the Union jack, waved side by side with the Stars and Stripes. The British fleet was arriving.
>
> A thrill of expectancy and suppressed excitement filled the air. 'When are they due?' 'Where can we best see them arrive?' was on the lips of every passerby.
>
> For three hundred days, the British fleet has ridden the seas, lead by the mighty *Hood*, the world's greatest battleship, in command of Vice Admiral Sir Frederick Field, K.C.B.-C.M.G.
>
> Through storm and sunshine these huge protectors of Great Britain have tossed and traversed three great oceans, the Atlantic, Indian and lastly, the glorious blue Pacific, our ocean that washes the sandy shores of this city.
>
> From noon thousands of people on foot and in automobiles climbed the steep hills above the harbor, and waited with strained eyes for the first glimpse, looking towards the Golden Gate.
>
> Tiny white sailing craft and fussy motor launches dotted the bay, whilst every ocean going vessel was dressed in honor.
>
> Planes circled daringly above, vying with the white winged gulls.... [S]uddenly out of the blue grey fog that had folded around the heads, majestically and slowly,

H.M.S. Hood sailed into the bay, followed by the five warships in single file. The spectators held their breath, then simultaneously from a thousand throats, rose a deafening cheer.

Britain's fleet had arrived. Above, planes circled in formation like huge graceful birds. At the Gate, one plane dipped low, dropping on the deck of the Hood a floral key to open wide the Golden Gate and the hospitable hearts of the San Francisco people. Impressively with a world of dignity, the ensign floating in the breeze, the armada steamed up the bay to Man-o-war Row, where America's flagship, U.S.S. *California* greeted the travellers.

Turning from the British fleet, our eyes rested on the protectors of USA, far away, anchored in the swift rising fog. They looked like eerie phantoms, a final ray of sunshine caught the magnificent U.S.S. *California* as H.M.S. *Hood* fired her first salute.

The British Lion reared her arrival in a salute of seventeen guns, answered by a similar welcome of friendship from USA flagship. Then the greeting whistles and screams from the Ferry Building, boats and craft.[17]

The arrival of the squadron marked the first time in forty years that a British squadron had dropped anchor in the territorial waters of the continental United States.[18] The mayor of San Francisco, James Rolph, delivered a message of welcome to the men of the squadron:

Your presence with us today will, we trust, make a pact between the British-speaking races even closer. We take pride in your magnificent ships, which we feel will never be used except in the defence of world peace. We surrender our city unto you. We capitulate.[19]

In response to the words of Mayor Rolph, Field replied:

We come to your city in peace and friendliness, remembering that our two countries stood side by side, to defend the right and bring peace to the world. In presenting us with the key to your city, you have found the key to our hearts.[20]

During the time it was at anchor, the squadron was placed at 'At Home' for Britons who resided in the area. In the meantime, hospitalities and courtesies were extended to the squadron. In adherence to the Prohibition laws of the United States, the ships of the squadron were still 'dry'. While at San Francisco, however, it became readily apparent that the efforts of the squadron to adhere to Prohibition greatly outstripped those of their hosts ashore. Geoffrey Wells recalled one such incident, which occurred in the Bohemian Club.

'I guess you boys will have a drink' said one of our hosts producing, as the conjurer does the rabbit, a bottle of whiskey which he passed to the bar attendant who therewith dispensed whiskey and sodas. We received sympathy for our stocks on

Ferry buildings in San Francisco alight during the squadron's visit. Note the White Ensigns hanging from the street lamps. (*Empire Photographic Publishing, Steve Locks*)

board being locked up and it became apparent that the only dry community in the district was the British ships. There were some that did not believe that we had not bottles in our cabins. Our reason for not having any was that it was not allowed. This absolutely baffled the American mind![21]

At 6.30 a.m. on 11 July, the squadron weighed anchor and proceeded out of San Francisco Bay. The following day, the First Light Cruiser Squadron, minus HMAS *Adelaide*, parted company with Field's flag as they set course for Callao, the first stop on a tour of South America. As they steamed past the battlecruisers and *Adelaide*, the First Light Cruiser Squadron cheered ship.

On 12 July, the First Light Cruiser Squadron parted company with the battlecruisers and HMAS *Adelaide*. HMS *Delhi* is seen here dipping the flag of Rear Admiral Brand as members of the ship's company gathered along the forecastle cheer as the ships part company. (*IWM Q83368*)

HMS *Delhi* leading the First Light Cruiser Squadron and dipping her flags as she passes the *Hood* prior to Field leaving. (*Empire Photographic Publishing, Steve Locks*)

9

South America

While throughout the cruise the squadron had frequently split for a handful of days or weeks in order to visit a multitude of ports, the descriptions of which have been interwoven throughout, due to the component elements of the Special Service Squadron sailing to two different destinations, interweaving their respective exploits is no longer possible. This chapter, therefore, will detail the tour made of South America by the ships of the First Light Cruiser Squadron while the subsequent chapter will pick up on the voyage of the battlecruisers and HMAS *Adelaide*.

Having parted company with Field's flag by cheering ship, the First Light Cruiser Squadron proceeded south for fifteen days before arriving at Callao, Peru. The weather during the voyage was perfect and cool, even after crossing over the equator. During the voyage, the men aboard the ships were engaged in daily rounds of ship borne routine. A number of gunnery and torpedo exercises were conducted before the dog watches saw various bayonet competitions, boxing matches, and fencing tournaments.

Callao was reached at 8 a.m. on 26 July amid thick weather that obscured the hills from view. As the squadron dropped anchor, the Peruvian cruiser *Coronel Bolognesi* saluted Brand's flag. A fast-paced entertainment programme followed. A ball was held by Pedro Gamio, the Peruvian foreign minister, to which sixteen officers were invited. Games of football proved to be particularly popular, with the teams fielded by the squadron meeting with favourable reports in the local press. Such was the openness of the squadron's game that the press mused as to whether the squadron had been filled with professional players before departing England. The Peruvians were surprised therefore to learn that all of the officers and men were almost all serving with the Atlantic Fleet.

Two parties of officers were taken on a trip up to Rio Blanco on the Lima–Huancayo railway, which until the opening of the Qinghai-Tibetan railway in 2006 was the highest railway in the world, where a height of 15,600 feet was reached by the parties.

Peruvian Independence Day occurred on 28 July. To mark the occasion, the squadron was dressed all over and at sunrise, noon, and sunset, twenty-one-gun salutes were fired. A short 'Te Deum' service was held in the cathedral to mark the occasion. The 'Te Deum' was attended by Brand, his staff, and the captains of the cruisers. The president of Peru, Augusto Leguía, as a mark of respect, insisted that the representatives of the squadron should take a place of honour immediately behind him during the walk from the palace to the cathedral and also at the march past which was to follow. A naval brigade of seamen and Marines partook in the march past, being assigned a place of honour in the procession. That evening, Leguía attended a dinner hosted by Brand aboard HMS *Delhi*. Also in attendance at the dinner was the British ambassador.

Brand, his staff, and the captains of the cruisers along with nineteen officers were guests at a lunch held by the minister of marine. A jovial function, two bands played alternatively throughout. An amusing incident occurred when a toast was proposed to the health of King George V. At this point, the enthusiasm of the bands overcame discretion and one struck up 'God Save the King' while the other struck up 'Rule Britannia'.

On 31 July, the squadron weighed anchor and departed Callao for Coquimbo, Chile. Messages of welcome were sent to the squadron from the British communities at Antofagasta and Iquique which contained requests that a ship from the squadron might be dispatched to visit them. Reluctantly, Brand had to refuse their requests. As at Callao, the squadron was well received when it dropped anchor at Coquimbo amid thick fog. A salute was fired into the fog, which heralded the arrival of the squadron. Already at anchor when the First Light Cruiser Squadron arrived was the cruiser *Chacabuco* and five destroyers. A lunch was given aboard the *Chacabuco* by the Chilean naval officers. In return, the squadron held dinners aboard HMS *Delhi* and *Danae* for the Chilean navy. Other events held while at Coquimbo included a dinner aboard the *Chacabuco* for Brand, his staff, and the captains of the cruisers, and a ball held in honour of the squadron. In addition to this, Brand entertained the governor of Coquimbo, the intendant of the province, and the commanding officers of the Chilean naval vessels in the port at an official lunch.

Departing Coquimbo, HMS *Dauntless* and *Dragon* sailed to Talcahuano while the *Delhi* and *Danae* proceeded to Valparaiso, where upon their arrival, the British ships fired a salute to the country. In reply, the Chilean cruiser *Blanco Encalada* fired a salute to Brand's flag of thirteen guns. The squadron received a warm, hospitable welcome at Valparaiso. The visit was to be but a short one, a fact which was deplored by one and all. The weather at Valparaiso was bad, nevertheless, an entertainment programme was put through which was enjoyed by all. One event that was held was a rugby match which after a desperate struggle saw the squadron emerge triumphant by four points.

While at anchor, Brand, Captain Austin of HMS *Danae*, four commissioned officers, and a party of men landed to place wreaths at the monuments of Blanco Encalada and Lord Cochrane. This was followed by a ball held at the Vina del Mar, which was attended by the whole of the British community and a large number of Chilean civilians and naval officers.

On 8 August, Brand travelled via train to Santiago to call upon the president of Chile, Arturo Alessandri. At Santiago, a lunch was held for the Brand at the English Club. Upon his return to Valparaiso, the squadron was placed 'At Home' in the Naval Club, which was loaned to the squadron for the purpose.

Meanwhile, HMS *Dauntless* and *Dragon* had visited Talcahuano. While there, Captain Round-Turner of HMS *Dauntless* had received a letter from the commander-in-chief of the Chilean Navy, Vice-Admiral Huerta, which stated:

Dear Captain Round-Turner,

As I have knowledge that your Squadron is going to pass over the sacred ground of the Battle of Coronel where the British maintained, as always, the traditions of their Navy, doing their duty and sacrificing their lives in the defence and honour of their Country, I have the honour to send to you a wreath by which the Chilean Navy wishes to express its profound admiration, and at the same time its homage to the brave Britishers of Admiral Cradock's Squadron on the spot where the battle took place.

Sincerely and Faithfully yours,

T. Huerta.[1]

Departing Talcahuano, *Dauntless* and *Dragon* rendezvoused with *Delhi* and *Danae*, and on 10 August, the squadron passed over the site of the Battle of Coronel where on 1 November 1914, the British West Indies Squadron, under the command of Rear Admiral Sir Christopher Cradock, was engaged by the German East Asia Squadron under the command of Vice-Admiral Maximillian von Spee. Outmatched and outgunned, the West Indies Squadron was annihilated. Over the site, a memorial service was held for Admiral Cradock and the officers and men under his command. As the service was conducted, the snow-capped peaks of the Andes stood out clearly in the sunlight. Wreaths were dropped astern in memory of those who lost their lives during the battle. The service was concluded with a hymn and the national anthem.

As the squadron continued on its way, a wireless signal was received from Punta Arenas indicating the pleasure with which the people there were looking forward to the squadron's arrival. The weather, however, became extremely rough. The upper decks became awash and water found its way into the wardroom of HMS *Delhi*. The squadron was driven off course by the weather. Such were the conditions that Brand, with great reluctance, decided to abandon the visit and to avoid the Strait of Magellan, and to instead take his ships around Cape Horn. The Strait of Magellan can be a treacherous body of water as Sir Francis Drake found out in August 1580 when he was faced with a storm which lasted for fifty-two days.

The violent storm without intermission, the impossibility to come to anchor; the want of opportunitie [*sic*.] to spread any sayle [*sic*.]; the most mad seas; the lee shores; the dangerous rocks; the contrary and most intolerable winds; the impossible passage out; the desperate tarrying there; and inevitable perils on every side, did lay before us so small likelihood to escape present destruction, that if the special providence of God himselfe [*sic*.] had not supported us, we could never have endured that woefull state.[2]

During the passage, while Drake's *Golden Hinde* made it through successfully, the *Elizabeth* also succeeded in making it through the passage but with great struggle while the *Marigold* floundered with all hands.

It was a similar such storm that was encountered by Brand and the First Light Cruiser Squadron. A heavy gale blew, whipping up mountainous waves that broke across the stern of the ships and travelled along their length. The squadron was fortunate that the wind and sea, at the height of the storm, were from dead astern. Snow began to fall as the squadron rounded Cape Horn. Between the snow squalls were intervals of sunlight during which the crews of the cruisers were presented with an excellent view of the Cape's bold, jagged headland which rose sheer out of the water. As the signal to alter course northwards was hauled down aboard *Delhi*, a small group aboard the cruiser started to sing 'Rolling Home' for after months at sea, the squadron was heading the general direction of Britain.

During the morning of 16 August, as the squadron faced the bracing cold wind that blew off Tierra del Fuego, HMS *Dauntless* and *Dragon* once more detached to make port calls; HMS *Dauntless* proceeded to the Falkland Islands while *Dragon* set a course for Bahia Blanca, Argentina. HMS *Delhi* and *Danae*, meanwhile, continued on through the rough head-sea bound for Buenos Aires.

HMS *Dauntless* proceeded to the Falkland Islands and dropped anchor at Port Stanley where a dance was held in the city hall for 700 residents from across

HMS *Delhi* rounding Cape Horn. (*Empire Photographic Publishing, Steve Locks*)

the islands as well as 150 men from the cruiser. The governor of the islands, Sir John Middleton, and his wife, Lady Middleton, entertained officers from the cruiser at Government House and were among the dignitaries of Port Stanley who were welcomed aboard *Dauntless* to a lunch held by Captain Round-Turner. The stay at the Falklands was brief and *Dauntless* soon put to sea bound for the river Plate and Montevideo where she was joined by *Dragon* following her visit to Bahia Blanca. Bahia Blanca was, at the time, the largest grain-exporting port in Argentina. Some 70 per cent of the grain exported from the port was carried in vessels flying the Red Ensign while the railways in the area were all ran by Englishmen. Every day that HMS *Dragon* was alongside, hundreds of the ship's company were taken out into the country by members of the British community. Shooting parties were organised for the men while a dinner was held at the Argentine Club for officers from the ship and a dance organised at the Hotel Atlántico. The cruiser was opened to visitors with many children being shown over the ship.

At Montevideo, 25 August was observed as a national holiday, the day marking ninety-nine years since Uruguay had claimed independence from the empire of Brazil. An official reception was held on board the ships for Sir Claude Malet, the British ambassador to Uruguay, and his wife before the two ships were placed 'At Home'.

Meanwhile, HMS *Delhi* and *Danae* had dropped anchor at Buenos Aires. Heavy fog had delayed the passage of the ships up the River Plate and it was not until 12 p.m. on 21 August that the cruisers arrived at Esenada Roads. The *Delhi* and *Danae* were alongside for ten days during which time hospitalities were lavished upon the crews and time was permitted to see something of the country. A ball was held by the British community at the Plaza Hotel at which there were a thousand guests. The Hurlingham Club, meanwhile, provided an outlet for almost every kind of sport. A detachment of 120 men drawn from the two ships marched through the city streets and placed a wreath on the monument to Almirante William Brown. The salute rendered by the Brigade was taken at the Presidential Palace by President Marcelo Torcuato de Alvear and Brand. The march past left the great impression on those who witnessed it.

The visit of the squadron to Buenos Aires coincided with the tour of South America being made by the crown prince of Italy, Umberto di Savoia (later Umberto II, the last king of Italy). On 29 August, the crown prince was present at an 'At Home' event held aboard the Italian cruiser *San Giorgio* which had also dropped anchor in the harbour. Brand along with Captains Pipon and Austin were invited aboard the *San Giorgio* and were presented to the Italian prince.

While alongside, leave was given to the crews. The behaviour of the liberty men was exemplary and no patrols were landed and no complaints were received from the local authorities. The two ships were opened up to visitors and during their time alongside they were visited by 14,800 people.

Departing Buenos Aires on 31 August, HMS *Delhi* and *Danae* rendezvoused with HMS *Dauntless* and *Dragon* before proceeding as a squadron to Rio de

Admiral Brand at Buenos Aires. (*Empire Photographic Publishing, Steve Locks*)

Janeiro. The squadron arrived off Rio on 3 September. Off the Brazilian coast, the squadron was met by two destroyers of the Brazilian navy which provided an escort into the harbour. Having provided an escort, the destroyers cheered the ship before departing.

Brazilian Independence Day was 7 September. To mark the occasion, the ships were dressed and twenty-one-gun salutes were fired at sunrise, noon, and sunset. During the course of the day, 500 men from the squadron joined 2,000 men of the Brazilian navy and Marines for a march through the city. A series of sporting competitions were held between the squadron and the Brazilian navy. The Brazilian navy distinguished itself at athletics and water sports and beat the squadron heavily at cricket. A number of football matches were also played, during which things were more even.

Soon the squadron's stay at Rio was over and the ships weighed anchor and put to sea. Out in the South Atlantic, they set a course north for the Cape Verde Islands, the final stop before they returned home.

10

'A Halo of Splendour'

Having parted company with the First Light Cruiser Squadron, the *Hood*, *Repulse*, and *Adelaide* were to conduct their own tour of the Caribbean and eastern Canada. Having parted company with Brand's command, the battlecruisers and *Adelaide* encountered some of the hottest weather of the cruise. Exercises filled up the days until 22 July when, sailing independently ahead of the *Hood* and *Repulse*, HMAS *Adelaide* arrived at Balboa, Panama. The battlecruisers reached Balboa the following day. While at anchor, the stores of the ships were replenished and mail was brought aboard before the ships began their transit of the Panama Canal to re-enter the Atlantic.

Entering the first of the twelve locks on 23 July, the ships were guided through the lock chambers by mules, electric locomotives named after the mules that had traditionally been used to cross the isthmus of Panama, which ran along the lock walls. Everyone was impressed by the quiet and efficient manner in which the canal staff performed their duties and the high state of efficiency which was maintained. Shortly before 3 p.m. on 23 July the ships of the squadron secured in the Pedro Miguel lock for the night and until 5 p.m. were opened up to visitors. The ships resumed their passage at 8 a.m. the following morning. As she transited the Panama Canal, the *Hood* gained the distinction of being the largest vessel to transit the passage. As she proceeded through the locks which lifted and dropped her with as much ease as does a lock on the river Thames a pleasure craft, she had less than thirty inches of clearance. Exiting the Gatún Locks, the *Hood* exited the Panama Canal and emerged into the Caribbean. The cost of her passage through the canal totalled $22,399.50, a figure worked out at $0.50 per ton plus towing fees.[1] In today's money, the cost to the British government for the *Hood's* transit through the Panama Canal would be approximately £390,434.91. The *Repulse's* transit through the canal came to a total of $17,679.50.

'A Halo of Splendour'

HMAS *Adelaide* alongside the coaling wharf at Balboa, Panama. (*Empire Photographic Publishing, Steve Locks*)

Above left: HMS *Hood* approaching the Miraflores Lock of the Panama Canal. (*Empire Photographic Publishing, Steve Locks*)

Above right: HMS *Hood* approaches the first lock at the Pacific end of the Panama Canal, 23 July 1924. (*Empire Photographic Publishing, Steve Locks*)

Above: HMS *Hood* entering the Miraflores Lock. (*Empire Photographic Publishing, Steve Locks*)

Left: An officer monitors the gap between the port side of the *Hood* and the wall of the Miraflores Lock. Between herself and the lock walls, *Hood* had less than 30 inches of clearance. (*Empire Photographic Publishing, Steve Locks*)

'A Halo of Splendour'

The gates of the Miraflores Lock opening to allow the *Hood* to enter Miraflores lake. (*Empire Photographic Publishing, Steve Locks*)

HMS *Hood* leaving the Miraflores Lock. (*Empire Photographic Publishing, Steve Locks*)

Electric mules stand by ready to help pull HMS *Repulse* through the Miraflores Lock. (*Empire Photographic Publishing, Steve Locks*)

An electric mule climbs the wall of one of the locks as it helps pull the *Repulse* through the locks. Eight mules were required to tow the *Repulse*. (*Empire Photographic Publishing, Steve Locks*)

HMS *Repulse* leaving the Miraflores Lock. (*Empire Photographic Publishing, Steve Locks*)

HMS *Hood* approaching the Pedro Miguel Lock. (*Empire Photographic Publishing, Steve Locks*)

HMS *Hood* entering the Pedro Miguel Lock of the Panama Canal. (*Richard Toffolo*)

Above left: HMS *Hood* in the Pedro Miguel Lock of the Panama Canal. As she transited the Panama Canal, the *Hood* gained the distinction of being the largest vessel to transit the passage.

Above right: HMS *Hood* in the Panama Canal. (*Author's Collection*)

'A Halo of Splendour'

Admiral Field looking on with binoculars in hand as the *Hood* works her way through the Pedro Miguel Lock. (*Empire Photographic Publishing, Steve Locks*)

HMS *Hood* being towed through the Culuebra Cut from the Pedro Miguel Lock. (*Empire Photographic Publishing, Steve Locks*)

HMS *Hood* in the Panama Canal Zone, 24 July 1924. (*NH 60452, US Naval History and Heritage Command*)

The view from the *Hood* as she is towed through the Culuebra Cut. (*Empire Photographic Publishing, Steve Locks*)

'A Halo of Splendour'

Right: The shadow of the spotting top of HMS *Hood* projected against the side of the Culuebra Cut. (*Empire Photographic Publishing, Steve Locks*)

Below: Crewmembers aboard the *Hood* crowd the forecastle to view the scenery as *Hood* works her way through the Panama Canal. (*Empire Photographic Publishing, Steve Locks*)

Above: HMS *Hood* entering the Gatún Locks of the Panama Canal, 24 July 1924. (*68147984, National Archives, Washington D.C.*)

Below: View from HMS *Hood* as she enters the first of the three Gatún Locks. (*Empire Photographic Publishing, Steve Locks*)

Right: HMS *Hood* photographed from astern descending the Gatún Locks of the Panama Canal.

Below: Men aboard the *Hood* watch one of the mules than run along the side of the locks to guide the ships through the lock chambers. (*Empire Photographic Publishing, Steve Locks*)

Members of the *Hood*'s crew photographed as they stand atop the conning tower taking photographs as the ship transits the Panama Canal. (*Empire Photographic Publishing, Steve Locks*)

Looking aft aboard HMS *Hood* as she leaves the first of the Gatún Locks. On the left of the photograph is the emergency dam. (*Empire Photographic Publishing, Steve Locks*)

Above left: The view from HMS *Hood* as the gates of the last of the Gatún Locks opens at the end of the ship's transit through the Panama Canal. (*Empire Photographic Publishing, Steve Locks*)

Above right: HMS *Repulse* passing through the second of the Gatún Locks. (*Empire Photographic Publishing, Steve Locks*)

Looking forward aboard the *Repulse* as she passes through the Gatún Locks. (*Empire Photographic Publishing, Steve Locks*)

HMAS *Adelaide* leaving the Gatún Locks. (*Empire Photographic Publishing, Steve Locks*)

In the Caribbean, the ships set a course for Jamaica. During the early evening of 25 July, *Adelaide* left the line with engine issues and the following morning the battlecruisers arrived off Kingston. A total of four days were spent at Jamaica. Having secured alongside, at 1.56 p.m. *Hood* fired a seventeen-gun salute, and a little over thirty minutes later, a swimming party and field gun crew were landed from *Repulse*. The following day saw normal shipborne routine followed until 10.30 a.m., when a religious service was held before the ships were opened to visitors during the course of the afternoon. Additional men, including small arms companies, landed to participate in a ceremonial march through the streets of Kingston on 28 July. While at anchor, the men partook in a number of activities including a naval derby which, among other things, saw the men partake in donkey races at Chapelton. The ships remained at anchor and were opened to visitors until 30 July when the squadron departed.

The routine preparations for sea were made during the early morning amid a heavy squall that blew in from the south-east. At 2.50 a.m., boats were hoisted and the awnings which had been erected over the decks were furled. Finally, at 9.15 a.m., anchor was weighed and at 9.30 a.m., the *Hood* preceded the *Repulse* and *Adelaide* out of harbour.[2]

At sea, the squadron set a course for Halifax, Canada. During the voyage to Halifax, a number of activities were conducted to keep the crews occupied. On the quarterdeck of the *Repulse*, Marines were drilled, while full power trials were conducted, sea boat crews were exercised, and action stations drills were held. On 1 August, the *Hood* conducted a torpedo firing exercise before on 4 August, she and the *Repulse* conducted high-angle and smoke shell firings.[3]

Right: The beginning of the naval derby. (*Empire Photographic Publishing, Steve Locks*)

Below: (*Empire Photographic Publishing, Steve Locks*)

Above: HMS *Hood* photographed coming up astern of HMAS *Adelaide* as she conducts full-power trials during the journey between Kingston and Halifax. (*Empire Photographic Publishing, Steve Locks*)

Left: HMS *Hood* during torpedo running exercises. (*Empire Photographic Publishing, Steve Locks*)

'A Halo of Splendour'   283

The squadron dropped anchor at Halifax on 5 August. The arrival of the squadron into anchor was delayed by thick fog. Once alongside, the weather deteriorated further. The warm, tropical weather to which the squadron had become accustomed over the preceding weeks was now a distant memory. The tropical heat gave way to the cold while rain and fog alternated with one another. The poor weather at Halifax led to many of the planned outdoor sporting events and games being abandoned. While this detracted somewhat from the visit of the squadron, the activities that were held were enjoyed by all. The weather broke for a ceremonial march through the city which once more saw people lining the streets cheering the Naval Brigade as it marched by.

Spirits were further dampened aboard HMAS *Adelaide* with the loss of one of her crewmen, Shipwright Albert Scott, who died on board at the age of twenty-eight, shortly before the ship dropped anchor in Halifax. Scott was subsequently buried at Halifax.

The visit of the squadron coincided with a city carnival that was held in celebration of the 175th anniversary of the founding of Halifax. Members of the squadron took an active part in these activities. On 7 August, Edward Macdonald, the Canadian minister of national defence, arrived in Halifax from Ottawa to welcome the squadron on behalf of the government. Four days later, Macdonald held a public dinner for Field, his staff, and the captains of the ships. Further hospitalities were extended to the squadron by the people of Halifax which were returned to the fullest possible extent by the squadron. While alongside, the ships were opened to visitors. During the ten days alongside, approximately 20,000 people were welcomed aboard and shown over the ships.

The squadron departed Halifax on the morning of 15 August amid fine, clear weather. The next stop for the battlecruisers and *Adelaide* was to be Quebec on the St Lawrence River. It had been intended that the squadron would arrive at Quebec at around 1.30 p.m. on 18 August; the weather, however, put paid to these plans. Dense fog was encountered on 17 August as the squadron made its way up the St Lawrence River. Owing to the fog, the squadron was forced to temporarily drop anchor 14 miles off Becquette Island Light. Visibility did not improve until the afternoon of the 18th. On account of the tide, the *Hood* and *Repulse* were prohibited from passing the Lower Traverse Light vessel no later than 7.15 a.m. Unable to make the passage into Quebec until the following morning, the squadron spent the night of 18 August in Murray Bay where a number of the men under the command of General James Murray had settled following the Siege of Quebec. Weighing anchor at 7 a.m., the squadron worked up to 15 knots as it passed the Cape Traverse Light Vessel and made its way through the Beaujei Channel before dropping anchor at Quebec beneath the historic walls of the fortress around 1.20 p.m.[4]

Large crowds had assembled on the terrace that stood beneath the imposing walls and towers of the Chateau Frontenac to welcome the squadron. Having secured, *Hood* fired a thirteen-gun salute to the lieutenant-governor of Ontario, Narcisse Perodeau. Perodeau along with the premier of Quebec, Louis-Alexandre

Above: Halifax Harbour with HMS *Hood* and *Repulse* at anchor. (*Empire Photographic Publishing, Steve Locks*)

Left: The grave of Shipwright Albert Scott of HMAS *Adelaide* at Halifax who died aboard the cruiser the day the squadron arrived in Halifax. (*P02766.015, Australian War Memorial*)

Taschereau, the general officer commanding, Brigadier-General J. P. Landry, and Mayor Joseph-Octave Sampson called on Field. Following these formalities, Field landed with Captain Im Thurn, members of his staff, Captain Parker, and Captain Stevenson whereupon they received an address from Mayor Sampson at King's Wharf, during which he spoke of the honour that had been conferred upon Canada by the dispatch of the squadron. Continuing, Sampson went on to proclaim:

> As Mayor of Quebec, I may be allowed to say that our city has always been proud of its French origin, but its citizens have always endeavoured to maintain the *Entente Cordiale* with their English-speaking fellow citizens. United for ever, since the tragic days of Wolfe and Montcalm, we have fully enjoyed the liberties guaranteed under the Treaty of Paris. Under the British Colours, we now rank among the free nations, and our trade and commerce have trebled the power and influence of our dear country, the Dominion of Canada. Let us continue in peace the success achieved by our predecessors. On a much larger scale we must work together for the benefit of the community.[5]

Meanwhile, a Toronto newspaper voiced the sentiments of Canadians of British origin, paying focus to the *Hood*:

> In her mass and speed and perfection of armament the *Hood* symbolizes the valorous determination of war-weary Britain to maintain intact for the good of mankind the far-flung Empire she has built up through the centuries. It is this symbolism which lifts the *Hood* out of the machine, and irradiates the great grey hulk with a halo of splendour, so that the Briton who watches her majestic course finds himself humming snatches of 'Land of hope and glory' and breathing the prayer 'God that made thee mighty, make thee mightier yet!'[6]

The following day, HMAS *Adelaide* proceeded into the tidal basin while the *Repulse* proceeded alongside No. 1 pier. At 7.48 p.m. that day, aboard the *Hood*, Field struck his flag as he departed the battlecruiser to embark upon a week-long tour of Ottawa, Toronto, and Montréal. During this period, command of the squadron was devolved to Captain Parker aboard the *Repulse*.

Field travelled by rail to Ottawa aboard a sleeping and dining car large enough to accommodate his entire party which was supplied by the Canadian National Railways on behalf of the Canadian government. At Ottawa, Field was met by the Canadian Prime Minister Mackenzie King. Also present at the station to greet Field were the aide-de-camp to the governor-general, naval and other military officials, and civic officials including Samuel Harris, the president of the Navy League of Canada, who had previously been on hand to welcome the squadron to Victoria. Following the formalities at the station, Field and his party proceeded to Government House to call upon the governor-general, General Lord Byng. That same evening, a dinner was held at the Ottawa Country Club.

Above: HMS *Repulse* (foreground) and HMS *Hood* (background) on the St Lawrence River during the squadron's visit to Quebec. (*2019-016-621, Lytton Family, Saanich Archives*)

Left: The archbishop of Quebec, Cardinal Louis-Nazaire Bégin, welcoming the officers and men of HMS *Hood*, *Repulse*, and HMAS *Adelaide*. (*P32, S4, P24, Bibliothèque et Archives nationales du Québec*)

The following day, a dinner was held by the governor-general which was attended by principal ministers of state and Field and his party. Immediately after the dinner, Field left Ottawa for Toronto. Field was seen off at the station by the governor-general, the prime minister and the minister of defence. At Toronto, Field was warmly received and was invited to open the Annual Canadian National Exhibition. Following conducting the opening ceremony in the Exhibition Grounds, amid a crowd of thousands, Field received the salute of 5,000 soldiers, sailors, and ex-servicemen who had saw active service during the First World War and in earlier conflicts. The march was led by the naval contingent. Simultaneous with Field's visit, 150 officers and men from the squadron were invited to the city to be guests of the city for a week. Two field gun crews—one drawn from the *Repulse* and the other from the *Hood*—were included in the party along with their guns. Two field gun crews composed of ratings from the Royal Canadian Navy were also invited to be guests of the exhibition. Each night, the field gun crews provided a display. A competition between the crews was also held with a silver cup to be presented to the winners. Out of this, the gun crew of the *Repulse* emerged victorious.

On 25 August, Field was received by a guard of sea scouts as he attended a ceremony in which he was given the honour of laying the corner stone of the Earl Beatty Junior and Senior Public School. Field and his party paid a visit to the city of Hamilton where they were guests of the Hamilton Navy League. From Hamilton, Field and his party journeyed to Montréal before returning to Quebec where Field once more hoisted his flag aboard the *Hood* at 10 p.m. on 27 August.

While visiting Ottawa, Toronto, and Montréal, Field had to deal with questions relating to the comments he had made while in Vancouver which had continued to cause a stir. Field's comments had sparked debate in the national press, which adopted a partisan tone and linguistic divide which characterised Canadian politics. In the cities visited by the squadron, support for Field was evident with supporters adopting a tone of Britishness and united empire. This was not something which was surprising for these cities were generally more conservative and Anglophone, placing a greater reliance on trade with Britain and the rest of the empire. The *Halifax Herald* reminded its readers that Nova Scotia had a historical connection to the navy, reiterated the importance of transatlantic shipping to the regional economy and rose to Field's defence asking its readership, 'is anyone so mean of spirit as to think that Canada should for all time depend on the Mother Country's fleet for protection of Canada's shipping?'[7]

The newspaper was careful to also articulate a future vision of a commonwealth in which Canada would stand alongside Britain as an equal partner, stating, 'if Canada must have full nationhood within the Empire, Canada must take full nationhood seriously'.[8] The *Daily Colonist* justified Field's words but also went on to add the caveat, 'he emphasises that whatever Canada may do is purely a question for Canada'.[9] These staunch proponents of empire framed the question of naval defence as an inherently Canadian one, making it a question of destiny, one in which Canada was in charge of her own destiny and free to rise to a standing on an equal footing with Britain and other Dominions in a commonwealth.

The site of the Annual Canadian National Exhibition. (*Empire Photographic Publishing, Steve Locks*)

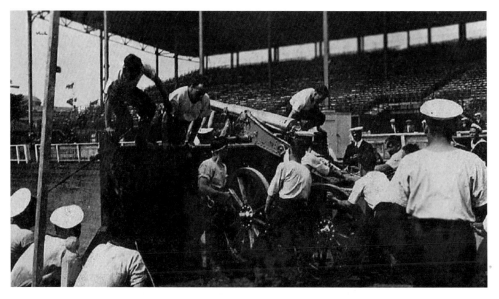

The field gun crew from HMS *Repulse* during a demonstration at the Annual Canadian National Exhibition in Toronto. (*Empire Photographic Publishing, Steve Locks*)

The field gun crew of HMS *Repulse* who emerged victorious from the competition held between the gun crews and were awarded a silver cup. (*Empire Photographic Publishing, Steve Locks*)

Those on the other side of the debate viewed Field's words as a tasteless and ill-conceived stunt the purpose of which was to cajole Canada into the arms of imperialist warmongers.[10] In the *Montréal Gazette* Field's words were described as 'off course' and warned that his words would detract from the intended message of imperial unity. The *Montréal Gazette* went on to state its hope that 'the presence of the Squadron in Canadian waters will hereafter be unattended by injudicious excursions into the field of domestic political controversy'.[11] The newspaper *Le Devoir* labelled the cruise of the Special Service Squadron a 'propaganda tour' and urged the Canadian authorities to remind Field of 'his limited purview for the betterment of Anglo-Canadian relations'.[12] Other Francophone papers were equally critical, nevertheless, the Francophone protests lacked an explicitly anti-British tone. Instead, the Special Service Squadron became another footnote in the national debate on Canadian autonomy, imperial responsibilities, and globalism which presaged the 1931 Statute of Westminster, establishing the legislative independence of the Dominions from the British parliament.[13]

Meanwhile, in Quebec, the squadron was hospitably entertained by the city's population. On 21 August, a ceremonial march through the city streets was held. 'At Home' events were held aboard the *Repulse* on the 22nd and aboard the *Hood* on the 30th. From 25 August until the 27th, the *Repulse* held a series of children's

HMS *Hood* in front of the Château Frontenac, Quebec. (*P428, S3, SS1, D7, P134/Fonds L'Action catholique / Croiseur de bataille "HMS Hood" à la hauteur du Château Frontenac/ Photographe non identifié, Bibliothèque et Archives nationales du Québec*)

HMS *Hood* on the St Lawrence River in front of the Citadelle of Quebec and Château Frontenac. (*P428, S3, SS1, D7, P132/Fonds L'Action catholique/Croiseur de bataille "HMS Hood" à la hauteur de la Citadelle/Photo C. P. R., Bibliothèque et Archives nationales du Québec*)

HMS *Hood* at anchor on the St Lawrence River. (*P428, S3, SS1, D7, P133/Fonds L'Action catholique/Croiseur de bataille "HMS Hood" à la hauteur du Château Frontenac/Photo C. P. R., Bibliothèque et Archives nationales du Québec*)

'A Halo of Splendour'

HMS *Hood* lying at anchor in the centre of the St Lawrence River, Quebec, during her visit to the city between 19 August and 2 September 1924. In the photograph, and in the ones on the previous pages, Field's flag can be seen flying from the foremast. It is likely that this photograph and the preceding ones were taken between 28 August and 2 September. (*P428, S3, SS1, D7, P37/Fonds L'Action catholique/Croiseur de bataille "HMS Hood" sur le fleuve Saint-Laurent / Photo C. P. R., 1924*)

A young boy dressed in a naval uniform sits astride a 15-inch gun aboard HMS *Hood*. (*Empire Photographic Publishing, Steve Locks*)

parties, all of which were well received. On 26 August, the French sloops *Ville D'Ys* and *Regulus* transited along the St Lawrence River past Quebec *en route* to Montreal. The French ships rendered Field's flag a fifteen-gun salute, which was returned by the *Hood*. Between these activities, the ships of the squadron were opened to visitors.

For the crews of the ships, it was not just the entertainment programme that filled their time. While at anchor, time was taken to both paint the ships and clean the ships, to make and mend clothes, conduct drills, undertake diver exercises, and test lifeboats. On 29 August, a squadron ball was held aboard *Hood* with a smaller dance also held aboard the *Repulse*.[14] The last function at Quebec was a farewell dinner held at the Garrison Club, at which 150 military and civilian officials alongside distinguished individuals were present. During the speeches made at the dinner, the chairman of the Garrison Club, Brigadier-General Landry referred to the presence of HMAS *Adelaide* and expressed his hope that on the next occasion that a squadron embarked upon a cruise around the empire that it would include a vessel of the Royal Canadian Navy.

During the mid-afternoon of 2 September, the squadron began to prepare to depart Quebec. At 3 p.m., the *Repulse* and *Adelaide* were unmoored and left the wharf before the *Hood* weighed anchor half an hour later. The squadron departed Quebec shortly before 4 p.m., departing the city in line ahead at 13 knots. Proceeding down the river, anchor was dropped for the night off the island of Orleans to await more suitable tidal conditions for the passage past the traverse light vessels. The squadron got underway once more at 7.30 a.m. the following morning. As the ships proceeded down the St Lawrence River, the banks of the river gradually receded from one another as the river widened to become a vast estuary which eventually gave way to the Atlantic Ocean. The squadron was now bound for what would be its final stop before returning to Britain, Topsail Bay, Newfoundland.

Topsail Bay, more commonly known as Topsail Bight, lies in the south-east of Conception Bay. The bay was reached on 6 September and was to be the squadron's anchorage for fifteen days. Something of a lonely anchorage, Topsail Bay had been selected as an anchorage for the simple reason that there was not enough room in the harbour at St John's to accommodate the *Hood, Repulse* and *Adelaide*. Already at anchor at St John's when the ships of the squadron arrived was the light cruiser HMS *Constance*.

The time spent at Topsail Bay provided the crews with an opportunity to collect themselves and to prepare for their return to Britain, and with that, to the normal business of naval life. Excursions were made to St John's 14 miles away. To facilitate the excursions, the government of Newfoundland laid on special trains free of charge for the crews while some of the local populace placed their cars at the disposal of the officers and men. The bars and clubs of St John's threw open their doors to the men of the squadron while a number of entertainment activities were organised by Sir William Allardyce, the governor of Newfoundland. The activities organised included late evening functions, as well as fishing and shooting excursions, the close season being curtailed for the squadron's benefit for a few days.

A ceremonial march through St John's was held on 10 September involving sailors and Royal Marines and the ships were opened to visitors. Tragedy, however, was not far away and an incident involving a car in which six people including two officers from HMS *Constance* lost their lives led to the temporary suspension of activities and cast gloom over the latter part of the squadron's visit. On 18 September, both *Hood* and *Repulse* landed field gun crews while *Hood* also landed a band for the funerals of the officers from HMS *Constance* who were buried at St John's. Three days earlier, on 15 September, the crew of the *Hood* posed over the forward turrets and forecastle for a crew photograph. This was followed on 19 September by a 'Miss World' competition aboard *Hood*. Meanwhile, those aboard the *Repulse* conducted numerous exercises as the ship began to slip back into naval routine.

On 15 September 1924, while in Topsail Bay, the crew of HMS *Hood* congregated on the forecastle and atop the forward turrets for a crew photograph. Note Joey the wallaby in the front row. (*HMS Hood Association*)

11

Return of the Squadron

During the afternoon of 21 September, the *Hood*, *Repulse*, and *Adelaide* weighed anchor and departed Topsail Bay. As the squadron got underway at 4 p.m., the band of the *Hood* was struck up, playing 'Rolling Home'.[1] Once underway the three ships fell into line astern, led by the *Hood*, and proceeded out into the Atlantic, setting a course for Britain. The *Hood*, *Repulse*, and *Adelaide* made their passage across a calm Atlantic; the swell had subsided and the wind died down. The sky was grey with cloud but the horizon remained clear. Across the horizon, a variety of steamers making their own way across the Atlantic were visible. Shortly before the three ships put to sea, Field sent a signal to the Admiralty in which he requested permission to attempt to break the record for crossing the Atlantic. The Admiralty refused permission, informing Field that an attempt to break the record would be a waste of fuel.[2]

As the ships proceeded across the Atlantic, the crews were engaged in a variety of activities, including the cleaning and painting of the ships. Divisions were exercised, a brief gunnery programme was conducted, sea boat crews were exercised, and men were drilled. The crossing did not, however, pass entirely without incident. When in the mid-Atlantic, HMS *Hood* suddenly shook violently. Captain Im Thurn was called to the bridge and an investigation launched which offered no explanation for the curious and sudden violent shaking. While the cause was never explained, one theory that was put forward was that the ship had hit a whale.[3]

Meanwhile, the First Light Cruiser Squadron had concluded its tour of South America and had proceeded through the Atlantic to the Cape Verde Islands where anchor was dropped for a short period. At 3 p.m. on 28 September, off Lizard Point, lookouts aboard the *Hood* sighted the First Light Cruiser Squadron, which rejoined Field's flag ten minutes later. The sight of the cruisers rejoining the flag generated interest among the officers of the *Hood* as recalled by V. C. Scott O'Connor.

Naval officers, who are more artful than their men, keep up a very good show of being unsentimental; and they have a little vocabulary of bad words for all such manifestations, but when the First Light Cruiser Squadron came into sight after an absence from the Vice-Admiral's flag of eighty days, they looked … uncommonly

HMS *Hood* passing in front of Kelly's Island, Conception Bay, on 21 September 1924. During the afternoon of 21 September, the *Hood*, *Repulse*, and *Adelaide* weighed anchor and departed Newfoundland to return across the Atlantic. (*867 10.12.011, Memorial University of Newfoundland*)

interested ... the wardroom door suddenly flew open as if a hurricane had pushed it in, and the President of the Mess appeared with a peculiar sort of look on his face, and called out in a loud voice 'The *Delhis*', it really did look as if there was a certain amount of sentiment about.[4]

The ships of the First Light Cruiser Squadron took up cruising stations alongside the battlecruisers shortly after rejoining Field's flag. At 4.05 p.m., HMS *Danae* and *Dragon* passed through the lines and cheered ship before detaching from the squadron to take up a course for Sheerness. Twenty-five minutes later, the *Repulse* and *Adelaide* also passed through the lines and cheered ship before parting company with Field's flag to make for Portsmouth. HMS *Hood* with *Delhi* and *Dauntless*, meanwhile, continued on to Cawsand Bay. Shortly before 9 p.m., the *Hood* secured alongside No. 4 Berth in the Bay. The following morning, at 4.30 a.m., the harbourmaster of Devonport was embarked aboard the *Hood* to serve as a pilot. A little over an hour later, the battlecruiser had weighed anchor and proceeded into Devonport where she stopped alongside the No. 6 Berth at Keyham Yard at 6.35 a.m. whereupon ammunition lighters began to secure alongside.

At 9.30 a.m., a guard of honour and the ship's band were paraded for the commander-in-chief, Plymouth, Vice-Admiral Sir Richard Phillimore, before the mayor of Plymouth was piped aboard to deliver an official welcome to Field following completing the cruise. The ceremonies were not over, however.

Members of the Admiralty arrived at Devonport to congratulate Field on the success of the cruise and to deliver the news that the King had made him a Knight Commander of the Most Distinguished Order of St Michael and St George while Captain Im Thurn was to be made a Companion of the Order. That afternoon, wives, sweethearts and families crossed the gangways from the quayside and boarded the battlecruiser for a special reception. Among them was R. O'Sullivan, the daughter of one of *Hood*'s petty officers who remembered, 'My dad gave a whistle and Joey, the wallaby, came bounding along. He nuzzled around my dad's pocket until he took out his tobacco pouch and gave him a pinch of tobacco. Joey was addicted to it'.[5]

HMS *Repulse* and *Adelaide*, meanwhile, were still at sea in the English Channel making their approach to Portsmouth. At 11.50 a.m. that day, the two ships stopped at Spithead to embark pilots. At noon, the *Repulse* fired a seventeen-gun salute to the commander-in-chief, Portsmouth, Admiral Sir Sydney Fremantle. Proceeding into harbour, at 12.45 p.m., the *Repulse* secured alongside the Southern Railway Jetty after which ammunition lighters secured alongside to disembark the ship's ammunition. Having dropped anchor at Portsmouth, the crew of HMAS *Adelaide* assembled on the forecastle of the cruiser for a crew photograph.

One by one, the First Light Cruiser Squadron dropped anchor and secured alongside, bringing to an end the cruise of the Special Service Squadron.

A group portrait of the ship's company of HMAS *Adelaide* mustered together on the forecastle following the ship's arrival in Portsmouth at the end of the cruise. The ship would operate in British waters before departing Portsmouth for Sydney on 7 April 1925. (*P02646.005, Australian War Memorial*)

Epilogue

The cruise of the Special Service Squadron has been referred to as 'a new undertaking' as it was 'specifically a demonstration of naval power', rather than a pure goodwill or royal tour.[1] Following the squadron's return to Britain, on 27 September 1924, *The Times* declared, 'The Squadron has done great work, a work of which none living may measure the scope and the full consequence. It has been on a mission; it has sown the seed of Empire loyalty'.[2]

Despite this, however, the enduring legacy of the cruise of the Special Service Squadron is less clear cut. The Admiralty contracted journalist V. C. Scott O'Connor to produce a commemorative book which depicted the empire 'in an Orientalist trope reminiscent of Victorian travel writing'.[3] O'Connor's book was very much a product of the time, which as Daniel Owen Spence and John C. Mitcham have pointed out, characterised non-British subjects as 'mere ethnographical displays'.[4] This fact was highlighted by such sentences as 'a man would have had to have a hard heart not to be touched by this spectacle of an untutored and, for all its disguises, primitive human nature', and the description of Fijian chiefs 'only two generations removed from cannibalism … it would appear, however, from the records available, that it is quite possible for a man to be very civil to another whom he proposes to eat'.[5]

In addition to the account written by O'Connor, the Admiralty and the Royal Colonial Institute co-sponsored a cinematic account of the cruise which was released in 1925 under the title *Britain's Birthright*. The film formed part of the wider empire series of films produced during the 1920s and included scenes of indigenous populations entertaining sailors and performing for the camera crews.[6] The film, however, has been described as a 'commercial failure'.[7] In the first instance, the Admiralty struggled to find a filmmaker who was prepared to support the venture which suggests that at the time the enterprise, the Royal Navy and possibly even the empire itself as subject matters were not deemed to be popular topics. It has been suggested that a key reason that lay behind this were advances in technology, namely powered flight and in particular aircraft which were drawing public attention away from the sea and with that the navy.[8]

Further to this, *Britain's Birthright* was not popular abroad. The film was 'refused by all the Dominions' and was only shown by private enterprise. This is somewhat surprising given the numbers of people who turned out to greet the ships and their crews, particularly in Australia, and the number of people who were welcomed aboard and shown around the vessels. This reaction serves to suggest that the novelty factor of the squadron dropping anchor was more of a draw for the citizens of the Dominions and colonies as opposed to imperial sentient and links to 'the Mother Country'.[9] One of the key reasons behind the film being refused by all the Dominions lies in the Americanisation of the film industry; it has been written that 'in some Dominions the theatres are very largely in the control of American interests'.[10] In its representation of foreign locals and in its formal style, the film is typical of the imperial films produced during the interwar period.

The cruise raised questions over the ethics of colonialism while also setting a precedent for the use of ships as symbolic bonds to unite divergent notions of identification.[11] During the 1920s and 1930s, a number of other showing the flag missions and tours would be undertaken.

All of the ships that formed part of the Special Service Squadron remained in service following the empire cruise and saw service during the Second World War. Of the eight vessels that formed part of the squadron, half would be lost during the course of the Second World War. HMS *Hood* was the first of the former ships of the squadron to be lost when she was hit in the magazine and suffered a cataclysmic explosion when a shell detonated her aft magazines as she engaged the German battleship *Bismarck* in the Denmark Strait on 24 May 1941. Of her then complement of 1,418, there were only three survivors.[12] The loss of life aboard the *Hood* made it the second largest individual maritime disaster sustained by the Royal Navy during the war.[13] Prior to the Second World War, the *Hood* had spent the remainder of the interwar period on showing the flag exercises and played a role in British efforts to check Italy following her invasion of Abyssinia and during the Spanish Civil War.

HMS *Dunedin* was the second ship from the squadron to be lost. Following replacing HMS *Chatham* as flagship of the New Zealand Division, *Dunedin* remained in New Zealand until 1937 during which time she provided assistance to the town of Napier following the Hawkes Bay earthquake. During the Second World War HMS *Dunedin* was involved in the hunt for the *Scharnhorst* and *Gneisenau* following the sinking of HMS *Rawalpindi*. The ship was lost on 24 November 1941 in the central Atlantic to the east of St Paul's Rocks when she was torpedoed by *U-124*. Out of the ship's complement of 486, four officers and sixty-three men survived.

HMS *Repulse* was the third ship to be lost from the squadron and was also lost in 1941. In October 1941, the *Repulse* was providing escort to convoys in the Indian Ocean. Selected to form part of Force Z alongside the battleship HMS *Prince of Wales*, the two ships sailed to Singapore where a naval base had been completed in 1938, to act as a deterrent force against Japanese aggression. Putting to sea on 9 December following reports being received of a Japanese invasion

Epilogue 299

force approaching Malaya, on 10 December both the *Prince of Wales* and *Repulse* were attacked by thirty-four torpedo and fifty-one high-level bombers and sunk. Crippled by the Japanese air attacks, the *Repulse* took on water and capsized to port and sank at 12.23 p.m. with the loss of 508 men.[14]

HMS *Dragon* was the fourth ship of the Special Service Squadron to not survive the Second World War. Having returned to Britain, following the cruise, *Dragon* saw service in British waters before being detached first to the China Station and then the America and West Indies Station in the 1930s. In 1938 she joined the Reserve Fleet. At the outbreak of the Second World War, HMS *Dragon* was attached to the Seventh Cruiser Squadron and participated in the hunt for the pocket battleship *Admiral Graf Spee*. The ship saw action during the allied efforts to capture Dakar in late 1940 before taking up convoy escort duties in the Atlantic until November 1941 when she sailed to the Indian Ocean and escorted convoys to Singapore. HMS *Dragon* would be the last warship to leave Singapore before the fortress surrendered to the Japanese on 20 January 1942.

On 15 January 1943, the ship was handed over to the Polish navy and commissioned as ORP *Dragon*. Refitted, ORP *Dragon* operated out of Scapa Flow providing escort to convoys bound for the Soviet Union. The ship saw action off the Normandy beaches, shelling German positions around Sword beach and providing fire support off Juno beach. The ship returned to Britain on 18 June 1944 as an escort to HMS *Nelson* which had struck a mine. On 7 July, she returned to the area off Caen where she provided offshore fire support to allied forces. The following day, at 5.40 a.m., she was struck by a German Neger manned torpedo which killed twenty-six members of her crew. Despite the efforts of the damage control team, following an inspection of the damage which concluded that the damage was repairable, and despite still being afloat, it was decided to abandon the ship. On 16 July, *Dragon* was decommissioned and towed to Arromanches where on 20 July she was scuttled to form part of the artificial breakwater for the Mulberry Harbour.

Following her return to Britain at the end of the cruise of the Special Service Squadron, HMS *Delhi* was paid off before recommissioning as part of the First Cruiser Squadron with the Mediterranean Fleet in January 1925. Following a brief interlude on the China Station and a return to the Mediterranean, the beginning of the 1930s saw *Delhi* attached to the America and West Indies Station. Returning to Europe, *Delhi* operated off Spain during the Spanish Civil War and assisted with the collection and transport of refugees. The outbreak of the Second World War saw *Delhi* deployed in the North Sea operating against German merchant vessels. Following service as part of the northern patrol, 1940 saw her operate against Vichy and Italian forces in the Mediterranean before participating in the allied assault on Dakar. Damaged on 20 November 1942 in Algiers Bay when her stern was blown off by a bomb dropped by an Italian aircraft, she returned to Britain for repairs. Recommissioned in April, in September she provided support for the Allied landings at Salerno and later Operation Dragoon, the Allied invasion of Southern France. Damaged by a German torpedo attack in February

1945 which damaged her rudder, following the war, HMS *Delhi* returned to Britain and was laid up. Assessed as uneconomic to fully repair as an aged design in a rapidly downsizing Royal Navy, she was mothballed and sold on 28 January 1948 to be broken up.

Following the cruise of the Special Service Squadron, HMAS *Adelaide* remained in British waters until January 1925 when she began her return voyage to Australia by way of the Mediterranean, Ceylon, and Singapore. Service in Australian waters followed until June 1928 when the ship was paid off into reserve. Modernised in 1938, which saw the ship converted from coal and oil burning to solely oil burning, the ship was recommissioned in 1939. With the outbreak of war in Europe, HMAS *Adelaide* was deployed on convoy escort duties in Australian waters. In February 1945, *Adelaide* was reassigned to serve as a tender to the naval base HMAS *Penguin*. Decommissioned from service in May 1946, HMAS *Adelaide* was gradually stripped of her equipment before being sold in January 1949 to be broken up.

For a period following the cruise, HMS *Danae* served in home waters before being transferred to the Mediterranean between 1927 and 1929 after which she was withdrawn to Britain for a refit and modernisation. Returned to active service in 1930, HMS *Danae* left Devonport for Halifax from where she joined the Eighth Cruiser Squadron on the America and West Indies Station. Service in the Pacific followed with the outbreak of the Second Sino-Japanese War in 1935 seeing *Danae* deployed to escort evacuation convoys from Shanghai to Hong Kong. Returning to Britain, HMS *Danae* was placed into reserve before being mobilised in July 1939 as the clouds of war gathered over Europe. Initially seeing service attached to the Ninth Cruiser Squadron in the South Atlantic and Indian Ocean, in March 1940, *Danae* was attached to the Malaya Force which conducted patrols in the area around the Dutch East Indies and Singapore. While in the Far East she was transferred to the China Station and was reunited with HMS *Dauntless* on convoy escort duty in the Yellow Sea. Paid off to undergo a refit at Cape Town, the *Danae* returned to service in July 1943. Participating the Normandy landings where she provided support in the area off Sword Beach, alongside ORP *Dragon*.

Following the loss of ORP *Dragon*, at the beginning of October 1944 HMS *Danae* was leased to the Polish navy. Crewed mostly by the surviving part of ORP *Dragon*'s crew, HMS *Danae* was commissioned into the Polish navy as ORP *Conrad*. From February 1945, the *Conrad* operated out of Scapa Flow and was withdrawn from service in April to undergo repairs on a damaged turbine. By the time the *Conrad* was released from dockyard control, the war in Europe was over. Attached to a destroyer flotilla, she was briefly stationed in Wilhelmshaven and until the end of 1945 served as a transport ship ferrying Polish Red Cross assistance to Denmark and Norway. Returning to Rosyth in January 1946 for operations with the Home Fleet, in September that year, she was returned to the Royal Navy. Renamed *Danae* once more, the ship was placed in Care and Maintenance. Paid off, in January 1948, HMS *Danae* was sold for scrap and was ultimately scrapped in March 1948 at the Vickers-Armstrong shipyard in Barrow.

Epilogue

Service in the Mediterranean followed the cruise of the Special Service Squadron for HMS *Dauntless*. Transferred to the America and West Indies Station, between 1931 and 1933, *Dauntless* saw service with the South American Division before being reassigned to the Third Cruiser Squadron in the Mediterranean in 1934. Returning to Britain in 1935, the *Dauntless* was paid off into reserve, to be recommissioned for service with the Ninth Cruiser Squadron at the outbreak of war. In December 1939, the ship was transferred to the China Station for operations in the Indian Ocean against German merchant vessels. In February 1942, *Dauntless* returned to Britain to undergo a refit at Portsmouth after which she was transferred to the Eastern Fleet. Ordered to Simonstown, South Africa, *Dauntless* was utilised as a training ship before being reduced to the Reserve Fleet in February 1945. The ship was ultimately sold to be broken up in 1946.

The cruise of the Special Service Squadron was designed to reassure the empire and send a message to the world regarding the continued relevance of British sea power and strength:

> The reliance on traditional ideas of imperial unity and the cultural manifestations of Britnshness undercut the cruise's objectives in places such as Canada and South Africa. Equally, the response from some colonial nationalists demonstrated the limits of naval rituals and 'invented traditions' in the aftermath of the Wilsonian era. Ultimately, the navy's historic voyage was an exercise in imperial propaganda based on a vision of the British Empire on which the sun was rapidly setting.[15]

The rhetoric of imperial unity that was espoused by overseas Britons of Britishness, racial solidarity and a common maritime heritage, reflected fading Victorian ideas of Britain. While the empire was at its peak and Britain was still the top global power, the empire on which the sun never set was rapidly approaching twilight.

Nevertheless, as an event, the Cruise of the Special Service Squadron was undeniably impressive and an achievement. During the course of the cruise, the squadron sailed 38,153 miles during which the equator was crossed six times. A total of 1,936,717 people visited the ships while they were alongside; HMS *Hood* alone was visited by 752,049 people.[16] In addition to this, 37,770 individuals were entertained on board the ships at parties and dances.[17] It was a journey never to be repeated by a modern naval force.

Endnotes

Introduction

1 'Deployment of HMS Queen Elizabeth and Carrier Strike Group will "fly flag for Global Britain"', Sky News, 26 April 2021, news.sky.com/story/deployment-of-hms-queen-elizabeth-and-carrier-strike-group-will-fly-flag-for-global-britain-12287281, accessed 15/11/2021.
2 'UK Carrier Strike Group Assembles for the First Time', 5 October 2020, *Royal Navy* (2020), royalnavy.mod.uk/news-and-latest-activity/news/2020/october/05/201005-hms-queen-elizabeth-carrier-strike, accessed 18/11/2021.

Chapter 1

1 Knowles, D., *Yamato: Flagship of the Japanese Imperial Navy* (Stroud: Fonthill Media, 2021), p. 11.
2 *Ibid.*, pp. 12–13.
3 Albertson, M., *They'll Have to Follow You Home!: The Triumph of the Great White Fleet* (Mustang: Tate Publishing & Enterprise LLC, 2007), p. 14.
4 Knowles, *op. cit.*, p. 13.
5 Stille, M., *Imperial Japanese Navy Battleships 1941–1945* (Oxford: Osprey Publishing Ltd, 2008), p. 8.
6 Knowles, *op. cit.*, p. 13.
7 *Ibid.*
8 Gewarth, R., *Twisted Paths: Europe 1914–1945* (Oxford: Oxford University Press, 2012), p. 39.
9 Knowles, *op. cit.*, p. 14.
10 Gewarth, *op. cit.*, p. 39.
11 *Ibid.*
12 *Ibid.*, pp. 39–40.
13 Parker, J., *Task Force: Untold Stories of the Heroes of the Royal Navy* (London: Headline Book Publishing, 2003), p. 108.
14 Connelly, M., 'Battleships and British Society, 1920-1960', *International Journal of Naval History*, Vol. 3, No. 2 (2004), p. 2.
15 Smith, S. M., *'We Sail the Ocean Blue': British Sailors, Imperialism, Identity, Pride and Patriotism c. 1890 to 1939* (Portsmouth: University of Portsmouth, 2017), p. 117.
16 Kennedy, P. M., *The Rise and Fall of British Naval Mastery* (London: Penguin, 2017), pp. 267–268.
17 Friend, J., 'Destroyer Flag-Flying Visits, Civic Ceremony, Empire and Identity in Interwar Britain', *British Journal for Military History*, Vol. 7, No. 2 (2021), p. 102; Rüger, J., *The*

Great Naval Game: Britain and Germany in the Age of Empire (Cambridge: Cambridge University Press, 2007), p. 255.

18 Smith, *op. cit.*, p. 121.

19 *Ibid.*, p. 123; Bell, C., *The Royal Navy, Seapower and Strategy Between the Wars* (Palo Alto: Stanford University Press, 2000), p. 163; Agar, A., *Showing the Flag: The Role of the Royal navy Between the Wars* (London: Evans Brothers, 1962), p. 17.

20 Rüger, *op. cit.*, p. 259.

21 Smith, *op. cit.*, p. 123.

22 *Ibid*, p. 117.

23 Wise, J., *The Rise of the Royal Navy in South America, 1920–1970* (London: Bloomsbury, 2014), p. 3.

24 Friend, *op. cit.*, p. 102.

25 Mitcham, J. C., 'The 1924 Empire Cruise and the Imagining of an Imperial Community', *Britain and the World*, Vol. 12, No. 1 (2019), p. 69; Smith, P. C., *The Battle-Cruiser HMS Renown, 1916-1948* (Barnsley: pen and Sword, 2008), pp. 19–20.

26 Smith, *op. cit.* (2008), pp. 20 and 27.

27 Agar, *op. cit.*, p. 25.

28 Friend, *op. cit.*, pp. 108–109.

29 ADM 116/2219.

30 O'Connor, V. C. S., *The Empire Cruise* (London: Riddle, Smith & Duffus, 1925), pp. 5–6; Knowles, D., *HMS Hood: Pride of the Royal Navy* (Stroud: Fonthill Media, 2019), p. 103.

31 Mitcham, *op. cit.*, p. 71.

32 ADM 116/2219.

33 *Ibid.*

34 *Ibid.*

35 *Ibid.*

36 *Ibid.*; Smith, *op. cit.* (2017), p. 127; Wise, *op. cit.*, p. 21.

37 Harrington, R., '"The Mighty *Hood*": Navy, Empire, War at Sea and the British Imagination, 1920-60', *Journal of Contemporary History*, Vol. 38, No. 8 (2003), p. 179.

38 Smith, *op. cit.* (2017), p. 129.

39 *Ibid.*

40 Mitcham, *op. cit.*, p. 79.

41 Lyon, P., *Britain and Canada: Survey of a Changing Relationship* (London: Frank Cass and Company, 1976), p. 50.

42 *Ibid.*, pp. 50–51.

43 *Ibid.*, p. 51.

44 Eayrs, J., *In Defence of Canada Volume I: From the Great War to the Great Depression* (Toronto: University of Toronto Press, 1964), p. 179.

45 Amery, L., *My Political Life Vol. II: War and Peace 1914–1929* (London: Hutchison, 1953), p. 276; Lyon, *op. cit.*, p. 42.

46 Mitcham, *op. cit.*, p. 85

47 ADM 116/2219.

48 *Ibid.*

49 Taylor, B., *The End of Glory: War & Peace in HMS Hood, 1916–1941* (Barnsley: Seaforth Publishing, 2012), p. 23.

50 For more information on the Battle of Zanzibar, see: Farwell, B., *The Great War in Africa, 1914–1918* (New York: W. W. Norton, 1986); Halpen, P. G., *A Naval History of World War I* (Annapolis: Naval Institute Press, 1995); Edwards, B., *Salvo!: Classic Naval Gun Actions* (London: Arms and Armour Press, 1995).

51 Miller, C., *Battle for the Bundu: The First World War in East Africa* (London: Macmillan Publishing, 1974), p. 384; Taylor, *The End of Glory*, p. 23.

52 Woodburn-Kirby, Maj.-Gen. S., *The War Against Japan Volume I: The Loss of Singapore* (Uckfield: The Naval & Military Press, 2004), p. 1.

53 *Ibid.*, p. 2.

54 *Ibid.*
55 *Ibid.*, p. 3.
56 *Ibid.*, p. 6.
57 *Ibid.*
58 ADM 116/2219.
59 Harrington, *op. cit.* (2003), p. 179.
60 ADM 116/2219.
61 Harrington, *op. cit.* (2003), p. 179.
62 ADM 116/2219.
63 *Ibid.*
64 *Ibid.*
65 *Ibid.*

Chapter 2

1 Knowles, D., *HMS Hood: Pride of the Royal Navy* (Stroud: Fonthill Media, 2019), p. 37.
2 Taylor, B., *The End of Glory: War & Peace in HMS Hood, 1916–1941* (Barnsley: Seaforth Publishing, 2012), p. 1.
3 Knowles, *op. cit.* (2019), p. 38.
4 *Ibid.*, p. 40.
5 *Ibid.*, pp. 55–56; ADM 186/249.
6 Knowles, *op. cit.* (2019), pp. 82 and 84.
7 Smith, P. C., *The Battle-Cruiser HMS Renown, 1916–1948* (Barnsley: pen and Sword, 2008), p. 5.
8 *Ibid.*, p. 6.
9 *Ibid.*
10 *Ibid.*, p. 7.
11 *Ibid.*, p. 12.
12 Burt, R. A., *British Battleships of World War One* (Annapolis: Naval Institute Press, 1986), p. 294.
13 Smith, *op. cit.* (2008), p. 13.
14 Newbolt, H., *History of the Great War Based on Official Documents Vol. V: Naval Operations* (Nashville: Battery Press, 1996), pp. 173–176; Burt, *op. cit.*, p. 302; Campbell, N. J. M., *Battle Cruisers: The Design and Development of British and German Battlecruisers of the First World War Era* (Greenwich: Conway Maritime Press, 1978), p. 64; Halpen, *op. cit.*, p. 377; Bennett, G., *Naval Battles of the First World War* (Barnsley: Pen and Sword, 2005), p. 251.
15 Roberts, J., *Battlecruisers* (Annapolis: Naval Institute Press, 1997), p. 123; Bastock, J., *Australia's Ships of War* (Cremorne: Angus and Robertson, 1975), p. 35.
16 Burt, *op. cit.*, p. 302.
17 HMS *Dragon* Log Book, 1 August 1919–21 July 1920.
18 'HMS *Dragon* at Riga, 17 October 1919', hmsdragon1919.co.uk, accessed 4/10/2021.
19 Cassells, V., *The Capital Ships: Their Battles and Their Badges* (East Roseville: Simon and Schuster, 2000), p. 6.
20 *Ibid.*, p. 5.
21 *Ibid*; Perryman, J., 'Ships Named *Adelaide*', *Semaphore* (Sea Power Centre, 2015), p. 1.
22 Royal Australian Navy, 'HMAS *Adelaide* (I)', navy.gov.au (2019), navy.gov.au/hmas-adelaide-i, Accessed 05/10/2021.
23 Cassells, *op. cit.*, p. 6; Perryman, *op. cit.*, p. 1.

Chapter 3

1 Heathcote, T., *The British Admirals of the Fleet 1734–1995* (Barnsley: Pen and Sword, 2002), p. 74.

Endnotes

2 *Ibid.*

3 Silbey, D., *The Boxer Rebellion and the Great Game in China* (New York: Hill and Wang, 2012); Harrington, P., *Peking 1900: The Boxer Rebellion* (Oxford: Osprey Publishing, 2001).

4 *Supplement to the London Gazette*, 15 September 1916, No. 29751, p. 9064.

5 Heathcote, *op. cit.*, p. 75.

6 *Ibid.*

7 Knowles, D., *HMS Hood: Pride of the Royal Navy* (Stroud: Fonthill Media, 2019), p. 369.

8 *Ibid.*, p. 99.

9 ADM 196/44/156.

10 Burt, R. A., *British Battleships of World War One* (Annapolis: Naval Institute Press, 1986), p. 230.

11 Campbell, J., *Jutland: An Analysis of the Fighting* (London: Conway Maritime Press, 1998), p. 16.

12 ADM 196/44/62.

13 *The Times*, 24 June 1893; Hough, R., *Admirals in Collision* (London: Hamish Hamilton, 1959).

Chapter 4

1 O'Connor, V. C. S., *The Empire Cruise* (London: Riddle, Smith & Duffus, 1925), p. 13.

2 IWM 24934.

3 Smith, S. M., *'We Sail the Ocean Blue': British Sailors, Imperialism, Identity, Pride and Patriotism c. 1890 to 1939* (Portsmouth: University of Portsmouth, 2017), p. 133.

4 *Ibid.*, pp. 132–133.

5 Taylor, B., *The End of Glory: War & Peace in HMS Hood, 1916–1941* (Barnsley: Seaforth Publishing, 2012), p. 23.

6 Most of what follows concerning the movement of the ships has been drawn from records held at the National Archives in Kew. The records consulted are: ADM 1/8662, ADM 53/78914, ADM 53/78915, ADM 53/82492, ADM 116/2219, and ADM 116/2220.

7 Knowles, D., *HMS Hood: Pride of the Royal Navy* (Stroud: Fonthill Media, 2019), pp. 104–105.

8 Benstead, C. R., *Around the World With the Battle Cruisers* (London: Hurst and Blackett, 1925), p. 2.

9 Mitcham, J. C., 'The 1924 Empire Cruise and the Imagining of an Imperial Community', *Britain and the World*, Vol. 12, No. 1 (2019), p. 82.

10 *Ibid.*, p. 83; ADM 116/2254.

11 Mitcham, *op. cit.*, p. 83.

12 *Ibid.*, pp. 83–84.

13 O'Connor, *op. cit.*, pp. 41–43.

14 Smith, *op. cit.* (2017), p. 127.

15 Mitcham, *op. cit.*, p. 78.

16 O'Connor, *op. cit.*, p. 48.

17 Smith, *op. cit.* (2017), p. 128.

18 Knowles, *op. cit.* (2019), p. 107.

19 Mitcham, *op. cit.*, p. 81.

20 *Ibid.*

21 O'Connor, *op. cit.*, p. 65.

22 *Ibid.*, pp. 69–71.

Chapter 5

1 *Times of Ceylon*, 18 January 1924.

2 Knowles, D., *HMS Hood: Pride of the Royal Navy* (Stroud: Fonthill Media, 2019), p. 109.

Empire Cruise

3 Smith, S. M., 'We Sail the Ocean Blue': British Sailors, Imperialism, Identity, Pride and Patriotism c. 1890 to 1939 (Portsmouth: University of Portsmouth, 2017), p. 129.

4 Ghani, S. M., 'My Visit to the Battle-Cruisers H.M.S. Hood and Repulse', Force Z Survivors Association (2019), forcez-survivors.org.uk/schoolboy.html, accessed 28/10/2021.

5 O'Connor, V. C. S., The Empire Cruise (London: Riddle, Smith & Duffus, 1925), pp. 109–110.

6 Knowles, op. cit. (2019), p. 109.

7 Smith, op. cit. (2017), p. 130.

8 Mitcham, J. C., 'The 1924 Empire Cruise and the Imagining of an Imperial Community', Britain and the World, Vol. 12, No. 1 (2019), p. 69.

Chapter 6

1 O'Connor, V. C. S., The Empire Cruise (London: Riddle, Smith & Duffus, 1925), p. 125.

2 Ibid.

3 Norman, A., HMS Hood: Pride of the Royal Navy (Stroud: The History Press, 2009), p. 37.

4 Knowles, D., HMS Hood: Pride of the Royal Navy (Stroud: Fonthill Media, 2019), P. 141.

5 Ibid., p. 168.

6 Ibid., pp. 168–169.

7 Ibid, p. 173.

8 Harrington, R., '"The Mighty Hood": Navy, Empire, War at Sea and the British Imagination, 1920–60', Journal of Contemporary History, Vol. 38, No. 8 (2003), p. 181.

9 Batchelder, A., 'The Mighty Hood and the Melbourne Cricket Club', HMS Hood Association (2020), hmshood.com/history/empirecruise/cricket.htm, accessed 28/10/2021.

10 Today Canberra is the capital of Australia. On 1 January 1901, the federation of Australia was achieved which was followed by a long dispute over whether Sydney or Melbourne should be the national capital. A compromise was reached in which it was decided to build a new city to serve as the capital city in New South Wales, the only condition being that the new capital be at least 100 miles from Sydney. The capital city was founded and formally named Canberra on 12 March 1913. While Canberra was constructed Melbourne was to be the temporary seat of government. Thus Melbourne served at the seat of government for Australia until 9 May 1927 when the Commonwealth Parliament moved to Canberra with the opening of the Provisional Parliament House. For more information on this, see Davison, G., Hirst, J., MacIntyre, S. (eds), The Oxford Companion to Australia (Oxford: Oxford University Press, 1998); Fitzgerald, A., Canberra in Two Centuries: A Pictorial History (Torrens: Clareville Press, 1987); Wigmore, L., Canberra: History of Australia's National Capital (Canberra: Dalton Publishing Company, 1971).

11 The Argus, 17 March 1924.

12 Sun News Pictorial, 17 March 1924.

13 Mitcham, J. C., 'The 1924 Empire Cruise and the Imagining of an Imperial Community', Britain and the World, Vol. 12, No. 1 (2019), p. 74.

14 Ibid.

15 Ibid.

16 Ibid.

17 Batchelder, op. cit.

18 Taylor, B., The Battlecruiser HMS Hood: An Illustrated Biography, 1916–1941 (Barnsley: Seaforth Publishing, 2015), p. 71.

19 O'Connor, op. cit., p. 179.

20 Mitcham, op. cit., p. 72; Sydney Morning Herald, 19 March 1924.

21 ADM 116/2254.

22 The Sporting Globe, 19 March 1924.

Endnotes 307

23 *The Argus*, 21 March 1924.
24 *The Sporting Globe*, 21 March 1924.
25 Bradford, E., *The Mighty Hood* (London: Hodder & Stoughton, 1977), p. 78.
26 O'Connor, *op. cit.*, p. 179.
27 Smith, S. M., *'We Sail the Ocean Blue': British Sailors, Imperialism, Identity, Pride and Patriotism c. 1890 to 1939* (Portsmouth: University of Portsmouth, 2017), p. 136.
28 *Ibid.*
29 *Ibid.*, p. 137.
30 *Ibid.*
31 *Ibid.*, pp. 136–137.
32 *The Argus*, 1 April 1924; *Daily Telegraph*, 28 March 1924.
33 Smith, *op. cit.* (2017), p. 138.
34 O'Connor, *op. cit.*, p. 188.
35 *Ibid.*, pp. 191–192.
36 *Ibid.*, p. 192.
37 *Ibid.*, pp. 192–193.
38 *Ibid.*, p. 193.
39 Cassells, V., *The Capital Ships: Their Battles and Their Badges* (East Roseville: Simon and Schuster, 2000), p. 6.

Chapter 7

1 O'Connor, V. C. S., *The Empire Cruise* (London: Riddle, Smith & Duffus, 1925), pp. 209–210.
2 *Ibid.*, p. 210.
3 *Ibid.*
4 *Ibid.*, p. 211; Knowles, D., *HMS Hood: Pride of the Royal Navy* (Stroud: Fonthill Media, 2019), p. 142.
5 Coles, A., Briggs, T., *Flagship Hood: The Fate of Britain's Mightiest Warship* (London; Robert Hale, 1988), p. 36.
6 Taylor, B., *The Battlecruiser HMS Hood: An Illustrated Biography, 1916–1941* (Barnsley: Seaforth Publishing, 2015), p. 72.
7 Coles, Briggs, *op. cit.*, p. 36.
8 *Ibid.*, p. 37.
9 O'Connor, *op. cit.*, p. 213.
10 Coles, Briggs, *op. cit.*, p. 37.
11 O'Connor, *op. cit.*, p. 214.
12 *Ibid.*, pp. 214–215.
13 *Ibid.*, p. 216.
14 *Ibid.*

Chapter 8

1 Taylor, B., *The End of Glory: War & Peace in HMS Hood, 1916–1941* (Barnsley: Seaforth Publishing, 2012), p. 25.
2 Mitcham, J. C., 'The 1924 Empire Cruise and the Imagining of an Imperial Community', *Britain and the World*, Vol. 12, No. 1 (2019), p. 81; ADM 116/2256.
3 O'Connor, V. C. S., *The Empire Cruise* (London: Riddle, Smith & Duffus, 1925), pp. 230–231.
4 *Ibid.*, p. 232.
5 *Ibid.*, pp. 236–237.
6 *Ibid.*, p. 237.
7 Knowles, D., *HMS Hood: Pride of the Royal Navy* (Stroud: Fonthill Media, 2019), p. 142.
8 O'Connor, *op. cit.*, p. 238.

308   *Empire Cruise*

9 *Ibid.*, p. 242.
10 Mitcham, *op. cit.*, p. 79.
11 *Ibid.*
12 O'Connor, *op. cit.*, pp. 244–245.
13 An officer of the Royal Navy, George Vancouver is best known for his 1791–1795 expedition which at various times included two and four vessels and circumnavigated the globe making contact with five continents. The primary aim of the expedition was to improve British knowledge of the Southern Pacific and to take back from the Spanish land and property at Nootka Sound which had been confiscated from British fur traders, and to establish a formal British presence there. The expedition saw Vancouver explore and chart North America's north western Pacific coastal regions, including the coasts of what are now British Columbia, Alaska, Washington and Oregon. Not only is Vancouver city and Island named after George Vancouver, so too is Vancouver, Washington. In addition to this, Mount Vancouver on the border of Canada and the United States between Yukon and Alaska as well as Mount Vancouver, New Zealand are both named for him.
14 O'Connor, *op. cit.*, pp. 248-249.
15 Jones, J. R. (ed.), *William 'Billy' Mitchell's Air Power* (Honolulu: University Press of the Pacific, 2004), p. 3.
16 Taylor, B., *The Battlecruiser HMS Hood: An Illustrated Biography, 1916–1941* (Barnsley: Seaforth Publishing, 2015), p. 74; Gruner, G. F., *Blue Water Beat: The Two Lives of the Battleship USS California* (Palo Alto: Glencannon Press, 1996), p. 72.
17 Marquiss-Munro, P., 'The Visit of the British Fleet', *The Wasp* (19 July 1924), *City Museum of San Francisco*, sfmuseum.org/hist11/britishfleet.html, accessed 19/09/2021.
18 Knowles, *op. cit.* (2019), p. 143.
19 Bradford, E., *The Mighty Hood* (London: Hodder & Stoughton, 1977), p. 85.
20 Marquiss-Munro, *op. cit.*
21 Taylor, *op. cit.* (2015), p. 74.

Chapter 9

1 O'Connor, V. C. S., *The Empire Cruise* (London: Riddle, Smith & Duffus, 1925), pp. 270–271.
2 Howarth, D., *A Brief History of British Sea Power: How Britain Became Sovereign of the Seas* (London: Robinson, 2003), p. 148.

Chapter 10

1 Knowles, D., *HMS Hood: Pride of the Royal Navy* (Stroud: Fonthill Media, 2019), p. 143.
2 ADM 53/82492.
3 *Ibid.*; ADM 53/78915
4 ADM 53/78915
5 O'Connor, V. C. S., *The Empire Cruise* (London: Riddle, Smith & Duffus, 1925), p. 258.
6 *Ibid.*, pp. 258–259.
7 Mitcham, J. C., 'The 1924 Empire Cruise and the Imagining of an Imperial Community', *Britain and the World*, Vol. 12, No. 1 (2019), p. 79.
8 *Ibid.*, p. 80.
9 *Ibid.*
10 *Ibid.*
11 *Montreal Gazette*, 3 July 1924.
12 Mitcham, *op. cit.*, p. 80.
13 *Ibid.*
14 ADM 53/78915; ADM 53/82492.

Endnotes 309

Chapter 11

1 Coles, A., Briggs, T., *Flagship Hood: The Fate of Britain's Mightiest Warship* (London; Robert Hale, 1988), p. 40.
2 *Ibid.*
3 *Ibid.*
4 O'Connor, V. C. S., *The Empire Cruise* (London: Riddle, Smith & Duffus, 1925), p. 266.
5 Coles, Briggs, *op. cit.*, p. 41.

Epilogue

1 Harrington, R., '"The Mighty *Hood*": Navy, Empire, War at Sea and the British Imagination, 1920-60', *Journal of Contemporary History*, Vol. 38, No. 8 (2003), p. 176.
2 *The Times*, 27 September 1924; Smith, S. M., *'We Sail the Ocean Blue': British Sailors, Imperialism, Identity, Pride and Patriotism c. 1890 to 1939* (Portsmouth: University of Portsmouth, 2017), p. 126.
3 Mitcham, J. C., 'The 1924 Empire Cruise and the Imagining of an Imperial Community', *Britain and the World*, Vol. 12, No. 1 (2019), p. 82.
4 *Ibid.*; Spence, D. O., *A History of the Royal Navy: Empire and Imperialism* (London: I. B. Tauris, 2015), p. 140.
5 O'Connor, V. C. S., *The Empire Cruise* (London: Riddle, Smith & Duffus, 1925), pp. 31 and 222.
6 Mitcham, *op. cit.*, p. 83.
7 Bell, C., *The Royal Navy, Seapower and Strategy Between the Wars* (Palo Alto: Stanford University Press, 2000), p. 168.
8 Smith, *op. cit.* (2017), p. 126.
9 *Ibid.*
10 *Ibid.*
11 Friend, J., 'Destroyer Flag-Flying Visits, Civic Ceremony, Empire and Identity in Interwar Britain', *British Journal for Military History*, Vol. 7, No. 2 (2021), p. 108.
12 For more information on the loss of HMS *Hood* see Knowles, D., *The Battle of the Denmark Strait: An Analysis of the Battle and the Loss of HMS Hood* (Stroud: Fonthill Media, 2019).
13 The single largest disaster suffered by the Royal Navy was the loss of HMS *Glorious*, which was lost on 8 June 1940 when she was sunk by the German battleships *Scharnhorst* and *Gneisenau*. 1,515 men died aboard HMS *Glorious*. The single largest maritime disaster suffered by Britain occurred during the Second World War and was the loss of RMS *Lancastria* which was sunk by German air attack on 17 June 1940. Exactly how many people died in the sinking of RMS *Lancastria* is undetermined; the *Lancastria* Association names 1,738 people known to have been killed while a 2005 estimate placed the true figure at somewhere between 3,000 and 5,800 with some estimates suggesting 6,500 people perished.
14 For more information on the loss of HMS *Repulse*, see Middlebrook, M., and Mahoney, P., *Battleship: The Loss of the Prince of Wales and the Repulse* (London: Allan Lane, 1977).
15 Mitcham, *op. cit.*, p. 88.
16 Coles, A., Briggs, T., *Flagship Hood: The Fate of Britain's Mightiest Warship* (London; Robert Hale, 1988), p. 41; Knowles, D., *HMS Hood: Pride of the Royal Navy* (Stroud: Fonthill Media, 2019), p. 161.
17 Coles, Briggs, *op. cit.*, p. 41.

Bibliography

Archival Sources

ADM 1/8662/111: Special Service Squadron, Empire Cruise. Table money and Flag allowances. Question of its operation on all occasions when the Light Cruisers are detached from the Battle Cruisers (Kew: The National Archives)
ADM 53/78914: HMS *Hood* Ship's Log, 15 May 1923-30 April 1924 (Kew: The National Archives)
ADM 53/78915: HMS *Hood* Ship's Log, 1 May 1924-18 April 1925 (Kew: The National Archives)
ADM 53/82492: HMS *Repulse* Ship's Log, 10 December 1923-28 November 1924 (Kew: The National Archives)
ADM 104/111: Register of Reports of Deaths: Ships (Kew: The National Archives)
ADM 116/2219: Empire Cruise – Special Service Squadron Vol. I (Kew: The National Archives)
ADM 116/2220: Empire Cruise – Special Service Squadron Vol. II (Kew: The National Archives)
ADM 116/2254: Special Service Squadron: Letters of Proceedings (Kew: The National Archives)
ADM 118/682/17941: Benger, Walter Francis (Kew: The National Archives)
ADM 196/44/62: Alister Francis Beal Service Record (Kew: The National Archives)
ADM 196/156/118: Alfred Douglas Punshon Service Record (Kew: The National Archives)
ADM 196/44/156: Henry Wise Parker Service Record (Kew: The National Archives)
IWM 24934 William Frederick Stone (London: Imperial War Museum)
IWM 34640 Edward Tomas Williamson (London: Imperial War Museum)

Literature

Agar, A., *Showing the Flag: The Role of the Royal Navy Between the World Wars*, (London: Evans Brothers, 1962)
Albertson, M., *They'll Have to Follow You Home!: The Triumph of the Great White Fleet* (Mustang: Tate Publishing & Enterprise LLC, 2007)
Amery, L., *My Political Life Vol. II: War and Peace 1914–1929* (London: Hutchison, 1953)
Arthur, M., *True Glory: The Royal Navy 1914–1939* (London: Hodder and Stoughton, 1996)
Bastock, J., *Australia's Ships of War* (Cremorne: Angus and Robertson, 1975)
Bell, C., *The Royal Navy, Seapower and Strategy Between the Wars* (Palo Alto: Stanford University Press, 2000)
Bennett, G., *Naval Battles of the First World War* (Barnsley: Pen and Sword, 2005)

Bibliography

Bennett, G. H., *The Royal Navy in the Age of Austerity 1919–22: Naval and Foreign Policy Under Lloyd George* (London: Bloomsbury Publishing, 2016)

Benstead, C. R., *Around the World With the Battle Cruisers* (London: Hurst and Blackett, 1925)

Bradford, E., *The Mighty Hood* (London: Hodder & Stoughton, 1977)

Burt, R. A., *British battleships of World War One* (Annapolis: Naval Institute Press, 1986)

Campbell, J., *Jutland: An Analysis of the Fighting* (London: Conway maritime Press, 1998)

Campbell, N. J. M., *Battle Cruisers: The Design and Development of British and German Battlecruisers of the First World War Era* (Greenwich: Conway Maritime Press, 1978)

Cassells, V., *The Capital Ships: Their Battles and Their Badges* (East Roseville: Simon and Schuster, 2000)

Chesneau, R. (ed.), *All the World's Fighting Ships 1922–46* (New York: Mayflower Books, 1980)

Coles, A., Briggs, T., *Flagship Hood: The Fate of Britain's Mightiest Warship* (London; Robert Hale, 1988)

College, J. J. *Ships of the Royal Navy: A Complete Record of All the Fighting Ships of the Royal Navy* (London: Casemate, 2010)

Connelly, M., 'Battleships and British Society, 1920–1960', *International Journal of Naval History*, Vol. 3, No. 2 (2004)

Davison, G., Hirst, J., MacIntyre, S. (eds.) *The Oxford Companion to Australia* (Oxford: Oxford University Press, 1998)

Eayrs, J., *In Defence of Canada Volume I: From the Great War to the Great Depression* (Toronto: University of Toronto Press, 1964)

Edwards, B., *Salvo!: Classic Naval Gun Actions* (London: Arms and Armour Press, 1995)

Farwell, B., *The Great War in Africa, 1914–1918* (New York: W. W. Norton, 1986)

Fitzgerald, A., *Canberra in Two Centuries: A Pictorial History* (Torrens: Clareville Press, 1987)

Friedman, N., *British Cruisers: Two World Wars and After* (Barnsley: Seaforth Publishing, 2010)

Friend, J., 'Destroyer Flag-Flying Visits, Civic Ceremony, Empire and Identity in Interwar Britain', *British Journal for Military History*, Vol. 7, No. 2 (2021), pp. 102–121

Gewarth, R. *Twisted Paths: Europe 1914–1945* (Oxford: Oxford University Press, 2012)

Gilbert, R., *Warships of Australia* (Adelaide: Rigby, 1977)

Gordon, W. R., 'Special Service Squadron World Cruise, November 1923 to September 1924. Being extracts from the diary of Midshipman W. R. Gordon', *The Naval Review*, Vol. 13, No. 1 (1925) pp. 108–114.

Gruner, G. F., *Blue Water Beat: The Two Lives of the Battleship USS California* (Palo Alto: Glencannon Press, 1996)

Halpen, P. G., *A Naval History of World War I* (Annapolis: Naval Institute Press, 1995)

Harrington, P., *Peking 1900: The Boxer Rebellion* (Oxford: Osprey Publishing, 2001)

Heathcote, T., *The British Admirals of the Fleet 1734–1995* (Barnsley: Pen and Sword, 2002)

Hough, R., *Admirals in Collision* (London: Hamish Hamilton, 1959)

Howarth, D., *A Brief History of British Sea Power: How Britain Became Sovereign of the Seas* (London: Robinson, 2003)

Jones, J. R. (ed.), *William 'Billy' Mitchell's Air Power* (Honolulu: University Press of the Pacific, 2004

Kennedy, P., *The Rise and Fall of British Naval Mastery* (London: Penguin, 2017)

Knowles, D., *The Battle of the Denmark Strait: An Analysis of the Battle and the Loss of HMS Hood* (Stroud: Fonthill Media, 2019)

Knowles, D., *HMS Hood: Pride of the Royal Navy* (Stroud: Fonthill Media, 2019)

Knowles, D., *Yamato: Flagship of the Japanese Imperial Navy* (Stroud: Fonthill Media, 2021)

Lenton, H. T., *British and Empire Warships of the Second World War* (Annapolis: Naval Institute Press, 1998)

Lyon, P., *Britain and Canada: Survey of a Changing Relationship* (London: Frank Cass and Company, 1976)

MacKenzie, J. M., *Propaganda and Empire: The manipulation of British Public Opinion, 1880–1960* (Manchester: Manchester University Press, 1985)

Marder, A. J., *The Anatomy of British Sea Power* (New York: Octagon Books, 1976)

Middlebrook, M., Mahoney, P., *Battleship: The Loss of the Prince of Wales and the Repulse* (London: Allan Lane, 1977).

Miller, C., *Battle for the Bundu: The First World War in East Africa* (London: Macmillan Publishing, 1974)

Mitcham, J. C., 'The 1924 Empire Cruise and the Imagining of an Imperial Community', *Britain and the World*, Vol. 12, No. 1 (2019), pp. 67–88

Moldt, J., *Britannia Ruled the Waves: An Imagological Analysis of the Battleship as a Cultural Image of the British Empire, 1905–1960* (Aalborg University, 2019)

Newbolt, H., *History of the Great War Based on Official Documents Vol. V: Naval Operations* Nashville: Battery Press, 1996)

Norman, A., *HMS Hood: Pride of the Royal Navy* (Stroud: The History Press, 2009)

O'Connor, V. C. Scott, *The Empire Cruise* (London: Riddle, Smith & Duffus, 1925)

Osbourne, E. W., *Cruisers and Battle cruisers: An Illustrated History of their Impact* (London: ABC-Clio, 2004)

Parker, J., *Task Force: Untold Stories of the Heroes of the Royal Navy* (London: Headline Book Publishing, 2003)

Peden, G. C., *Arms, Economics and British Strategy: From Dreadnoughts to Hydrogen Bombs* (Cambridge: Cambridge University Press, 2007)

Perryman, J., 'Ships Named *Adelaide*', *Semaphore* (Sea Power Centre, 2015)

Roberts, J., *Battlecruisers* (Annapolis: Naval Institute Press, 1997)

Roskill, S., *Naval policy Between the Wars Vol. I: The Period of Anglo-American Antagonism, 1919–1929* (New York: Walker & Company, 1968)

Rüger, J., *The Great Naval Game: Britain and Germany in the Age of Empire* (Cambridge: Cambridge University Press, 2007)

Silbey, D., *The Boxer Rebellion and the Great Game in China* (New York: Hill and Wang, 2012)

Smith, P. C., *The Battle-Cruiser HMS Renown, 1916–1948* (Barnsley: Pen and Sword, 2008)

Smith, S. M., 'We Sail the Ocean Blue': British Sailors, Imperialism, Identity, Pride and Patriotism c. 1890 to 1939* (Portsmouth: University of Portsmouth, 2017)

Spence, D. O., *A History of the Royal Navy: Empire and Imperialism* (London: I. B. Tauris, 2015)

Spence, D. O., *Colonial Naval Culture and British Imperialism, 1922–67* (Manchester: Manchester University Press, 2015)

Stille, M., *Imperial Japanese Navy Battleships 1941-1945* (Oxford: Osprey Publishing Ltd, 2008)

Taylor, B., *The Battlecruiser HMS Hood: An Illustrated Biography, 1916–1941* (Barnsley: Seaforth Publishing, 2015)

Taylor, B., *The End of Glory: War & Peace in HMS Hood* (Barnsley: Seaforth Publishing, 2012)

Thomas, R. D., 'Empire, Naval Pageantry and Public Spectacles', *Mariner's Mirror*, Vol. 88, No. 2 (2002), pp. 202–213

Wigmore, L., *Canberra: History of Australia's National Capital* (Canberra: Dalton Publishing Company, 1971)

Whitley, M. J., *Cruisers of World War Two: An International Encyclopaedia* (London: Cassell, 1995)

Wise, J., *The Role of the Royal Navy in South America, 1920–1970*, (London: Bloomsbury, 2014)

Woodburn-Kirby, Maj.-Gen. S., *The War Against Japan Volume I: The Loss of Singapore* (Uckfield: The Naval & Military Press, 2004)

Bibliography

Newspapers

The Argus
Montreal Gazette
The Sporting Globe
Sun News Pictorial
Sydney Morning Herald
The Times
Times of Ceylon

Webpages

Batchelder, 'The Mighty *Hood* and the Melbourne Cricket Club', *HMS Hood Association* (2020), hmshood.com/history/empirecruise/cricket.htm, Accessed 28/10/2021.

'Deployment of HMS Queen Elizabeth and Carrier Strike Group will "fly flag for Global Britain"', Sky News, 26 April 2021, news.sky.com/story/deployment-of-hms-queen-elizabeth-and-carrier-strike-group-will-fly-flag-for-global-britain-12287281, Accessed 15/11/2021.

Ghani, S. M., 'My Visit to the Battle-Cruisers H.M.S. *Hood* and *Repulse*', Force Z Survivors Association (2019), forcez-survivors.org.uk/schoolboy.html, Accessed 28/10/2021.

Marquiss-Munro, P., 'The Visit of the British Fleet', *The Wasp* (19 July 1924), *City Museum of San Francisco*, sfmuseum.org/hist11/britishfleet.html, Accessed 19/09/2021.

Royal Australian Navy, 'HMAS *Adelaide* (I)', navy.gov.au (2019), navy.gov.au/hmas-adelaide-i, Accessed 05/10/2021.

Royal Navy, 'UK Carrier Strike Group Assembles for the First Time', 05 October 2020, *Royal Navy* (2020), royalnavy.mod.uk/news-and-latest-activity/news/2020/october/05/201005-hms-queen-elizabeth-carrier-strike, Accessed 18/11/2021.

Smith, S., 'British Sailors and Prohibition: the experience of going "dry" in the USA during the Empire Cruise', Port Towns and Urban Cultures, 2015, porttowns.port.ac.uk/britishsailors-prohibition/, Accessed 25/09/2021.

Index

Abyssinia 298
Addison, Rear Admiral Albert 156
Adelaide 123-127
Adelaide, HMAS 39-40, 49, 163-164,
181, 190, 194-195, 201, 211-212, 221,
224, 226, 229-231, 243-244, 258-260,
266-267, 280, 282-286, 292, 294-296,
300
Admiral Graf Spee 299
Admiral-Class 28
Agar, Captain August 15
Ahi, Berenice 213
Akagi 11
Albany 120, 122-123
Albion, HMS 42
Albemarle, HMS 42
Allardyce, Sir William 292
Alessandri, Arturo 262
Algiers Bay 299
Alvear, Marcelo Torcuato 264
Al-Said, Sayyad Khalifa Bin Harub 67, 69
Amagi 11
Amery, Leo 15-17, 19-20, 25
Andes 262
Anglo-Japanese Alliance 22
Apia 211
Aquitania, RMS 27
Argentina 263-264
Armstrong Whitworth 33-34, 37-39
Arromanches 299
Astraea, HMS 46
Atago 11
Atlantic Ocean 10, 22-23, 31, 51, 211, 256,
265-266, 292, 294-295, 298-300
Auckland 190, 193, 195, 201-205, 207-208
Austin, Captain Francis 46-47, 134, 261, 264

Australia 5, 9, 12, 15-19, 22-24, 39, 84-85,
87-88, 98, 105, 131-133, 136, 142, 154,
175, 190, 193, 298, 300
Australia, HMAS 27, 32, 132, 179-180, 184
Austria-Hungary 41

Bahia Blanca 263-264
Balboa 266-267
Baltic Sea 30, 33, 35, 38
Bapaume 194
Barfleur, HMS 41
Barham, HMS 27
Barrow 300
Barwell, Sir Henry 123
Batchelder, Alf 129
Beal, Captain Alister 48-49
Beatty, Admiral Sir David 15, 17, 28, 44, 287
Beaumont Hamel 194
Benger, Able Seaman William 82
Benstead, Lieutenant Charles 51, 129, 202
Bentinck, Rear Admiral Sir Rudolph 61
Beqa 208, 210
Bellerophon-Class 46
Bellona, HMS 43
Benbow, HMS 45
Bermuda 16, 21, 35
Bismarck 298
Bismarck Archipelago 22
Black Sea 5
Blake, General at Sea Robert 226, 237
Blanco Encalada 261
Blenheim, HMS 43
Bluebell, HMS 83
Bluff 201
Blundell, Midshipman George 201
Bombay 16, 21

Boston 21
Boxer Rebellion 41
Brand, Henry, 1st Viscount 43
Brand, Henry, 2nd Viscount 43
Brand, Rear Admiral Sir Hubert 43-44, 59,
    61, 64, 70, 77-78, 83, 88, 99, 101-102,
    104, 122-123, 131, 133, 179, 184, 188,
    201-202, 206, 210, 213, 238, 259-266
Brand, Lady Norah 123
Brazil 9, 264-265
Bridges, Sir Tom 124, 127
Brisbane 179, 184-191
Britannia, HMS 41, 43, 48-49
British Columbia 4, 223, 252, 308
British Empire Exhibition 21
Brock, Captain Osmond de Beauvoir 49
Brownrigg, Captain Sir Douglas 43
Bruce, Stanley 136, 156, 175
Brunton, Sir William 175
Buenos Aires 263-265
Buffalo, HMS 124
Bunbury 122, 127
Burma 15
Burrard Inlet 226-230
Bushell, Frederick 147, 154

Cadmus, HMS 84
California, USS 257
Callao 258, 260-261
Cameroon 12
Camperdown, HMS 49
Canada 12, 15-16, 19-21, 24, 36-37, 216,
    221, 226, 242, 266, 280, 285, 287, 289,
    301
Cape Verde 265, 294
Carlisle, HMS 83
Caroline Islands 22
Cape Horn 262-263
Cape Town 55-56, 61-62, 66, 98, 300
Caribbean 24, 266, 280
Cawsand Bay 295
Cerberus, HMS 49
Ceres, HMS 44
Ceylon 9, 15, 21, 67, 74, 76, 300
Chacabuco 261
Chapelton 280
Charlton, Matthew 175
Chatham, HMS 190, 194-195, 207, 298
Cherwell, HMS 43
Chile 9, 261-262
China 9, 16, 22, 41, 83
Christchurch 190, 195, 200
Christmas Island 85, 87
Clydebank 27, 30-31, 33

Cochrane, HMS 46, 48
Cockatoo Island Dockyard 39-40
Collier, Able Seaman William 201
Collingwood, Vice-Admiral Cuthbert 226, 237
Colombo 21
Conrad, ORP (See HMS *Dragon*)
Constance, HMS 41, 292-293
Contest, HMS 43
Cooke, John 88
Conception Bay 292, 295
Concord, USS 67
Coolidge, President Calvin 213
Coquimbo 261
Coronel, Battle of 262
Coronel Bolognesi 260
Coryndon, Sir Robert 70
Courageous, HMS 32
Cradock, Admiral Christopher 262
Creswell, HMAS 156-157
Crete 5

Dafoe, J. W. 20
Daily Colonist 223, 287
Dakar 299
Danae, HMS 17, 26, 33-34, 46, 51, 62,
    64-65, 70, 73-75, 77, 85-86, 109, 118,
    127, 135, 143, 145, 154, 156, 184, 186,
    190, 195, 200, 221, 261-264, 295, 300
Danae-Class 17, 19, 33-34, 36-37
Danzig 39
Dar el-Salem 70-71
Dauntless, HMS 17, 26, 33-36, 46, 50, 62,
    64-65, 70-71, 74-75, 77, 85, 118, 154,
    178, 184, 187, 189, 190, 201, 215, 221,
    255, 261-264, 295, 300-301
Defiance, HMS 41-42
Delhi, HMS 17, 19, 37-38, 46, 50, 58,
    62, 64-65, 70-71, 74-75, 77, 84, 93,
    96-98, 108-109, 111, 117, 122, 127,
    135, 138, 141-142, 144-145, 154-156,
    164, 179, 184-187, 190, 195, 200, 202,
    215, 220-221, 255, 259, 261-264, 295,
    299-300
Demerara 21
Denmark 300
Denmark Strait 298
Devonport 26, 29, 49-51, 122, 295-296, 300
    Dockyard 26, 39
De Chair, Admiral Sir Dudley 156
De Robeck, Admiral Sir John 50
Dragon, HMS 17, 26, 33, 36, 48, 51, 62,
    70-71, 84-85, 87, 154-156, 173, 187,
    189-191, 195, 200, 221-222, 261-264,
    295, 299-300

Drake, Sir Francis 226, 237, 262-263
Dreadnought, HMS 41
Duncan, HMS 42
Duncan-Class 49
Dunedin 19, 21, 38-39, 190, 201
Dunedin, HMS 17, 19, 38-39, 49-50, 77, 85, 127, 154, 173, 184-185, 188, 190, 201, 207, 298
Durban 62, 64-66
Durban Light Infantry 64, 66
D'Eyncourt, Sir Eustace Tennyson 27-28

East London 66
Edinburgh 39
Edward VII, King 43
Edward VIII, King 15, 21, 36
Egypt 9
Elizabeth 263
Elswick 37-38
Encounter, HMS 49
England 74, 123, 136, 175, 212, 260
English Channel 51, 296
Esquimalt 21, 221-222, 225-226, 252, 255
Excellent, HMS 46

Fairbairn, Captain Bernard 46, 48, 100
Fairbairn, W. M. 46
Falkland Islands 263-264
Farrington, Governor Wallace 39
Ferguson, Lady Helen 39
Ferguson, Sir Munro 39
Field, Vice-Admiral Sir Frederick 25-26, 41-42, 44, 50-51, 55, 61, 66-67, 69-70, 77, 79, 81, 83, 88, 98-104, 122-123, 127, 131-133, 136, 156, 165, 190, 194-195, 200-202, 205, 207, 210-211, 213, 223, 226, 236, 238-239, 242, 244, 256-260, 273, 283, 285, 287, 289, 291-292, 294-296
Fiji 208, 210-211
Fisher, Admiral John 30-31
First World War 6, 9, 11-12, 14, 19, 22-23, 27, 33, 35, 37, 42-44, 49, 84, 133, 287
Foster, Henry 190
France 41, 133, 299
   Vichy 299
Franklin, J. T. 88
Freetown 51, 53-55
Fremantle 84-85, 87-90, 92-98, 104-106, 108-109, 111-123
Fremantle, Admiral Sir Sydney 296
Fuller, Sir George 175

Gallipoli 194

Gamio, Pedro 260
Gandhi, Mahatma 21
Geddes, Sir Auckland 24
Georgetown 21
George V, King 42, 50, 61, 194, 211, 213, 261
Germany 11, 22, 41
   Empire 22
Gibraltar 5, 9
Glenelg 124-126
Gneisenau 298
Golden Hinde 263
Good Hope, HMS 43
Goodwin, Captain Frank 212
Griffon, HMS 43
Gran Canaria 51
Great Britain 5, 7, 9, 11-12, 19-20, 22, 36, 38, 41-42, 50, 61, 66, 84, 98, 125, 133, 136, 175, 205, 207, 211, 213, 223, 226, 256-257, 263, 285, 287, 292, 294, 297, 299-301
   Colonial Office 17-18, 55
   Committee of Imperial Defence 23
   Foreign Office 17-18, 24
   Treasury 12, 17-18
Great White Fleet 9-10
Greenacre, Walter 64
Greenock 29, 36
Grenville, Admiral Sir Richard 226, 237
Guam 5, 22
Guillemard, Sir Laurence 83
G3 Battlecruiser 11

Halifax 36, 280, 282-284, 300
Hamilton 287
Hamilton, Rear Admiral Frederick 43
Hampton Roads 9-10
Harrhy, Able Seaman William 184, 189
Harris, Samuel 285
Harwich 33, 36
Haughty, HMS 45
Hawaii 9, 24, 210-213, 215-216, 219, 221
Hawkins, HMS 17, 83-84
Hawthorn, Leslie and Company 39
Hayward, Reginald 223
Hebburn 39
Hecla, HMS 45
Heligoland Bight, Battle of 32
Hercules, HMS 45
Herron, HMS 49
Hickson, Major Gerald 147
High Seas Fleet 12, 27, 32
Hobart 142, 147-155
Hodges, Rear Admiral Sir Michael 25

Index

Hong Kong 23, 300
Honolulu Maru 154-156
Hood, HMS 6-7, 16-19, 24, 26-29, 33,
 42, 44, 50-52, 54-56, 58, 62, 66-69,
 71, 76, 79-85, 87-91, 94-96, 99-100,
 108-113, 115, 119-120, 122-127,
 129-131, 133, 135-142, 146-154,
 156-157, 159-168, 173-174, 176-177,
 179, 181, 190, 192-197, 200-205, 208,
 210-218, 221-228, 231-232, 234, 236,
 239, 242-247, 249-251, 256-257, 259,
 266-269, 271-280, 282-287, 289-296,
 298, 301
Hood, Rear Admiral Horace 28
House of Commons 43

Immortalité, HMS 48
Imperial Conference 16-17, 20, 23
Imperieuse, HMS 41
Im Thurn, Captain John 44, 67, 69, 83, 88,
 102, 236, 285, 294, 296
Indefatigable, HMS 28
India 12, 15-16, 19, 21-23
 National Congress 21
Indian Ocean 23, 62, 67, 74-75, 298-301
Inflexible, HMS 27
Ingles, Captain John 22
Intervention War 12
Invincible, HMS 28-29
Ipoh 77-78
Iraq 12
Iron Duke-Class 45
Italy 5, 41, 264, 298

Jamaica 24, 280
James, Sir Frederick 79, 84
Japan 5, 9, 11, 15, 22, 41, 136
Jarrow 34-35
Jaseur, HMS 42
Jellicoe, Admiral Sir John 15, 19, 27, 31-32,
 190, 193-195, 200-202, 205, 207
Jerram, Admiral Thomas 42
Jervis Bay 40, 156-157, 179
Johore, Sultan of 83
John Brown and Company 27, 30-31, 33
Jutland, Battle of 28-29, 32, 42, 45, 190,
 193

Kaiser, SMS 32
Kaiserin, SMS 32
Kia Peng, Choo 81
Kandy 74
Kelantan, Sultan of 83
Kenya 21, 70-71

Keyes, Commander Adrian 221
Keyes, Admiral Sir Roger 15-16, 18, 24
Kiel 43
King, Mackenzie 19-20, 285
King George V, HMS 42
Kingston 280, 282
King's African Rifles 70-71
Königsberg, SMS (1905) 22
Königsberg, SMS (1915) 32
Krakatoa 85-86
Kuala Kangsar 77
Kuala Lumpur 77, 79-82

Lake Preston 105, 110
Lambton, Captain Hedworth 48
Landry, Brigadier-General J. P. 285, 292
Layfield, Marine Henry 84
League of Nations 22, 175, 223
Leguía, Augusto 261
Leveson, Admiral Sir Arthur 83-84
Leviathan, HMS 46
Le Devoir 289
Loder-Symonds, Captain Frederick 21, 24
London 12, 20, 51
Lowestoft, HMS 46, 49
Lusitania, HMS 27

MacDonald, Edward 283
MacDonald, Ramsey 136
Mackensen-Class 27
Madden, Admiral Sir Charles 42
Magellan, Strait of 262
Malacca 83
Malaya 77, 82-83, 299
Malaysia 5
Malcolm, General Sir Neill 83-84
Malet, Sir Claude 264
Malta 22
Manchuria 22
Mariana Islands 22
Marigold 263
Maritzburg 64
Marquiss-Munro, Phyllis 256
Marshall Islands 22
Mary, Queen 212
Maryland, USS 11
Massey, William 50, 195, 207
Maxwell, George 81
McDonald, Vice-Admiral John D. 213
McMaster, Andrew 223
Mediterranean Sea 16, 22-23, 29, 41,
 299-301
Melbourne 127, 129-138, 140-145, 147
Mersey, HMS 22

Messines 194
Mexico 9
Middleton, Sir John 264
Minotaur, HMS 41
Mitchell, Sir James 88, 98
Mitchell, Brigadier General William 256
Mombasa 21, 70-71
Montevideo 264
Montreal 24, 285, 287, 292
Mossell Bay 66
Murray, General James 283

Nairobi 70-72
Napier 195, 199, 201, 298
Nathan, Matthew 184
Nauru 22
Nelson, HMS 299
Nelson, Vice-Admiral Horatio 226, 237
Newcastle Upon Tyne 37 39
Newdigate, Sir Francis 88
Newfoundland 15-16, 36, 292, 295
Newport 24
New Guinea 22
New South Wales 43, 156, 175
New York 12, 24
New Zealand 5, 9, 12, 15-16, 19, 21-24, 50,
    136, 190, 193-194, 200, 202, 205-208,
    210, 298
New Zealand, HMS 15, 19
Nichol, Walter 223
North Sea 32-33, 36, 299
Norway 300
Nova Scotia 287
No. 13 Class 11
N3 Battleship 11

Oakley, Corporal B. 80-81
Oman 5
Ontario 21, 283
Orkney Islands 12
Ottawa 283, 285, 287
Ottoman Empire 12
Owen, William 226, 236-239

Pacific Ocean 9, 11, 19, 22-23, 132-133,
    179, 210, 252, 256, 267, 300
Pahang, Sultan of 79
Palestine 12, 194
Palmers Shipbuilding and Iron Company 34-35
Panama 266-267
    Canal 16, 266-267, 274-279
Paris Peace Conference 22
Parker, Captain Henry 45, 50, 62, 67, 83,
    88, 102, 104, 147, 236, 252-253, 285

Passchendaele, Battle of 194
Patrician, HMCS 221
Pegasus, HMS 22
Penelope, HMS 46
Penfield, Mark 201
Penguin, HMAS 300
Perodeau, Narcisse 283
Perth 88, 98, 102, 105, 108
Peru 9, 260-261
Petersfield, HMS 83
Pinjarra 105
Pipon, Captain James 46-47, 59, 64, 264
Philippines 9
Phillimore, Vice-Admiral Sir Richard 295
Plymouth 51, 295
Plowman, Sir George 64
Popham, Lieutenant Arthur 49
Portsmouth 24, 32, 50, 295-296, 301
Port Alfred 66
Port Elizabeth 66
Port MacDonnell 127
Port Stanley 263-264
Port Swettenham 77, 79-82
Pretoria 56, 61
Prince of Wales, HMS 298-299
Princess Margaret 20
Princess Royal, HMS 49
Punshon, Signal Boatswain Alfred 136, 142,
    146
Punta Arenas 262

Queen Elizabeth, HMS 5
Queen Elizabeth-Class 27, 29
Queen Mary, HMS 28
Queensland 184, 190
Quebec 24, 283, 285-292
    Siege of 283

Ramillies, HMS 32
Ransome, Lieutenant Charles 142
Rawalpindi, HMS 298
Regulus 292
Renown, HMS 15, 18, 21, 31-32, 36
Renown-Class 30
Repulse, HMS 16-17, 24, 29-33, 45, 50-51,
    53, 56, 60, 62-63, 66-68, 71, 74, 79-85,
    88, 92-94, 114, 116, 121, 124, 127,
    129-130, 135-136, 141-142, 146-147,
    156, 158-159, 162-163, 166, 168, 174,
    177-179, 181, 190, 193-195, 198-199,
    201-203, 210, 212, 214, 219-224, 226,
    228, 230, 232-233, 236, 242-244,
    247-248, 251-252, 266, 270-271,
    279-280, 283-289, 292-296, 298-299

Reuter, Admiral Hans Hermann Ludwig 32
Rhode Island 24
Rhodesia 66
Richardson, Major General Spafford
    210-211
Riga 36
Rio Blanco 260
Rio de Janeiro 29, 33, 264
Rivers
    Clyde 29
    Murray 105
    Plate 264
    St. Lawrence 283, 286, 290-292
    Thames 266
Robe 127
Robinson, Admiral Samuel S. 252
Rolph, James 257
Roosevelt, President Theodore 9-11
Rosetta Head 127
Rose-Innes, Sir James 61
Rosyth 29, 32, 300
Rotorua 205-206
Round-Turner, Captain Charles 46-47, 64,
    70, 262, 264
Royal Australian Air Force 131, 156
Royal Australian Navy 18-19, 40, 49, 132,
    163, 175, 194, 226
Royal Canadian Navy 287, 292
Royal Colonial Institute 297
Royal Marines 55, 66, 70, 84, 147, 169,
    171, 184, 210, 224, 293
Royal Navy 5, 9, 11-12, 14-15, 17, 19,
    22-23, 26-29, 39, 41-46, 49-50, 61,
    66-67, 83-84, 98, 124, 133, 147, 175,
    205, 297-298, 300
    Admiralty 14-15, 17-26, 28, 32, 42,
    44-45, 48-51, 55, 123, 136, 211, 242,
    294, 296-297
    America and West Indies Station 299-301
    Atlantic Fleet 33, 35-36, 38, 45, 50, 260
    Battlecruiser Fleet 44
    Battlecruiser Squadron 28-29, 32, 42
    Channel Squadron 41, 48
    China Station 41-42, 84, 299-301
    Eighth Cruiser Squadron 300
    Fifth Light Cruiser Squadron 33, 36
    First Battle Squadron 33, 42
    First Battlecruiser Squadron 32
    First Cruiser Squadron 32, 43, 299
    First Light Cruiser Squadron 32-33,
    35-36, 38, 44, 51, 56, 62, 64-66, 70-71,
    77, 79, 83, 122, 127, 158, 179, 184-185,
    190-191, 201, 210, 212, 214, 220-222,
    225-226, 258-261, 263, 266, 294-296

Force Z 298
    Fourth Battle Squadron 45
    Grand Fleet 27, 31-32, 42, 44-45, 190,
    193
    Home Fleet 45, 300
    Mediterranean Fleet 41-42, 44, 49, 299
    New Zealand Division 49, 190, 207, 298
    Ninth Cruiser Squadron 300-301
    Northern Patrol 299
    Reserve Fleet 299, 301
    Second Battle Squadron 42
    Second Cruiser Squadron 46
    Second Destroyer Flotilla 43
    Seventh Cruiser Squadron 299
    Sixth Light Cruiser Squadron 22
    South American Division 301
    Third Cruiser Squadron 301
    Training Squadron 41, 48
    UK Carrier Strike Group 5-6
    Volunteer Reserve 55, 64
Rundle, Captain Mark 147
Russell, Arthur 50, 56, 66, 80
Russia 12, 33, 41
    Civil War 33, 35, 38

Salerno 299
Salim, Sheikh Ali Bin 70
Salish Sea 221
Samoa 22, 208-212
Sampson, Joseph-Octave 285
Sandford, Commander Francis 62
San Francisco 16, 24, 252, 255-258
San Giorgio 264
Scapa Flow 12, 32, 299-300
Scharnhorst 298
Scott, Shipwright Albert 60, 283-284
Scotts Shipbuilding and Iron Company
    36-37
Seattle 16, 21
Second World War 298-299
    Mulberry Harbour 299
    Normandy Landings 299-300
Selangor, Sultan of 79
Severn, HMS 22
Sierra Leone 51, 54
Simonstown 62, 70, 301
Singapore 5, 16, 22-23, 83-85, 136, 175,
    298-300
    Keppel Harbour 23
    Naval Base 23, 175, 298
Sino-Japanese War 300
Shanghai 300
Shantung Peninsula 22
Spanish Civil War 298-299

320   *Empire Cruise*

Slater, Alexander Rushford 51
Smartt, Sir Thomas 61
Smith, McCallum 105
Smuts, Jan 61-62
Somme, Battle of the 194
South Africa 12, 16, 51, 55, 61, 64, 66, 301
South China Sea 5-6
Spithead 20, 296
Spooner, Commander C. A. 17-18
Starfish, HMS 49
Stevenson, Captain John 49, 285
Stevenson, Robert Louis 211
Stone, Leading Stoker William 50
Sturdee, Admiral Sir Frederick 45
St John's 36, 190, 292-293
St Kilda 131, 133
St Paul's Rocks 298
Summerall, Major General Charles P. 213
Sungei Potani 77
Suva 208, 210
Sydney 23, 39-40, 156, 158-174, 176-181, 190, 201, 296

Table Mountain 56
Tacoma 21
Taiping 77
Takao 11
Talcahuano 261-262
Tamrookum 184
Tanganyika 12
Taschereau, Louis-Alexandre 285
Tasmania 142, 147, 153
Temeraire, HMS 46
Tenerife 51
Tierra del Fuego 263
Tiger, HMS 27, 29, 31
Togo 12
Tokyo 43
Topsail Bay 292-294
Toronto 285, 287-288
Town-Class 39, 179
Transjordan 12
Trincomalee 16, 21, 67, 71, 74, 76
Trinidad 9
Tsushima, Battle of 9
Tudor, Admiral Sir Frederick 27
Twofold Bay 154

Umberto II, King 264
United States 9-12, 15, 19-20, 22, 24, 41,
    132, 212, 257
    Army Air Corps 212
    Congress 11, 24
    Pacific Fleet 252
Upolu 210
Uruguay 264
U-124 298

Vailima 211
Valparaiso 261-262
Vancouver 16, 37, 223, 226-234, 236, 239, 242, 244-245, 247-252, 287
Vancouver, Commander George 226, 237
Vancouver Sun 226
Vernon, HMS 41-42
Versailles, Treaty of 12
Verster, Ryno J. 61
Vickers-Armstrong 300
Victoria 221-226, 252, 285
Victoria, HMS 49
Victoria and Albert, HMY 44
Ville D'Ys 292
Virginia 9-10
Vivian, Commander John 147
Volage, HMS 48
Vulcan, HMS 44

Walker 33
Warspite, HMS (1884) 48
Warspite, HMS (1913) 48
Washington Naval Treaty 23, 132, 179
Wellington 190, 192-200
Wells, Lieutenant Geoffrey 51, 133, 208, 257
Western Samoa 208, 210-212
Westminster, Statute of 289
West Indies 24
Weymouth, HMS 49
Wilhelmshaven 300
Willunga 127-129
Wilson, President Woodrow 11
Winnipeg 252
Wood, Petty Officer George 74
Woolman, Wilfred 50, 84, 147, 154

Zanzibar 21-22, 51, 66-71